CHARLES V

CHARLES V

Otto von Habsburg

*Translated from the French
by Michael Ross*

PRAEGER PUBLISHERS

New York · Washington

BOOKS THAT MATTER

Published in the United States of America in 1970
by Praeger Publishers, Inc., 111 Fourth Avenue,
New York, N.Y. 10003

© 1967 by Librairie Hachette, Paris, France
English translation © 1969 by George Weidenfeld & Nicolson Ltd.,
London, England

Library of Congress Catalog Card Number: 76-100916

MAY 8 '72

Printed in Great Britain

CONTENTS

CONTENTS

LIST OF ILLUSTRATIONS

between pages 96–97

ACKNOWLEDGEMENTS

The publishers would like to thank the following for providing illustrations for this volume and for permission to reproduce them:

Giraudon, Paris, plates 1 and 2; Kunsthistorischen Museum, Vienna, plate 3; the Mansell Collection, plates 4, 6, 10, 11 and 13; the Radio Times Hulton Picture Library, plates 5, 7, 9 and 15; Bildarchiv Foto Marburg, plate 8; the British Museum, plate 12; Ampliaciones y Reproducciones Mas, plate 14.

Foreword

The conception held by posterity of the past is not one that is rigid or unchangeable like the immutability of death, on the contrary it undergoes almost infinite fluctuations. Despite this, history – that is to say the way we interpret the past – forms an integral part of the present, because it is on history that the present is based. This is why each succeeding generation views the past from a different angle, while different nations, cultures, and creeds interpret historical events from their own individual points of view, notwithstanding the fact that the historical facts of the case may be universally admitted.

Only in the Middle Ages did the west have a unitarian concept of history; at that time, the doctrinal ascendancy of the church was so great, and its age-old tradition so strong, that ideological, nationalist and even regional influences were of little account. This universal framework of thought was logically extended to cover every aspect of human life. When assessing a man as hero or villain one obeyed certain universal criteria and not partisan considerations or a conformity of race or belief. Learning formed a harmonious and ordered whole, and theology was the centre around which revolved philosophy, law, political science and even the natural sciences. With the decline of medieval Christianity, this unity was destroyed. Emancipated from transcendental philosophy, the natural sciences only recognised as true what man could measure, count and weigh; the inevitable corollary of this was legal, and therefore political autonomy. The proponents of absolute government resolutely turned their backs on the concept of the natural rights of man, while their totalitarian attitude led them to advance theories which verged on the absurd; philosophy followed a similar course. By the end of the eighteenth century, theology, formerly

A*

queen of the sciences, found itself in a position of stark isolation; it had almost become relegated to the role of a superstitious cult, which, it was generally expected, would sooner or later disappear altogether.

On the historico-political plane, the struggle between the emperors and the Roman pontiffs foreshadowed the end of an epoch. While the popes justified their pretensions to govern Europe by the divine origins of their function, the emperors claimed, by virtue of the special mission entrusted to them by the Almighty, to be not only equals of the popes, but sometimes even their superiors. Friedrich II of Hohenstaufen's bitter struggle with the papacy gave rise to one of the first of the ideological debates symptomatic of this new historical epoch; in it the arguments put forward, and particularly those employed on the imperial side, no longer related in any way to the medieval thought of previous generations. Jokob Burckhardt was right when he called Friedrich II the first modern ruler to be placed at the head of the empire.

The end of the Middle Ages saw the introduction of certain ideological concepts whose anti-Christian content was not immediately apparent. The pagan spirit of the Renaissance progressively changed man's attitude to nature and his destiny, and thus created a new image of history. The dawn of European nationalism caused the newly created nations to interpret the past (without always being aware of it) in a way which suited their goals in the future, and not, as before, in relation to the wider concepts of the *Orbis Europaeus Christianus* of the Middle Ages. As this evolution only took place gradually, however, the two worlds continued to exist side by side for a long time. Thus, towards the beginning of the sixteenth century, we find that while Renaissance humanism did not differ so very greatly from the deep-rooted beliefs of medieval Christendom, there was, at a political level, a clash between the old concept of a community of Christian peoples and the new nationalist ideology.

Charles of Burgundy, the last universal emperor of the west and the founder of a new empire overseas, belonged so far as his beliefs and philosophy were concerned to the Middle Ages. And it was as a representative of such old traditions as those of a western empire, a cultural commonwealth of Europe and Christian unity, that he remained often incomprehensible to his contemporaries – despite the fact that his supple and inventive mind was already formulating ideas characteristic of the new age. With the development of the new *idées-forces*, later centuries were incapable of grasping Charles v's conception of the world, a conception which was in any case regarded by the advocates of the new beliefs as typifying a way of thought completely opposed to their own.

His personal stature and true role in history were forgotten. Neither the counter-reformation, nor, with greater reason, the age of enlightenment did him justice. The memory of his devoutness alone was sufficient to shock the nineteenth-century world, poised as it was on the brink of attacking heaven itself. A century which accorded the state and race divine status, and had come to regard the concept of nationhood as paramount, could have nothing in common with this man who, born in Burgundy and brought up in the Netherlands, had become King of Spain – a country whose geographical position made it the link between Europe and the other continents – and had been able to assimilate that country's vital spirit so thoroughly. Such a century could have nothing in common with a sovereign who, while wearing the German crown, maintained, as King of the Romans, continuous relations with Italy; a man, too, who spoke and wrote fluently in French, Dutch, Spanish and German, and whose political horizon extended from the Americas to the Far East; evidenced by his interest in the fate of Indians of the Andes, his relations with the 'Shah Sophi' of Persia, and his search for the mythical Prester John. In a word, it was impossible for nineteenth-century ideologists, themselves unable to see the wood for the trees, to understand this man, the breadth of whose view could not be contained within the narrow confines of a fragmented Europe.

These preliminary comments already indicate why Charles's image, so blurred during the lifetime of previous generations, has suddenly regained its identity in our age and given rise to such increasing interest on the part of numerous historians. The ideas coming to the surface in this, the second half of the twentieth century, are surprisingly allied to those problems and concepts which preoccupied Charles. In fact after three centuries of schism and division we are returning gradually to a unity of movement and thought.

The rapid, often explosive, evolution of natural science demonstrates more and more clearly every day the existence of forces beyond our material world. Science is no longer, as it was around 1860, in conflict with the idea of the existence of a creator and prime-mover of the universe. This point of view will probably lead to science realising that all branches of human knowledge are related to one another. Heisenberg, speaking of the basic equation of matter, has been the first to formulate this new unity, while on a philosophic plane, Teilhard de Chardin has already glimpsed the possibilities in his attempts to establish a synthesis between faith and evolution. The concept of a united Europe, despite difficulties, proves that in politics too a new cycle is just beginning. Thus Charles v, once regarded as the last fighter in a rearguard action, is suddenly seen to have been a forerunner. In fact, we can find at some levels of our modern spiritual, technological and sociological revolution the same situations as those which formerly preoccupied medieval Christendom. Mankind, just as in the times of the emperor of the west and his predecessors, seeks above all for peace, unity and faith.

Friedrich Nietzsche, one of the great prophets of our spiritual revolution, wrote: 'We only want to serve history in as much as it serves our life.' A new generation is unlikely to benefit from the example of a Europe which became fragmented and finally destroyed itself in a terrible internecine war, leaving behind it nothing but schisms and the pseudo-religion of nationalism. Our generation will find its historical inspiration in the unitarian concepts which (albeit, rather naively) animated men in the Middle Ages, concepts last embodied in the person, mind and political views of Charles v.

All his life, the emperor fought for a united church and his most passionate hope lay in the convening of a council to preserve religious unity. He regarded the setback sustained by this project as the most unhappy in his career, for he came to realise, once the council had been assembled, that although it might put a check on any further schisms, it would only lead to a hardening of existing theological differences, especially in northern Europe.

In our own times, the whole world has followed with passionate interest the vicissitudes of another council. The ecumenical question has stimulated the minds and conversation of believers and unbelievers alike, and further reminded us of the efforts once made by the Emperor to convene a general council of church fathers to prevent a western schism. Today, the disastrous consequences of a divided church are recognised by all intelligent thinkers who, no matter what their creed, seek to find a remedy. Furthermore, four centuries ago, Charles had already seen one of the problems which was to preoccupy delegates at the Second Vatican Council; the problem of the place of the church in the modern world and how to reconcile the unchangeable tenets of the faith with the needs of successive new generations. It was not from opportunism that the sovereign had urged the Church of Rome to undertake its own reform, for he was sincerely convinced of the necessity for a spiritual revival from within. Today, when we see theologians and bishops severely criticising certain practices of the old church, and frankly condemning a number of past errors, we realise that in his hard struggle to achieve unity (even with some of the popes) the Emperor was acting out of a truly Christian spirit in every sense of the word.

Together with ecumenicity, European unity has become the major issue of our time and here again we see how closely linked Charles's ideas are with our own struggles today. Despite existing rivalries, the emperor never attempted to subjugate France, nor to impose German, Spanish or Italian domination. In fact, it never occurred to him to prefer one of his kingdoms above another, as can be seen from the way in which, long before the end of his reign, he had apportioned them among members of his family; in this he was attempting not to conquer or to dominate, but to establish the nations in a free community of equal partners. His ultimate aim was to create an alliance of peoples who, while retaining their own individual characteristics and laws, would be linked together by a united church and a common desire to defend the west against the forces of Islam – these had already penetrated into the heart of Central Europe, while in the Mediterranean their sailors were threatening the coasts of Christian states.

There is yet a third plane on which Charles anticipated our age, and this was his policy in the newly discovered territories. Far from wanting the populations of his overseas possessions to become the victims of colonial exploitation – in the sense given to 'colonialism' by nineteenth-century imperialist expansion – he wanted to afford them the means of raising their standards to the level of those in the mother country.

For us today, two great figures of the sixteenth century stand out as an example and an inspiration – they are Charles, the last universal emperor, and Philip II, who so faithfully preserved his paternal heritage. Looking at their lives and struggles, we can understand a little how, in spite of great differences, it might be possible to establish a united Europe and world peace, together with a Christian community and harmony between all believers. It is only thus that the order will be created that will protect us against the destructive forces of materialism. For today, when the all-powerful negative symbolised by the nuclear bomb, is in our own hands, we can only defend ourselves effectively against it by our moral strength. Our survival will depend upon a spiritual revival, all the more urgent because we have long since passed the point where man's evil actions were necessarily limited by his lack of control over his environment.

The author is deeply grateful to M. Jean Mistler, of the Académie Française, who suggested the idea of this book. From first to last he has been unfailingly generous with encouragement and invaluable advice, and his kindness in reading over the manuscript was further testimony to a long-standing friendship.

OTTO VON HABSBURG

I was not invested with the imperial crown in order to rule over yet more territories, but to ensure the peace of Christendom and so to unite all forces against the Turk for the greater glory of the Christian faith.

CHARLES V

I

The Ancestral Heritage

THE HOUSE OF AUSTRIA

The child born at Ghent on 24 February 1500 to Philip, Archduke of Austria, Duke of Burgundy, and his wife Joanna of Castile, was heir to a long and historic lineage, for the House of Habsburg – or, as it was to be called more and more frequently, the House of Austria – had played a leading part in world affairs for more than two centuries.

It was in 1273 that the Electors of Germany, partly because of pressure from the Roman Curia, elected a King of the Romans in order to end the long interregnum which followed the extinction of the Hohenstaufen dynasty. Their choice fell on Count Rudolf von Habsburg, a wealthy and beneficent minor noble, who, although not of the same rank as the imperial princes, enjoyed very considerable prestige.

This founder of the Habsburg dynasty succeeded in resolving a problem generally considered almost impossible: that of establishing order within the German Empire. Germany had in fact fallen into chaos and its name had come to indicate a geographical term rather than a state. In the eighteen years of his reign, Rudolf re-established the authority of the imperial crown and then went on to found a state based on law. The decisive turning point which was to assure his success was his victory over Ottokar II of Bohemia, the most powerful Prince of the Empire who had risen in revolt against the new order. Rudolf thus not only became the first Habsburg to ascend the imperial throne, but he also acquired for his House the Duchies of Austria and Styria, annexed by Ottokar when the Babenberg dynasty died out.

Ruldolf I demonstrated in his policies the guiding principles of government to be followed by his heirs in the centuries to come, and all his actions were sanctioned by treaties and by accepted legal rights.

He aimed to expand the power of the House of Habsburg, not by wars, but by intelligent political manœuvres and, better still, by diplomatic marriages. Generous towards his vanquished enemies, he was utterly ruthless to those who opposed his legally established rule. He regarded himself as king of all his people and not merely the ruler of a certain privileged class.

Rudolf, however, failed to ensure that the imperial crown remained in the possession of the Habsburgs. He could only have achieved this had he been formally consecrated as emperor, for under medieval law no King of the Romans – that is to say the elected successor of the emperor – could be chosen by his predecessor unless the latter had actually received the crown from the hands of the ruling Pontiff. A number of unfortunate accidents prevented Rudolf from obtaining the benefit of this sacred rite – which he constantly sought – and so he was never able to assure the election of his eldest son, Duke Albrecht of Austria. On his death, therefore, the choice of a successor to the imperial throne passed once again into the hands of the elector-princes.

Fearing the much increased power of the Habsburgs, the princes elected instead Count Adolf von Nassau, a petty noble. Almost immediately, however, war broke out between Albrecht and Adolf, and the latter being killed in the ensuing battle, Albrecht, as victor, was unanimously hailed as King.

Albrecht was to rule for ten years and his reign, in which he consolidated the power and influence of the crown, was one of the best of the period. But his death was an example of immanent justice – gaining the throne by violence, he lost it at the hands of an assassin. The murder was not a political act but one carried out by his nephew, Johann of Swabia, with certain adventurers, for reasons of personal revenge; believing himself to have been a victim of his uncle's injustice he sought to claim his rights. Albrecht was murdered within sight of Habsburg, the castle on the river Aar from which the family derived its name. This assassination was one of those unforeseeable acts which sometimes lead to a major revolution in political history, and throughout the course of the history of the House of Austria there were to be many such sudden and unexpected changes of fortune. But despite these moments of crisis, the succeeding generations always reverted sooner or later to traditional policies and managed to continue – sometimes in very different circumstances – the work of the man whose fate had left it uncompleted.

After Albrecht's death, the Electors chose as his successor the representative of another family, Count Henry of Luxembourg, who was to become known to history as Dante's emperor. This great Italian poet, the devoted partisan of the Ghibellini, dedicated all his genius and talent to this new king. But Dante's dream was not to be realised. Henry, although he succeeded in being crowned by the Pope, died too soon. It was rumoured that he had been poisoned, but such accusations were common in the Middle Ages and must not be treated too seriously; the sudden death of a political figure in those days, when medical diagnosis, then so primitive, failed to reveal the cause, was all too frequently attributed to poison.

The elections which followed led to a stalemate, and for years afterwards Albrecht's son, Friedrich of Austria, disputed the crown with his cousin, Ludwig of Bavaria. Finally, in 1322, Ludwig defeated his rival in the battles of Ampfing and Mühldorf and Friedrich became his prisoner. But in spite of this success, Ludwig was unable to resolve the innumerable problems that beset the empire; moreover, he was quite unable to force Leopold, Friedrich's younger brother, to acknowledge the royal prerogative of the House of Wittelsbach.

Friedrich himself offered to go to Austria to negotiate a peace, but, having been unable to win over Leopold, was forced to return to Germany and become a prisoner once again. Eventually the dispute was ended by a compromise, rare in the annals of history, with Ludwig accepting his former enemy and prisoner as co-regent. All acts of state, it was decided, were to be signed by both parties. This hybrid formula did not last long, for Friedrich died soon after, thus causing the House of Habsburg to lose the imperial crown once again.

When Ludwig died, another member of the Luxembourg dynasty ascended the throne. Under the title of Charles IV, Charles of Bohemia was to bring new glories to the crown and succeed in establishing his House as a strong power in the eastern part of central Europe. Until 1437 the crown of the Holy Roman Empire – with only one short interruption – remained in the possession of the House of Luxembourg. The Habsburgs seemed, once and for all, to have been driven back to the south eastern confines of Germanic Europe. Their sphere of influence in the Swiss states was weakened by continual struggles against the Confederates. One of the Dukes of Austria, Leopold III, even died in battle at Sempach, fighting against the Swiss peasants.

But in spite of these reverses and through all these difficult years,

3

the House of Habsburg never ceased to pave the way for its future by wise and patient policies. The most important figure of this period was Rudolf IV, son of Jeanne, an Alsatian heiress of the Counts of Pfirt, and son-in-law of Charles IV. In spite of his relatively short reign, Rudolf laid the foundations for the establishment of a great Austrian power in the Danube basin, and it was he, moreover, who conceived the idea of an Austrian State. This highly intelligent and ambitious ruler, strongly imbued with a sense of mission, founded the University of Vienna, an act which earned him the name of 'Rudolf the Founder'. He also laid the first stone of the Cathedral of St Stephen, which remains to this day the true symbol of Austria. Rudolf introduced what were almost revolutionary reforms for those times into government administration and public finance. As a politician he was extremely able and he concluded a treaty of succession with the House of Luxembourg which was to affect the course of history after his death. Thanks to him, Austria was finally assured a specially privileged place at the heart of the empire. While we must not forget that Rudolf's claims were derived from forged documents, we see that their consequences were nonetheless considerable. The *Priviligium Maius* not only constitutes a major political and diplomatic landmark in the closing years of the Middle Ages, a period when men were not over-scrupulous in their use of dubious historical 'facts' and debatable titles; but it also came to be regarded as the *Magna Carta* of Austrian independence. Later, a successor of Rudolf, the Emperor Friedrich III, ratified and incorporated this document into the legal code. Rudolf IV also succeeded in placing on top of the princely Austrian hat a symbolic crest, resembling a crown, which gave the dynasty a position analogous to that of the Elector-Princes. He was also the first to use the title Archduke, later carried by all the Habsburg princes, a title recognised by European dynastic protocol as superior in rank to that of any other uncrowned prince or ruler.

In spite of these political successes, the most important of which was the union of Austria with the Tyrol, the power of the Habsburgs was weakened from time to time, due to the practice of successively partitioning the dynastic domains between all the sons of reigning dukes, who all enjoyed equal rights under medieval law. There was also a period when the House of Austria was broken up into three ruling lines. The division can be understood in geographical terms. On the one hand there were the so-called Austrian Principalities of Upper and

4

Lower Austria, which together with the Duchies of Styria and Carinthia formed what was known as Inner-Oesterreich, and on the other, the Tyrol and the southern German possessions which extended as far as Alsace, and was termed Vorder-Oesterreich, or Further or Outer Austria.

Attempts to limit the inconvenience caused by these policies of partition were not lacking; general acknowledgement of the primacy of the senior branch of the House was recognised more than once. Finally the disappearance of the collateral branches left the door open to reunification. The so-called Austrian branch died out in 1457, the Tyrolean in 1496, leaving only the Styrian line. Moreover since 1439, the imperial crown had been secured by this Styrian branch after Albrecht of Austria had worn it for less than two years.

Albrecht, the second emperor of that name, was the son-in-law of Sigismund, last of the Luxembourg line of emperors. He had inherited under the will of the latter and by the earlier treaties of Rudolf IV, the crowns of Hungary and Bohemia. For the first time in history, the three kingdoms of the future Danubian monarch – Bohemia, Austria and Hungary, with the exception of the Duchies of Styria, Carinthia and Sudentenland – were united under one ruler. It now seemed that the large scale plans conceived by Ottokar II of Bohemia and Charles IV of Luxembourg were at last to be realised. It was then that Albrecht II, that dynamic and energetic monarch, died in an epidemic while fighting the Turks in Hungary.

Soon after his death his widow gave birth to a son, known to his contemporaries as Ladislaus Posthumus. Friedrich V of Styria, elected emperor under the name of Friedrich III, was not strong enough to maintain his rights as guardian of this young man, and when Ladislaus died unexpectedly at the age of seventeen, the Habsburgs lost the crowns of Bohemia and Hungary. The great Danubian empire started to break up. At Prague, as at Eszertgom, national kings mounted the throne, but none was successful in founding a dynasty. Towards the end of the fifteenth century, Bohemia and Hungary were reunited under a king of the Polish house of Jagellon, but were in fact, governed by a feudal oligarchy. The bourgeoisie suffered cruelly at the hands of the nobility, the legal system was disrupted and the State had no authority. It was this chaos, amounting almost to anarchy, that gave the increasingly powerful Turks an opportunity to obtain a foothold in Central Europe, and was to be the major problem for generations to come, a problem which was to be one of the main concerns of Charles v.

The imperial crown had passed from Albrecht II to Friedrich of Styria because the elector-princes regarded him as weak and easy to manipulate. But Friedrich in fact showed himself to be not only one of the most interesting of all the long line of Habsburgs, but also of all the rulers of the late Middle Ages. He combined in his character a lack of decision, almost amounting to sloth, and yet at other times showed an indomitable will and remarkable constancy in the defence of his own rights. In spite of the procrastination which so exasperated his associates, the emperor always seemed to know the exact moment and hour which called for action. At such times he astonished everyone by the quickness of his decisions. When a struggle was inevitable, he showed great courage and indefatigable energy – he seemed suddenly to be completely transformed, only to sink again into a state of lethargy once victory was attained.

When success in practical ventures was denied him, he consoled himself by his complete confidence in Divine Providence, which, according to him, had entrusted the business of ruling the world to the House of Habsburg. He embellished buildings and documents with five cabalistic letters – A E I O U – to which various interpretations have been given, some of which have been handed down to today. These five letters may stand for *Austria erit in orbe ultima*, or again *Austria extenditur in orbem universum*. Friedrich III loved to collect precious stones and talismans and had a pronounced taste for the fine arts. Whenever possible, he was a generous patron of the arts and he was well-read, even erudite, as can be seen from his correspondence with the humanist, Aeneus Sylvius Piccolomini, later to become Pope Pius II. Moreover, Friedrich was fully cognisant with most of the disciplines of his time, and also showed a great interest in occult sciences. He enjoyed good company and having selected his guests with great care, he often stayed up late at night with them discussing scientific matters and public affairs. On these occasions he showed himself a brilliant conversationalist, for he was remarkably well-informed and possessed an accurate knowledge of all the most important aspects of European politics.

During certain periods of his life, Friedrich was reduced to such financial straits that he was without the means to maintain a court. He then lived as a guest in the castles of his Styrian vassals and paid his debts with bills of exchange, often of doubtful validity. So seldom did he visit the 'real' Germany, that the elector-princes seriously considered deposing him, as they had deposed Wenceslas of Luxembourg in 1400.

However, towards the end of his reign an unprecedented event took place: it was not left to the emperor to choose a successor, but the Imperial elector-princes themselves insisted on electing a successor in good time to insure the continuity of the line. Thus Maximilian, Friedrich's only son, was elected King of the Romans almost against the wishes of his father. Friedrich guarded what remained of his power jealously. He had a profound sense of the pre-eminence and authority of the imperial crown, and for this reason he never hesitated to spend lavishly, in order to invest himself as the highest representative of Christendom, with all possible pomp. When he attended the Diet of Augsburg, accompanied by his young son, the brilliance of his train made a profound impression on the burghers of the city and on contemporary chroniclers. Wherever he went in public, despite his habitual modesty, he appeared as the Universal Monarch dreamed of by Dante. He was moreover, extremely popular; like most of his predecessors, he had the ability to speak to the common people in their own language. As an old man he visited Nuremberg, where he invited all the children to the fairground, gave them cakes and sweets and chatted to them for a long while, and the image of this benevolent old patriarch remained engraved for ever in the memory of the inhabitants of the city.

The emperor had chosen a wife from a distant country, Eleanor of Portugal, and he was married in Rome, where he was able to receive the imperial crown. He was in fact the last Holy Roman Emperor to visit the Eternal City. Eleanor presented him with a son, baptised under the name of Maximilian, but she was never able to live in the inclement climate of Austria, particularly that of Styria. She suffered greatly from homesickness and longed for the sunshine of her native country and the broad horizons of the Atlantic seaboard. Moreover, she could scarcely abide the poverty of her husband's court and the perpetual dangers of internal disorders and the ever-present Turkish menace.

At the beginning of his reign, Friedrich had been obliged to defend himself against his brother Albrecht and the burghers of Vienna, who laid siege to his Hofburg residence. The rebels offered the empress and the young prince a safe conduct to freedom but this the emperor refused

7

as being contrary to the traditions of his family and his code of honour. There is a legendary account of how finally the rebels allowed eggs and white bread to be introduced to the besieged garrison in order to feed the imperial child. The unshakeable confidence of the emperor was finally justified. At the last moment he was always saved, even in the most desperate situations. Of all the emperors, Friedrich's reign was the longest. He governed for fifty-three years – long enough to justify the claim of historians that he defeated all his enemies by surviving them.

On his death, in 1493, the position of the dynasty had radically altered, and the miraculous future of the House of Austria was already mapped. His old adversary, Matthias Corvin of Hungary was dead, his son Maximilian, King of the Romans, had driven back the Hungarians from the walls of Vienna and had even extended his frontiers beyond the St Stephen's kingdom. Even if Maximilian had not yet won the imperial crown, he was now assured of its inheritance by right of treaty. The continuity of the House of Habsburg as head of the Empire was guaranteed. But most important of all, Maximilian's Burgundian marriage had extended the Habsburg domains as far as the North Sea and the English Channel. By his union with one of the wealthiest heiresses in Europe, the axis of the Habsburg dynasty was removed from the Danube basin to the region between the rivers Meuse and Escaut. Vast perspectives were thus opened up

So we arrive at a turning point in history. A dynasty whose very existence had seemed threatened in the middle of the fifteenth century, now found itself, a generation later, in a position to rule the whole world. Of course Friedrich III could not foresee the importance of Christopher Columbus's voyage, but it is interesting to note that the discovery of the New World in 1492 took place during the reign of the old Emperor, already a legendary figure for most of his subjects.

Friedrich's tomb in the cathedral of St Stephen in Vienna, a masterpiece of Renaissance art, affords some idea of the true grandeur and dignity which surrounded this monarch in spite of the numerous setbacks to which he was subjected. These outward signs, however much they may be criticised, nevertheless represent a historical fact. Indeed, in this long reign we find the origins of an evolution in European politics which was not to become apparent until long after the death of the old monarch.

Maximilian's character was very different from that of his father.

All they had in common were extraordinarily well-developed powers of imagination and a love of art and pomp and ceremony. Unlike Friedrich III, Maximilian was always quick to make up his mind but he lacked constancy of purpose and changed his ideas easily when new and more tempting projects were presented to his fertile imagination. Even in his old age, he was always receptive to new ideas and adventurous schemes and, indeed, everything that the life and art of his times afforded. Maximilian could justly take as his motto Ulrich von Hutten's exclamation, 'Quel siècle, quelle science, quelle joie de vivre!' (What a century, what knowledge, what a wonderful life!)

The Emperor Maximilian had warm-hearted instincts and was noted for his physical courage. These two qualities led him into the most risky adventures, so much so, that his people and writers of the time bestowed on him the flattering title of 'last of the knights'.

His life often poses difficult problems for the historian. Opinions concerning his policies and his work are often at variance, but as far as his personality is concerned there is little argument. He was a sympathetic figure. Popular with all classes of society, and of all the Emperors since Rudolf I, the most loved, his name became a legend after his death. Stories concerning him are as numerous as they are flattering, such as the account of his miraculous escape from the Martinswand near Innsbruck. The emperor, while out hunting had become lost among steep mountain cliffs. Unable either to advance or retreat, all seemed lost when suddenly a youth appeared, who guided him down to safety by an unknown path only to disappear again at the foot of the rock.

By his marriage to Marie of Burgundy, the House of Austria became the House of Austria and Burgundy. This change did not merely entail a geographic displacement of the seat of power of the Habsburg dynasty, but the inheritance by the House of Habsburg of the ancient traditions of Burgundy. The language factor was also important since Maximilian already used French in his correspondence and in conversation with his children. This factor is reflected in the names given to Maximilian's son and grandson. Philip of Burgundy was the first Habsburg to be given the name of one of the great kings of ancient times, a name pleasing to the French and Burgundians. This name was to be perpetuated in the Spanish line of the Habsburgs. The son of Philip was christened Charles in memory of his paternal grandfather, Charles the Bold. This first name, traditional in the House of Valois,

9

and which perpetuates that of the earliest imperial ruler, was thus adopted by the House of Habsburg. This particular Charles, although the first of the name among the Dukes of Burgundy and Archdukes of Austria, is known to history as the Fifth, or Charles Quint, and in Spain as Carlos Quinto. Charles often emphasized the fact that he was a member of the royal family of France, and the tone and context of his words make it obvious that he was prompted by a genuine and profound sentiment, since the Burgundian Netherlands, where he was born, and Burgundy itself, lie between the two great eastern and western Frankish States – Gaul and Germany – and is a living synthesis of the physical and moral characteristics of two great western peoples. It would be impossible to understand the character and political dreams of Charles v if one were to disregard the influence of his maternal Burgundian background.

THE BURGUNDIAN FACTION

The great partition of the Empire effected at Verdun in the year 843 by the grandsons of Charlemagne and the sons of Louis the Pious, created a third state between the two Frankish Empires which at first sight seems artificial. To begin with, this state did not even have a name of its own, but was referred to by the name of its ruler – Lotharingia, or the Kingdom of Lothar – a name which was retained later, although it applied only to the territories tributary to the eldest son of Louis i.

This newly created state was very much a country of transition. From the mouth of the Meuse and the Rhine, it extended along the valley of the Meuse and the Saône and thence down the Rhône valley as far as the Mediterranean. It not only included ancient Burgundy which from the time of the Merovingians formed part of the Frankish Empire, but it also embraced Aquitaine in the south-west and Neustria, between the Loire and the Escaut; and in the east, the Germanic part of the Empire, at that time known as Austrasia.

The geographic name of Burgundy shifts and changes in the course of history, and does not by any means correspond exactly to territories occupied by Germanic and Burgundian peoples. Burgundians appeared for the first time on the Middle Rhine, and their passage there left a lasting impression. Later we find them beyond the Juras (Porte de Bourgogne) in what was formerly Gaul and Helvetia and in Roman

Narbonnensis, which later became Provence. In Provence, a Burgundian kingdom was founded, later divided into two parts – Upper Burgundy, which extended as far as Lake Leman, and Lower Burgundy, known as the Kingdom of Arles. This kingdom was, with Germany and Italy, the third partner in the Roman Empire. It became reattached to the imperial crown at the time of the Saliens and Hohenstaufen dynasty by rather tenuous links. By degrees, as the power of the Emperors declined, the Kings of France imposed their authority on the former Burgundian territories. During this period the name Burgundy was also applied to the regions further north. What later became the Duchy of Burgundy, one of the richest and most important fiefs of the French Crown, no longer possessed any territory on the Mediterranean but held lands situated between the Jura and the sources of the Seine, and it is this territory to which the name Burgundy is still applied.

Long before the time of Charles v, this Burgundy was again partitioned into the French Duchy of Burgundy and Franche-Comté, which became a fief of the German crown.

When the Dukes, who also held Franche-Comté in fief from Germany, acquired vast territories in the Low Countries, the name Burgundy was further extended to include the regions of the Escaut, Meuse and Rhine and thereafter the political and residential centre of the Ducal power was to be found in Brabant and Flanders. When the House of Austria appeared on the Burgundian scene, the designation 'Burgundy' applied less to the sloping vineyards of the Saône, than to the rich provinces on the coasts of the North Sea, and only the funerary crypt of the dukes remained in traditional territory – in the Charter-house of Dijon. It was only when the reign of the Habsburgs in the Low Countries had come to an end, that the name Burgundy was once more applied exclusively to the former Duchy.

What was the real reason for the importance of Burgundy; why was it termed the Middle Empire? The answer is to be found in its geographical position. It encompasses the lands on either side of the great road that runs from the North Sea to the Mediterranean; to the east it is bordered by the high chain of the Alps which separates the Germans from the Latins, and to the west by the Massif Central, both considerable natural barriers. Between these frontiers lies a country crossed by numerous rivers which made the Burgundian route one of the most convenient and therefore one of the busiest of thoroughfares; ships could navigate the Rhine, the Meuse and the Moselle, and, further south, beyond the watershed, the Saône and Rhône.

But apart from these waterways, the configuration of the country itself made it the natural route between western and central Europe. Whoever controlled this country, which extended from Maestricht to Liège and thence to Metz, Verdun and Lyons and as far south as Avignon and Arles, was in a position to play a dominant role in Europe, provided always he was not caught between the pincers of France and Germany. Throughout history, these two countries each in turn occupied or annexed the territories of the former Lotharingia, but every time, independent status was once more restored to this much disputed territory. Sometimes these two great neighbours had the wisdom to create a buffer zone and retreat behind their own frontiers to preserve the peace. Sometimes a third power, on establishing its influence over the Low Countries, attempted to establish a sphere of influence between these two power blocs, a policy followed by Spain and later by England.

From an economic and strategic point of view, nothing indicates more clearly the crucial importance of these territories, comprising Lotharingia, the Netherlands and Burgundy, than the fact that nearly every military campaign that has changed the destiny of Europe has been fought between the Meuse and the Saône, the English Channel and the Porte de Bourgogne. This has been a constant historical factor, and applies as much to Caesar's conquests of the German tribes and the Gauls, as to the decisive battles of the Second World War. Burgundy and the Low Countries, together with the plains of Lombardy and Bohemia and the country round Vienna, have always been among the great battlefields of Europe.

As soon as the Habsburgs set foot in Burgundy they seemed to have been carried away by its dynamic or *genius loci*. They not only inherited immense wealth and vast resources of power and cultural riches, but also a legacy of almost incessant wars with the Kings of France. The French kings were obliged to maintain control over this central region if they wished to preserve their own sovereignty; and by the end of the fourteenth century, England, too, had entered the power struggle. For her, the Low Countries constituted a bridgehead to the Continent which was essential for the protection of the British Isles.

But the vast territories of the Middle Empire were not only of military significance; they were above all the cradle of great civilisations.

Whether this was because here was the meeting ground of many races who mingled and benefited from the exchange, or whether the country itself was possessed of some intrinsic and mysterious virtue, as we seem to find in other lands where ancient cultures have flourished without any logical explanation, is difficult to decide.

Whatever the reasons, this border country between the western empire of the Franks, which was almost entirely Latin in character after the ninth century, and the eastern empire which remained Germanic, played a dominant role in the development of the languages, arts and literature of all Europe. Since the time of the Romans, there were to be found in this region important cultural centres, like Treves in the valley of the Moselle, while under the Merovingians and Carolingians, the brilliant reputation of such cities as Rheims, Verdun, Metz and Strasburg far exceeded their immediate provincial importance. It should be noted that the Carolingian dynasty itself (and many others) was Burgundian in origin since it was founded in the town of Heristal in the Liège area. It was at Strasburg, in the presence of their respective armies, that the sons of Louis the Pious swore a mutual oath of peace, and so that all men present could testify to this solemn covenant, Ludwig the German swore in French, and Charles the Bald in German. The text of this oath is linguistically one of the most important of the Middle Ages and is of primary value in the study of the origin of the German language. Most recent research into the subject suggests that it is written in the official administrative language of the Empire, and that the word *deut* (diet or assembly) refers in fact to the army of the Franks. The vigorous exchange of intellectual and cultural ideas between French and Germanic peoples was to lead to some remarkable achievements throughout Burgundy, using the word in its widest geographical sense.

Most of the great convents built during the time of the reform of the monasteries are to be found in Lotharingian territory. Albert Brinkmann, the historian of German civilisation, rightly stresses that the artistic forms which originated with the Cluniac movement attained a greater perfection in Burgundy than anywhere else. In his writings he traces the artistic evolution which culminated in the Gothic style. This reached its apogee in the region between Rheims and Paris, spread both east and west of the Middle Empire, and became an essential element in European culture.

It was in Mediterranean Burgundy that the art of the troubadours

13

was born. From there the art travelled northwards and also eastwards where, particularly at the end of the twelfth and beginning of the thirteenth centuries, it developed into the German *Minnesang*. The troubadour poetry was to have a decisive influence on much of medieval thought and in particular on the western concept of chivalry.

During the thirteenth century, a specifically urban culture replaced the knightly arts and poetry, a culture which also had its origins in Burgundy and lasted longer there than anywhere else. The wealthy merchant cities of the Low Countries constituted a financial and economic basis for an intensely intellectual mode of life.

With the foundation of the Habsburg Empire, Burgundian culture, already flourishing in the fourteenth century, spread throughout the whole world, even as far as South America. It was a happy synthesis of the elegance and refinement which marks the end of the age of chivalry and the new and vigorous spirit of the developing towns. Johan Huizinga in defining this period called it 'The autumn of the Middle Ages', a phrase which well suggests the abundant fruits of the period, together with the brilliance of autumnal colours, while hinting of the melancholy associated with the close of day.

The evolution of Burgundian chivalry was the result of a socio-economic phenomenon peculiar to this region. Elsewhere in Europe the nobles lived apart from the cities, shut away in their fortified castles, and the development of a monetary economy in Germany and in France from the beginning of the thirteenth century hastened their impoverishment and decline. An example of this can be seen in the German *Raubritter*, the robber-barons of the empire. But in Burgundy on the other hand the nobles were able to combine their aristocratic 'castle' existence with the culture of the cities, and they achieved a fusion of the two ways of life unique in Europe.

This typically Burgundian development was crowned by the foundation of the Order of the Golden Fleece. It was a knight, Philippe de Mézières, who first proposed the formation of a fraternity of knights – to be called 'The Passion of Christ' – whose aim would be the reviving of the ideal of the crusades. In 1396, after the defeat of the Christians in the battle of Nicopolos, he wrote to the Duke of Burgundy, Philip the Bold, inviting him to place himself at the head of this new order. Today on re-reading the texts of Philippe de Mézières, one discovers ideas and formulas similar to those which were in fact to be incorporated in the statutes of the Order of the Golden Fleece. The Duke was fired with enthusiasm for de Mézières' proposal, but death prevented him from pursuing it. John the Fearless in his turn took up the idea, and was on the point of completing arrangements for the formation of the Order when he was assassinated on 10 September 1419 on the bridge of Montereau.

Philip the Good, John's successor, was also fired by the ideals of the crusaders, and he at once despatched his knights to the Turkish Empire to seek out its weaknesses. Among all the Christian rulers, Philip the Good was the only one who attempted to help the Byzantine emperor in the eastern Empire's hour of agony. His fleet forced the Muslims to raise the siege of Rhodes, participated actively in the defence of the Dardanelles and even ventured beyond the Bosphorus into the Black Sea. It is not surprising, therefore, that it should be Philip who would realise the dream of Philippe de Mézières; for he hoped both that the glory and prestige of the Order would exalt the status of the Duke of Burgundy, and that he might himself become leader of a crusade.

The religious basis of the Order is shown by the inscription on the duke's tomb at Dijon.

POUR MAINTENIR L'EGLISE QUI EST DE DIEU MAISON
J'AI MIS SUS LE NOBLE ORDRE QU'ON NOMME LA TOISON.

The act of foundation itself, after so long a period of gestation, was a masterpiece of Burgundian diplomacy. Burgundy at the time was allied with England against the King of France, and the Duke of Bedford the English regent, wished to bestow the Order of the Garter on Duke Philip. But Philip felt that this gesture was taking things too far and one to be avoided without hurting his ally's feelings. It was for this reason that on his marriage to Isabella of Portugal, in January 1430 he hurried forward the foundation of the Order of the Golden Fleece, for he had managed to insert into its statutes an interdict forbidding any of its members to accept any other order established by a foreign ruler. About two years later, on 27 November 1431, the Golden Fleece was born, when for the first time the solemn chapter of the twenty-four knights nominated by the duke was convened at Lille. Founded originally with the idea of leading a crusade, the Order was soon to realise that such enterprises were a thing of the past; but on the other hand it found that it had a part to play within the framework of European politics that largely compensated for the loss of its original purpose. Thus during the last years of the Dukedom of Burgundy, the

Golden Fleece helped considerably to enhance the prestige of the country. As sovereign head of the Order, the duke was equal in rank to any of the great monarchs of the west, while the personal oath, which tied the knights to their founder, both reaffirmed their allegiance to Burgundy and established fruitful links beyond its frontiers. In fact, from the moment the order was established, knights from all over western Christendom were admitted to the Order. This oath also included a clause which was unique: the duke could not declare war without the consent of the Chapter. The supreme will of the state was thus subordinate to a supra-national organisation. One could hope therefore that the needs of all Christians would in future prevail over purely personal ambitions and that force would only be employed in a just cause. If in practice this clause was sometimes ignored, the idea in itself was of exceptional value.

On a more worldly level, the important festivals in Burgundy were generally associated with great tournaments characteristic of Burgundian chivalry. Although popular among all the nobility, these tournaments entailed serious sacrifices on their part, for not only were horses lost in the lists, but noble families often had occasion to mourn the loss of human lives. The proud and courageous Burgundian knights were eager to pit their strength against the Germans and French, and an incident during the Diet of Worms illustrates the kind of situation that this provoked. There, in front of the whole assembly, one Burgundian challenged all the German nobles and knights present. The Emperor Maximilian himself took up the challenge, and in an unforgettable hand-to-hand combat he managed to vanquish his vassal. It is probable, moreover, that it was in fact in Burgundy that Maximilian trained himself to become one of the most redoubtable jousters of his time. When later Charles v came to Spain with a numerous train of Burgundians, national xenophobia caused the Spaniards to turn against his followers but their prowess in tournaments gained them the respect of the Castilians, all of whom were warriors at heart. This provided the foundation for a stable and amicable relationship between the nobles of Spain and the Low Countries, a relationship which was to play an important part in the life of the Emperor.

At the close of the tournaments sumptuous banquets were given for all contenders. Unlike the customs of ancient chivalry, these Burgundian feasts combined the pleasures of the table with artistic and cultural displays. The spirit which pervades the 'Autumn of the Middle Ages' is evident in the culinary masterpieces and in the way the dishes were presented. The trade of the Low Countries ensured that Burgundian cooks were supplied with rare ingredients and spices from India and the Orient and just as the verses recited or sung were concerned with legends of antiquity or of early Christian times, so tradition and poetic fantasy were the favourite topics of conversation among the guests.

So in Burgundy we find united the three elements essential to the development of a truly cultured society – a sense of fundamental values, idealism, and sources of knowledge which were an integral part of the life of the community.

The Order of the Golden Fleece and its emblems associated with the Argonauts reflects thus the spirit of the period, a spirit which might be termed 'romantic'. The idea of a new crusade against the Infidel was always in the air. It had never entirely disappeared in Europe, but it was given new impetus at the beginning of the fifteenth century as a result of the growing Turkish menace in the East. The Turks had annihilated the Serbs at Kossova on the so-called Plain of Blackbirds in 1389, and almost in one blow the Balkan peninsula had been conquered. Then in 1396, the forces of Sigismund, King of Hungary, later to become the German Emperor, were crushed at the battle of Nicopolis on the Danube, and he himself only just escaped capture. A large number of knights drawn from the most illustrious families of western Europe had followed this king on his progress. The result of this battle demonstrably proved that western methods of fighting were no match for the new military art already practised by the Turks and had a profound influence on later developments of the period. Maximilian I and his grandson Charles V both profited by the lesson of Nicopolis. It forced them to create a modern army combining the virtues of chivalry with the requirements of a new epoch.

The Burgundian knights, however rich, courageous, ambitious and pious they might be, were never able to realise their dream of a holy war against the Turks; neither was the Order of the Golden Fleece any more successful in this respect. The only significant victory in the fifteenth century won by the forces of the west over Islam came at the battle of Belgrade 1456. This miraculous feat was accomplished by an army more suitably termed a horde, whose tactics were ludicrously at variance with the classic principles of warfare, and whose triumph was due to two things: the enthusiasm and almost fanatical faith inspired by the preaching of that great holy orator John of Capristan, and the ability of John Hunyadi.

The knights in their Burgundian castles still continued to talk of crusades, and after the fall of Constantinople in 1453 they took a collective oath to reconquer the Imperial Byzantine city. They never set out. Another dramatic event soon took place, however, which was to teach them the limitations of their armed forces; this was the crushing defeat of Charles the Rash by the Swiss. Maximilian on the other hand owed his victory over the armies of Louis xi at the Battle of Guinegatte in 1479 to a combination of knightly courage and modern tactics. In dismounting from his horse before the battle, an act which obliged every great noble to fight on foot with him among the infantry, he gave the foot soldiers the leadership they had up to now lacked; by his example he stressed the importance of a force which although despised by the knights was to become the ruling factor in battle.

The Emperor Maximilian was still a young man when, at the side of his father, he first met Charles the Rash and his Burgundian knights, and he was hardly more mature when he was summoned to Burgundy by his fiancée Marie. Charles v on the other hand, like his father Philip, was a Burgundian from infancy. He took part in the great processions of the knights, in their hunts, tournaments and feasts and spoke the same language as this cultivated élite. But more important from a political point of view, he shared their ideas and saw the world from the perspective of the Low Countries, where the great lines of power stretching from Paris and London, the Lower Rhine and Austria, all crossed.

From the beginning of its history until our own times Burgundy has preserved its individuality. It was an almost unique political phenomenon. Its frontiers bore little relation to geographical facts; its territories were scattered. For simplification's sake it can be described as being divided into two main regions, separated by the Duchy of Lorraine. Compared with other states at the end of the Middle Ages, Burgundy retained a certain degree of homogeneity, but the legal nature and origins of the titles, on which the rule of the dukes was based were extremely diverse. In 1363, the King of France, Jean ii, known as John the Good, had invested one of his sons, Philip the Bold, with the Dukedom of Burgundy. The Dukes of Burgundy thus formed a collateral branch of the French royal dynasty and were regarded as the first

18

vassals of the crown. This placed them on the same rank as the Kings of England, who held vast territories in fief from the King of France and were therefore tied to him by feudal bonds although in their role as sovereigns of their own country they were his equals. This situation, already complicated enough, was made even more difficult by the English aspirations to the Crown of France, an aspiration which was one of the determining causes of the Hundred Years' War.

Soon the Duchy of Burgundy in turn was to threaten the House of Valois. Philip the Bold, by his marriage with the daughter of the Count of Flanders and by his acquisition of Franche-Comté, a fief of the German Crown, had considerably enlarged his territorial dominions which now extended from the Channel coast to Lake Leman. The almost continuous rivalry between the elder and the cadet branches of the French royal dynasty developed into open hostility in 1407, when John of Burgundy murdered the Duke of Orleans, brother of the King of France. Common interests led to an alliance between England and Burgundy, and we find this pro-English policy becoming the 'leit-motiv' of Burgundian politics. The pattern was repeated during the reign of Charles v, in particular in the policy pursued by his aunt Marguerite of Austria as regent of the Low Countries.

In 1415 the Duke of Burgundy recognised Henry v of England as the lawful King of France; and then a few years later John the Fearless (1371–1419) was assassinated on the bridge of Montereau on his way to negotiate peace with the Dauphin. It is almost certain that the French prince was not responsible for the outrage committed by his followers, but nevertheless, the tension between the Houses of Valois and Burgundy, which had assumed the proportions of a vendetta since the assassination of the Duke of Orléans, was naturally aggravated by this renewed bloodshed. It was not until sixteen years later, in 1435, that a peace treaty was signed at Arras between Charles vii of France and Philip the Good.

The terms of this treaty were favourable to Burgundy. The most important concession obtained by the Duke was that large portions of his territories were freed from the suzerainty of the kings of France. Disputes over the legality of these concessions were later to play a major role in the conflicts between the Emperor Maximilian and Louis xi, and between Charles v and François i.

The greatest expansion of Burgundian territories, the high point in its history, occurred during the reign of Charles the Rash (1433–77).

The Duchy of Burgundy – if one can apply the term to all the territories ruled by the Burgundian dynasty – was then composed of fiefs of the crown of France, with their centre at Dijon; and of Flanders, Artois and Picardy, including the towns of Arras, Lille, Ypres, Ghent and Bruges. In addition to these, were added the German fiefs – Franche-Comté, with Besançon; and Brabant, together with Brussels, Louvain, Malines and Antwerp; and a further area which stretched as far as Bois-le-Duc on the Meuse, incorporating Hainault and the regions of Mons, Valenciennes, Namur, Luxemburg and Limburg. North of these territories, in the Rhine Delta, the Habsburgs also inherited from the Wittelsbachs the lands of Holland and Zealand, including the cities of Amsterdam, Leyden, Delft, Middelburg and the Hague. These territories were subdivided into ecclesiastical estates belonging to wealthy monasteries such as those of Cambrai, Liège and Utrecht, from which the Duke of Burgundy received considerable feudal dues.

A special case was that of the County of Guelder – or Gelderland – which still managed to retain its territorial independence although the ruling house was intimately connected with the Duchy of Burgundy. Later, under the Habsburgs, however, Gelderland was forcibly incorporated with the Netherlands.

The difficulties inevitable in such a maze of legal rights and titles are highlighted by the curious case of Flanders, which even after French suzerainty had been abolished by the Treaty of Arras, continued to retain the Parliament of Paris as its supreme court, for almost a century, an anomaly which was brought to an end by Charles v.

It would be futile to attempt to understand the essence of the Burgundy of those days in terms of nineteenth-century nationalism. The lack of territorial unity and the great difference on a constitutional level, might have made such an amalgamation of territories ungovernable, but there were certain links visible and invisible, which made Burgundy a perfectly viable political entity.

First and foremost, there were the dynastic ties. The personal loyalty of vassals to their sovereign, which was the foundation of the medieval political structure, and which existed long before the modern conception of sovereignty ever made its appearance, still played a major role in Burgundy. It is only towards the end of the fourteenth century that we find in Europe territorial loyalties gradually superseding personal allegiances. The Burgundian rulers seem to have understood this development at a very early date, and therefore created a powerful and modern administration as a link between the central government and its domains. From the beginning, the government was concerned to retain its homogeneity, a task made all the easier since most of the government officials came from the same territory: Franche-Comté. What is more, the House of Burgundy was able to appoint its numerous bastards – who in the Middle Empire, just as in France, enjoyed positions of great prestige – to episcopal sees, from which they were able to render important services to the dynasty. We thus find David and Philip of Burgundy, the illegitimate sons of Philip the Good, becoming bishops of Utrecht, while the Duke's brother, John of Burgundy, was himself bishop of Cambrai, and had all his children appointed to benefices. This custom was to change with the arrival of the Habsburgs. Their bastards, who anyway were less numerous than those of the Valois and Bourbons, were not given positions of importance even when they were assured of their future by being elected prebendaries.

Another important element in the Burgundian political system was the clergy. Their viewpoint and social position was similar to those of government officials whose legal constitution had much in common with that of the churchman. The clerics were interested in the stability of the state from a spiritual as well as a material point of view. This was particularly true of the clergy of the Netherlands. Modern and profoundly reformist in their thought, they were well aware that a great state containing wealthy merchant cities offered a much more fertile field for the development of new religious ideas than a small self-contained country, provincial in its outlook. This was particularly so in the way the growth of humanism and the spread of culture gave the country a sense of its place in history, even while the state itself remained undeveloped.

By degrees the culture of the nobility spread to the cities, influencing and generally acting as a stimulant to their inhabitants. The new school of painting thus had its first triumphs in Brussels, Bruges and Ghent. From the very outset, this school produced masterpieces such as the creations of Memling, a Rhenish artist who had settled in Flanders. Literary works at the beginning of the sixteenth century, for example the *Miroir des Dames* by the Chevalier Claude Bouton, published in 1520, were still written in the style of the court, but printing was soon to alter the whole character of literature. In such an atmosphere, where a community of thought prevailed in surroundings of freedom, humanism was bound to triumph and forge cultural links much stronger than any provided by purely political ideologies. It is therefore not surprising that German humanism found its finest flowering in the Low Countries as evinced by Erasmus of Rotterdam, one of Charles v's most respected councillors. Erasmus is a prime example of the humanist theologian, a man who was at one and the same time priest, teacher, writer, and politician (in the best sense of the word): in short, an *uomo universale*.

Fortunately, for the House of Habsburg, the betrothal of Maximilian to the heiress of Burgundy was already a *fait accompli* when Charles the Rash was killed before the walls of Nancy following the defeats of Morat and Granson. The interminable negotiations between the Emperor and the Duke which preceded this union of their families had been interrupted by frequent crises, but with the death of Charles the Rash, who left no male heir, this was now a thing of the past.

In the Low Countries the Estates took advantage of the occasion to force Marie of Burgundy, then only nineteen, to grant them the 'Great Privilege'. The city of Ghent, always one of the most turbulent of all the rich cities of Flanders, went still further in executing two of the late duke's councillors, Hugonet and Humbercourt, despite the pleas of the young Duchess. The city authorities had hoped by this brutal act, to weaken from the very start the authority of their young sovereign and her future husband. This event, however, was to have quite contrary results, for their actions acted as a spur in bringing Maximilian to the Low Countries. Until then he had delayed his departure mainly through lack of the necessary funds, but also because of a love affair which detained him in Austria. The Ghent authorities' show of strength recalled his obligations to him and aroused in him that spirit of adventure which was to be manifested throughout his life. Immediately he set out on a triumphal progress across the Rhineland, the acclamations of the crowds increasing from town to town as he reached the Low Countries, where he was greeted with tumultuous demonstrations of loyalty.

His popularity was due to his personal charm and appearance, to his gift for doing the right thing and to his chivalrous character, which corresponded with the Burgundian ideal, still very much alive in the country. On his arrival, Marie immediately fell deeply in love with him. The young people could not even wait for the day chosen for their marriage, but were married privately at midnight. Their life together was to be short but happy.

Maximilian's main task was to defend the rights of Marie against

Louis XI of France, who saw the death of Duke Charles as facilitating an attempt to conquer Burgundy. Louis was a dangerous enemy. An unscrupulous, crooked, scheming and energetic ruler, he was without doubt the most remarkable king of France since Philippe Auguste. His peers, the princes of Europe, called him 'the spider', and, plotting with infinite patience, he seemed determined to humble the neighbouring kingdoms just as he had subdued his great vassals. To stand up to this great king required all the reckless courage possessed by Maximilian. Contrary to all expectations, the latter was victorious at the battle of Guinegatte, due to his own personal bravery, and to the new tactics which he employed of using his knights to bolster the morale of the infantry. For the moment, at any rate, his wife's inheritance in Burgundy had been saved.

But the days following the battle of Guinegatte disclosed the weak points of the Burgundian structure – a weakness common to many other states of the period. The sovereign was unable to deploy his military forces as he chose, for the Estates showed little interest in helping their young prince to become, as they thought, too powerful, and therefore denied him the means to continue his struggle with the necessary force.

His early happiness was soon destroyed. At the age of twenty-four Marie died after a fall from a horse. Although pregnant she had insisted on going hunting, and after she had been thrown she refused immediate medical attention out of false modesty. Although in great pain for several days before her death – which she knew to be inevitable, she behaved with much fortitude. She died on 27 March 1482.

Maximilian remained in mourning for a long time, and it was not until much later that his political advisers dared suggest a new marriage to him. Finally he bowed to their arguments and married the Italian Maria Sforza of Milan. This unfortunate woman never ceased to suffer from the fact that the emperor jealously guarded the memory of his first wife and never displayed any affection for her.

Marie of Burgundy left two children; a son Philip, born in 1478, and a daughter Margaret, two years his junior. During the lifetime of his wife, the Estates had accorded certain sovereign rights to Maximilian as Prince Consort, but after 1482 he no longer had any legal claim except as the father of the legitimate heir, his four-year-old son. Soon the antagonism felt by some of the Estates towards him developed into open rebellion.

23

It is not easy to discover the true causes for the violent insurrections that broke out in towns like Ghent, Bruges, Louvain and Brussels, while others, such as Antwerp, and still more those in southern Burgundy, declared themselves for Maximilian. It is scarcely likely that they were prompted by economic motives; a much more plausible reason is that the burghers' love of liberty prevented them from recognising any sovereignty outside the framework of their own city. The rebellion reached its climax at Bruges in 1488. Maximilian, who had been elected King of the Romans and therefore successor to the imperial throne, was taken prisoner there and his life thus placed in danger. But here too he succeeded in impressing the infuriated mob by his personal courage and regal bearing. Finally, Friedrich III died, and the German princes, usually so slow in coming to the help of the crown, suddenly recollected their duty towards the emperor whom they had just elected and who now found himself directly threatened. The greater part of the Burgundian nobility also rallied to his cause, and Maximilian was freed and the rebellious towns forced to capitulate.

From this moment the rule of the Habsburgs was assured in Burgundy, and their position made all the stronger since the Archduke Philip, now a young man, had begun to exercise his own rights. Naturally, there were some Burgundians and Netherlanders who tried to use the young prince as a tool against the emperor, but it is interesting to note in this respect that father and son increasingly came to treat each other as equals.

From the moment of Friedrich III's death, in 1493, Maximilian exercised imperial authority although the title of *Romanorum Imperator electus* was not bestowed on him officially until later. He found his prestige enhanced by his new authority in Germany; but this was soon to be weakened by the imbroglio following his plans for marrying the heiress of Brittany. She had been married to the emperor by proxy, but in spite of the latter's protestations, she was seized from him soon after by the King of France. It took many diplomatic and military successes to restore Maximilian's prestige.

In the same year as Friedrich III died, Philip, then aged fifteen, was declared to have reached his majority. In 1494 he made his entry into Louvain in great pomp in the presence of the Estates and the chivalry of Burgundy. In 1496, the Infanta Joanna of Castile, his betrothed, arrived in the Low Countries. Just as Maximilian and Marie had fallen in love at first sight, so Joanna fell in love with Philip, reputed to be one of the handsomest men of his time. Again a marriage was arranged before the official date. The chroniclers of the time remark with amusement that it was the Infanta herself who could not wait for the consummation of the nuptials. In 1498 the young couple had a child, Eleanor, who was later to become a great influence in the life of Charles v. And then in 1500 Joanna at last gave birth to the long awaited male heir. He was baptised Charles, his grandfather's name.

Marguerite, the sister of Philip, had left for Spain by sea in 1497 in order to marry Don Juan the brother of Joanna. But in 1498 this prince died, and Philibert of Savoy became her second husband; but he too died within a short time. Marguerite, twice widowed at the age of twenty-four, decided never to marry again. She too was to play a major part in the life of her nephew.

By the death of her brother, Joanna became heiress to the Catholic Kings of Castile and Aragon, since in 1500, the year in which Charles v was born, the other future successor to the throne of Spain had died. This was Don Miguel, son of Joanna's eldest sister, the wife of the King of Portugal. Thus the potential heirs to the Spanish Empire were considerably reduced in numbers.

The eyes of all Europe – that is to say the princely courts, the church and the higher nobility – were turned naturally to Burgundy, where the young prince who was now making his first tentative steps, might one day inherit the most important territories in the whole world. Never since the days of the Hohenstaufen dynasty had there ever been such an opportunity for realising a universal empire as now, at the turn of the fifteenth and sixteenth centuries.

2

Childhood and Youth

THE EDUCATION OF A RULER

After Eleanor, and Charles of Burgundy, Joanna had four more children: Isabella, born in 1501; Archduke Ferdinand, born in Spain in March 1503; Marie who was born in Brussels in 1506, and lastly Catherine who was born in 1507 at Torquemada. Catherine was to have an unhappy youth, since being the youngest, she was obliged to accompany her mother to the castle of Tordesillas, where Joanna was confined under strict supervision, half prisoner, half invalid.

Joanna's husband, the Archduke Philip – who was recognised as Philip the First in line of Spanish kings, although he ruled only over Castile and not Aragon – died suddenly in 1506. The mystery surrounding the death of this young prince has never been completely solved. As nearly always in such cases, it was claimed that he had been poisoned. It was even hinted that Joanna's morbid jealousy motivated the crime. It has further been claimed that Joanna's madness was occasioned by her husband's infidelities. It is more than probable however, that even if Philip had practised all the husbandly virtues, he still would not have escaped his wife's censure. She constantly suspected him and hated him to be out of her sight. On the other hand it must be admitted that Philip did not exactly live the life of a hermit. But although these might have been grounds for quarrels between husband and wife, there is no reason to suppose that the young prince's death was due to anything but natural causes, and in fact only the inability of the doctors to make a diagnosis gave rise to these malicious rumours.

Once a widow, Joanna became completely demented. She would not permit herself to be separated from the body of her husband; his coffin accompanied her wherever she went and from time to time she insisted on having it opened. Her people were as frightened of her outbursts of grief as of her sudden rages. There was no solution except to place her in solitary confinement in the castle of Tordesillas.

This tragedy created serious difficulties for Spain, for although Joanna still remained queen she was incapable of ruling. The enemies of Ferdinand of Aragon were thus in a position to oppose him; their rights, they claimed, were vested solely in the sovereign queen, and indeed, even after the accession of Charles to the throne, the House of Austria continued to regard the poor demented woman, until her death in 1555, as the only legitimate ruler of the Catholic Kingdoms of Spain.

The infant Ferdinand was brought up at the court of his grandfather of Aragon. He was the favourite of the old king, who for a long while was to consider him as his successor, not only to the crown of Aragon, but of Castile as well. But in spite of his speculations concerning the child's future, the old king seemed persuaded he still had many more years to live. He took as his second wife Germaine de Foix – who was later to marry the Elector of Brandenburg – by whom he hoped to have a child.

Charles and his three sisters, Eleanor, Isabella, and Marie, then became wards of their aunt, the Archduchess Marguerite. When, on the death of Philip, the Estates of Burgundy invited Maximilian to nominate a regent, the latter had not hesitated for an instant, nor could he have made a better choice. Marguerite was the wisest of women and possessed one of the most astute political minds of her epoch. An outstanding figure of the House of Habsburg, she might well be considered the forerunner of the Empress Maria Theresa. She was probably less temperamental than the empress, but displayed the same characteristic acuity and realism. Very well informed and a woman of great energy, she combined, like her eighteenth-century descendant, the two most important qualities necessary to a sovereign: a capacity to judge men, and the courage to delegate authority only to those qualified to take responsibilities, and not to flatterers.

In 1504 Marguerite lost her second husband, to whose memory she erected one of the most remarkable monuments in all the world – the church of Brou, the masterpiece of Conrad Meit, of Worms. Henceforth the young widow had no other ambition than to serve her country and her family – Burgundy and the House of Habsburg. She had very precise ideas about what she considered to be wise policies. With unusual continuity of purpose, she managed to steer a straight course all her life, never setting political expediency above practical necessity. She understood the weaknesses of her period, an age when friendships and alliances were all too easily betrayed, when the most unexpected political unions followed one on the other, as though politics were no more than a game of chess. Marguerite regarded it as her duty to adhere to certain fundamental political principles, all the more necessary because of Maximilian's impulsive character. His enthusiasm for arranging new political unions was such that it required all Marguerite's sang-froid to avoid the pitfalls into which the brilliant, but dangerous, policies of her father might lead.

The basis of Marguerite's diplomacy was friendship with England. This was a policy helped by personal ties, for the memory of her grandmother, Margaret of York the wife of Charles the Rash, and her relationship to the Tudors, forged a sentimental link with the royal house of England. But this family connection was of only secondary consideration in comparison with the commercial interests of the Flemish merchant cities. For them an anglophile policy was of great importance as they were largely dependent on the English wool trade and any conflict with the English Crown would have disrupted their commerce. Marguerite, who always remained in close touch with her citizen subjects, espoused their cause because she too was equally convinced of the necessity of an alliance between the two great maritime powers. It is interesting to note than an analogous situation existed at the same time in Germany. Since the Middle Ages both the burghers and the Elector-Princes of Cologne led the pro-English faction; an initiative that later passed to the Hanseatic towns.

The House of Habsburg's involvement with Spain was an additional reason for the maintenance of friendly relations with England. The various journeys undertaken by the sovereigns and their envoys, in particular the redeployment of large groups of people which occurred under the reigns of Philip and Charles Quint, would have been impossible without England as a staging point. The essential lines of communication between the Netherlands and Spain were dependent on the goodwill of London, which explains the reason for the Spanish defeat in the Flemish war once the Armada had been destroyed. Finally, experience had taught that the strategic defence of the territories between the Escaut and the Meuse, so often the seat of war, was greatly helped when the seaboard flank of the Burgundian armies was supported by the English fleet.

Marguerite's greatest disappointment was when it became no longer possible to retain the friendship of England. The causes for this setback were less political than because of the personality and behaviour of Henry VIII.

But the Archduchess's sympathy for England did not lead her, however, to pursue an anti-French policy; on the contrary, together with the Burgundian nobles, she did everything in her power to keep the peace with France. To sum up the situation simply, it could be said that while the cities of the Netherlands wished for an alliance with England, the nobles on the whole were francophile. Such a combination of policies was generally favourable to peace; moreover, while the Burgundian knights still considered a crusade against the Turks as the essential duty of the West, they were not prepared to make war against fellow Christians, and in the meanwhile, the often bloody tournaments satisfied their craving for combat and provided an opportunity to show off their martial prowess.

The importance of the Burgundian family ties with the Royal House of France should not be underestimated, either in the case of Marguerite or of Charles. No blood relationship had previously existed between the Habsburgs and the Valois, and perhaps this was why Maximilian sometimes spoke of the 'hereditary' enmity between Burgundy and France. In a letter to the young Archduke Charles in 1513, he refers to the French as the *anchiens et encoures naturels ennemis de nostre maison de Bourgogne*. But in spite of the many deceptions he had suffered at the hands of France, Charles never ceased to regard the French as the natural allies of Burgundy. Marguerite, who in this case was fully in agreement with her nephew, recognised that the special mission of the House of Burgundy was to act as the intermediary between France, England and the 'German' Empire. One could even say that Marguerite was a progenitor of the idea for a Belgian state, although at that time the idea of a geographic national policy was not even born.

In the Netherlands, Marguerite did not establish her court in one of the grand cities of Flanders or of Brabant, but at Malines, where she built a palace which was to introduce a new style of architecture. Nor, as was the usual custom of Renaissance princes, did she erect a great monumental palace, but a building in a style much closer to our own days – rococo. It was spacious enough to house her court of young princes and the Chancellory of the Regency, but there was no trace here of the luxury and pomp of the residences of most other sovereigns.

From what is known of the furnishings of her palace, we know that it was in good taste, devoid of excessive luxury, that the tapestries and the Netherland pictures gave it an air of comfort, and the historical scenes which they depicted were object lessons to the young princes.

The education of Charles was based on a sensible balance between science and the usual physical training expected of a knight and warrior. Charles, however, was much more interested in equestrian exercises and feats of arms than in intellectual study. In this respect he was only following the family tradition for we are told that Maximilian showed absolutely no interest in book learning, but that from his earliest youth he surpassed all his companions in fencing and horsemanship. This ancestor, however, was of a much more robust constitution than his grandson. Contemporaries say that Charles was 'tender and delicate', and doctors anxiously asked themselves whether he had the stamina to survive his years of childhood. That he survived was not so much due to his physical constitution as to his iron will, which from his earliest youth had forcibly impressed contemporary writers, and although this was the dominant feature of his character it was tempered by his common sense.

Charles was brought up in the most carefully chosen company of young nobles. Germany was represented by Johan of Saxony and Friedrich von Furstenberg; Italy by Maximilian Sforza, and Burgundy by the youthful Balançon. His education and studies were under the general supervision of Adrien of Utrecht, a man with the very highest qualifications, doyen of St Pierre de Louvain and vice-rector of the university (and later to be elected pope). He was a member of the order of the Fraternity of the Common Life (*Les Frères de la Vie Commune*) and was thus a representative of the *devotia moderna*. He combined the piety of the Middle Ages with the humanism of the Renaissance and appreciated the need for the reformation of the Church. Adrien was assisted in his task by Robert of Ghent, Adrien Wiele, Juan de Anchiata, the erudite Luis Vaca, and, for physical exercises, Charles de Poupet, Seigneur de la Chaulx.

Apart from this close circle of tutors, there was one man who exercised a profound influence on Charles and who was responsible for forming his political ideas; this was the Chamberlain and Councillor Guillaume de Croy, Seigneur de Chièvres. This Burgundian nobleman had enjoyed the absolute confidence of the Habsburg family for a long time, and moreover, had won the esteem of the Valois. At the time he was summoned to supervise the education of the young prince, he already held an important place in Burgundian politics. De Croy was a man of wide interests, an able diplomatist and a farseeing statesman; he had, moreover, the gift of attracting all with whom he came in contact. Nothing proves better the qualities of this man than the exceptional devotion shown to him by the young prince over the course of many years. Guillaume de Croy was a true knight in the traditional sense of the word, devoid of any of the ostentation or frivolity that marked the behaviour of the majority of his peers. His intellectual austerity and the sobriety of his mode of life were due to his profound Christian beliefs and to the formative influence of humanism. It was these qualities that attached him to the young man who was already prone to melancholy and who, according to Pierre Martyr, had already the mannerisms of an old man when he was only sixteen years of age.

A by no means negligible role in the education of the young prince was also played by his chaplains, whose influence was predominantly Spanish. Among these priests was the great scholar, Cardinal Mota, who served Charles during the most decisive moments of his political career, Alfonzo Manriquez, Bishop of Badajoz, and Miguel Pavye, his father confessor. Nevertheless, on a final analysis, it was the counsels and influence of Adrien of Utrecht that dominated his whole religious life.

As was customary at that period, the future marriage of the young prince occupied everyone's thoughts from his infancy. Already by 1501, Claude de France, the daughter of Louis XII, had been chosen as his betrothed, though in fact she became the wife of his great rival, the Comte d'Angoulême, better known as François I. This was just one of a long series of similar marriage projects. In 1508, for example, Marguerite, in pursuance of her anglophile policy, conceived the idea of a marriage between the young Burgundian and Mary Tudor, daughter of Henry VIII. The negotiations for this dragged on for several years, simultaneously with other matrimonial plans.

After his eighth birthday Charles was no longer considered a child. The disputes that from then on centred around his person were all the more complex because the many different origins on which the rule of Burgundy was based meant that each part of the country had different legal statutes. One can see this in the incident that occurred during the war that broke out between England and France in 1513. Maximilian

31

had rashly offered his services to Henry VIII in consideration of a daily payment of one hundred ducats, and it was under these circumstances that while in command of an army of German and English troops, he won a victory over the French, again on the field of Guingatte. At the same time, however, his grandson Prince Charles, as a vassal of the French Crown, was summoned by Louis XII to take up arms on the side of France, though, because of his youth, his personal services were dispensed with. French pretensions to the suzerainty of Burgundy had in fact already been abolished for some time, though Paris still continued to claim its former feudal rights, if only symbolically.

Towards 1508, the Spanish – in particular Charles's maternal grandfather, Ferdinand of Aragon – began to take an interest in the young prince. Ferdinand sent two noblemen, Juan de Lanuza and Juan de Aragon, to the Burgundian court, where they lost no time in intriguing against Guillaume de Croy. They were unsuccessful, however, in undermining his authority, moreover it was soon discovered that these Aragonese had contacts with the French Court of so suspicious a nature that one of their companions, Diego de Castro, was arrested.

When Marguerite heard of this, she decided to clear up the whole affair once and for all. By the Decree of Lille of 15 October 1513, she appointed with exceptional diplomatic skill, a triumvirate to direct the policy of the young prince. This triumvirate consisted of Charles's two grandfathers, Maximilian and Ferdinand of Aragon, and Henry VIII, each of whom was obliged to exercise his function through an intermediary at the Burgundian Court. Maximilian's representative was the Count Palatine Friedrich, one of his most faithful supporters; Ferdinand nominated the Senor de Lanuza, who was already in the Netherlands and the King of England chose Floris d'Egmond, Lord of Isselstein.

In order to stress her friendship with England and also to revive the proposed marriage with Mary Tudor, Marguerite sent Charles on a state visit to England, a visit which was a great success, or at least seemed so at the time.

Shortly after the prince's return home, a serious crisis developed between the regent and her nephew. Marguerite, exasperated by the intrigues of the Castilians, ordered the arrest of Don Manuel, Lord of Belmonte, a highly important personage among the Spaniards in the Netherlands. However, this nobleman was a member of the Order of the Golden Fleece, which enjoyed certain unique privileges, in particular the right of trial by a special court. On learning of Manuel's imprisonment, the Knights of the Holy Fleece passed a solemn vote of censure on the Regent and sent her an official delegation to protest at her conduct. The regent was disagreeably surprised to find this delegation headed by the young archduke, who was opposed to his aunt, partly on principle as Knight of the Golden Fleece, and partly from personal motives. Marguerite was in no mood to comply with the demands of the delegation and when reminded of the special privileges of the Order, replied angrily that were she a man, she would force these noble lords to 'set their statutes to music'. In the end a compromise was reached, one which, while satisfactory to the nobles, at the same time preserved the authority of the crown, and accordingly, Don Manuel was sent back as a prisoner to the Emperor Maximilian, who immediately set him free.

The good relations between the members of the triumvirate were not to last long. Princess Mary of England, whose hand had long been promised to Charles, was married in 1514 to Louis XII of France who died a year later, to be succeeded by François d'Angoulême.

The power struggles of this period are reflected in the various marriages and broken marriage alliances of the princely families. A slight diminution in Guillaume de Croy's influence, for example, was enough to destroy the matrimonial plans of the two Habsburg princesses, Marie and Isabella, and Charles d'Egmond and the Duke of Lorraine. If these unions had taken place, the policy which Charles the Rash had pursued in regard to Lorraine would have been effected peacefully. Once these plans were abandoned, the eight-year-old Archduchess Marie was sent in 1514 to Austria, where very soon she was to become the central figure in Maximilian's last great marriage plan to unite the House of Habsburg with the Jagellon dynasty; meanwhile Archduchess Isabella was married by proxy to Christian II, King of Denmark.

On 5 January 1515, Charles of Austria was proclaimed as having reached his majority in the Hall of the Estates at the Court of Brussels. At the express wish of Ferdinand of Aragon, Charles's accession to the throne of Castile was to be postponed until he was twenty-five years old, a decision which allowed his grandfather to rule the Iberian peninsula for another ten years.

One of the first acts of the new régime was to send representatives to the coronation of François I of France. François in a letter, as superficially courteous as it was fundamentally arrogant, had summoned 'his most illustrious vassal, the Duke of Burgundy' to attend the ceremony in person. In sending his representatives Charles avoided an open breach with France, but at the same time pointedly but tactfully emphasised the wide difference between his own status and the pretensions of the French Crown. In spite of mounting tensions between the two rulers, Guillaume de Croy indefatigably pursued his pro-French policy, and in an attempt to improve relations, proposed a marriage between Charles and the Princess Renée, sister-in-law of François. This proposed alliance, however, had the effect of increasing the already existing tension between Charles of Burgundy and his grandfather Ferdinand of Aragon, since the latter was already manœuvring in Paris to obtain the hand of the young princess for his other younger and favourite grandson, Ferdinand. It was therefore a personal triumph for Guillaume de Croy when at the Peace of Paris, solemnised at Notre Dame on 2 April 1515, Charles was chosen as the husband-elect in place of his brother, although, as events proved later, the consequences of this alliance were as abortive as many other similar projected marriages between the Habsburgs and the Crown of France. But there was one Burgundian political marriage which had consequences impossible to envisage at the time – the marriage between the thirty-two-year-old widower Henry of Nassau and the Countess Claude de Chalon Arlay, who was later to inherit the independent principality of Orange when her brother Philibert de Chalon was killed fighting at Florence. The House of Nassau was thus established in Orange, the name of which it bore through the centuries to come. It is also of interest to note that coincidentally the prestige of the House of Nassau was further enhanced by Charles v's decision to appoint Henry of Orange as governor of Holland, Zealand and Friesland on the death of Jean d'Egmond. Later on the growth of power of the House of Nassau was to become a serious danger to the Habsburgs when Prince William of Orange defied Philip II.

In internal politics, the position of Guillaume de Croy was now firmly established in the eyes of the world when his former pupil appointed him as his privy councillor, side by side with Adrien of Utrecht and Jean de Souvage.

In spite of all vicissitudes and changing circumstances, the unshakeable political aim of both the Burgundian Estates and of Charles himself was to maintain an entente with France. It was for this reason that Charles's attitude was one of benevolent neutrality when François I, immediately after ascending the throne, found himself involved in a dangerous war with the Swiss who had marched on Milan, and caused him to write a few days after the battle of Marignano, on 23 September 1515, to François and his mother, Louise of Savoy, congratulating them on their victory and offering his services as mediator. Relations between the Netherlands and Aragon now appeared even more strained than relations between Burgundy and Paris. So much so indeed, that Adrien of Utrecht was sent to Spain by Charles, who needed a man of proven ability and one in whom he had complete confidence, to be on the spot. Suddenly, however, the situation changed. King Ferdinand of Aragon, though still an active man for his age, died long before he had anticipated. On 23 January 1516, in the Cathedral of Sainte Gudule in Brussels, Charles, Duke of Burgundy, Archduke of Austria, was proclaimed King of Castile and Aragon. The act of proclamation, moreover, recognised the dual nature of the sovereignty and it was with the cry of 'Long Live Their Catholic Majesties Doña Juana and Don Carlos', that the new king was greeted.

THE KING OF SPAIN

The vast Spanish kingdom of which Charles was now the ruler was historically, sociologically and ethnographically very different from his native Burgundy; so too was the Spanish conception of its mission in the world. Spain had only achieved national unity subsequent to the marriage of Ferdinand of Aragon to Isabella of Castile. Until then, each of these two kingdoms, during the course of many troubled years had developed their own widely divergent national characteristics and traditions.

The Kingdom of Aragon, with its Mediterranean seaboard, was naturally orientated towards the east and for a long time now it had been a maritime power of considerable importance, having conquered the Balearic islands, Sardinia, Sicily, and finally the Kingdom of Naples. We must bear the position of Aragon in mind in judging the Mediterranean policy of Charles v, which was to play such an important part in his reign. Aragon had always had very close contacts with France; there was a distinct similarity between the Catalan language and the language of the French people to the north of the Pyrenees, while beyond these mountains the County of Roussillon provided Aragon with a bridgehead to France. Aragonese folklore and customs moreover were largely influenced by their Mediterranean situation, by the busy, cosmopolitan sea ports, and by constant commercial exchanges with the south of France and southern Italy.

Castile on the other hand was a continental state, whose development had been profoundly influenced by the *Reconquista* – the reunification of Spain under the Christian Cross. Its character was reflected in the sombre austerity of its arid plateaux and in the harsh traditions of its people, whose hard, proud temperament had been moulded by centuries of constant war against the Moors, and for whom danger and privation were an everyday experience.

While certain parts of Aragon had from time to time belonged to France and Charlemagne's rule had extended as far south as the Marches of Spain on the banks of the Ebro, Castile, on the other hand, had for five centuries preserved the traditions of the Visigoths whose whole energies had always been directed towards the subjugation of the Moorish kingdoms of Cordoba and Granada and the ultimate *Reconquista*. Thus Castile remained continental, while Aragon was predominantly Mediterranean in character.

This difference in character explains why the two kingdoms for so long led separate existences and why their political union under the Catholic Monarchs did not result in an immediate amalgamation. Isabella's kingdom of Castile remained distinct from her husband Ferdinand's kingdom of Aragon and the knights and nobles of each kingdom jealously preserved their special privileges. But on the other hand, the ecclesiastical dignitaries wished to create a united Church of Spain, for only by this means could they remain independent of Rome and prevent the Curia from dominating the country by setting the Castilian bishops against the bishops of Aragon. There was another factor which encouraged the fusion of the two kingdoms. By Isabella's conquest of Granada in 1492 and the expulsion of the Moors from Europe, Castile's ports were thrown open to the Mediterranean; the eyes of Spain turned towards Africa and Cartagena now became a port of equal importance to those of Barcelona and Valencia.

But even more important for the future of Spain as a world power was the decision taken by Isabella of Castile under the walls of Granada in 1492, when she entrusted Christopher Columbus – a maritime adventurer of Genoese origin – with three ships to voyage to the Indies. For reasons which remain obscure, Columbus had left the service of Portugal and declared his readiness to seek the Land of Cockaigne, and the fabulously wealthy Indies, not by the eastern route round Africa, a route already familiar to Portuguese navigators, but by journeying westward. Such a voyage, within the limits of contemporary knowledge, was a voyage into the unknown – perhaps even a voyage to the edge of the world, if the still unproved theory that the world was round should be false. With its complete reliance on scientific theories this was indeed a bold venture. Columbus based his plans on the map of the world which the Florentine Toscanelli had designed from information supplied by Marco Polo. His only mistake was in calculating the circumference of the earth which led him to believe that he had reached India when in fact he had arrived at the West Indies; he believed too that the legendary Cipangy – the modern Japan – lay near the mouth of the Orinoco. Even the first *Conquistadores* who followed in the steps of Columbus did not realise his mistake. It was only on 23 September 1513, when a Spaniard, Vasco Nuñez de Balbao, reached the shores of the Pacific, that it was realised that this newly discovered country was in fact a continent that lay half-way towards India. It was not until nine years later that a Portuguese navigator, Fernand Magellan, financed and encouraged by Charles, brought back proof that the earth was a sphere, after a voyage of circumnavigation which had lasted from 1519 to 1522.

After Columbus's enterprise, Castile was able to take its place alongside Portugal as one of the great maritime nations of the world, and with surprising rapidity it became a serious rival to the country of Henry the Navigator, which for so long had led the world in voyages of discovery. Now Castile in its turn was able to share in the great conquests of the age, which more than any other discoveries were to enlarge the horizons of humanity. On 7 June 1494, Pope Alexander VI, by his famous act of arbitration, divided the new-found lands between Spain and Portugal. The line of demarcation which he drew, however, did not prevent future territorial disputes, for the maps he used were still far from accurate and resulted in many anomalies. Thus, part of the South American continent, which was situated further to the east than was at first believed, was ascribed to Portugal, whereas Spain, on the other hand, acquired the East Indies.

When the Venetian brothers, Cabot, following the forgotten Viking route, later explored and rediscovered the seaboard of North America, Spain's rights to these territories under the pope's ruling were in dispute. But although Spanish claims to these territories were speedily abandoned, the fact that this question was ever raised shows how world-embracing were the political problems facing Charles v.

The important part played by Spain in voyages of discovery and the lucky chance that, thanks to Columbus, opened up the most propitious route to the New World, led Spain to seek a union with Portugal. Moreover, Spain's interests in south Italy and in the control of the western Mediterranean, which dated from even before the *Reconquista*, were additional inducements to put an end to her rivalry with Portugal as much in Europe as in the newly discovered lands.

It was only natural that the powerful seaboard countries of Algeria and Morocco and the countries beyond should have profoundly influenced the Iberian peninsula. Throughout history, the south of Spain and north Africa were more often than not united both strategically and politically. Up to the time of the *Reconquista*, the Straits of Gibraltar were not so much a frontier as a bridge between the two continents. But the conquest of north Africa, which would have been a possibility immediately after the fall of Granada and at the time of the final offensive against the Moors, had to be postponed due to more pressing affairs in Europe. Nevertheless, defensive measures were still necessary to insure freedom of navigation between Spain and Naples and to safeguard the southern Iberian shores, which were constantly menaced by Barbary corsairs. Hence the establishment of the numerous Spanish bridgeheads along the Moroccan coast. In addition to these considerations of purely national interest, the great problems facing Christendom had to be taken into account: there were hopes for a future crusade, and on a European level, the planning of a continental strategy in the war against the Turks. Had it not been for the sudden impetus afforded to the ports of Seville and Palos by Atlantic navigation, Spain might well have been orientated towards the Mediterranean by the great seaport of Valencia.

In view of the leading role played by Italy in the political designs of Charles v, it would have seemed only natural that the monarch should govern his country, not from its geographic centre, but from one of the great cities of Aragon closer to Naples and Palermo. But his decision to establish the capital of the united kingdoms at Toledo, and later at Madrid, was the logical consequence of the growing importance of Gibraltar and the Atlantic. Also he wished the centre of government to be closer to the sea routes which stretched from Biscay, Santander and Corunna to Burgundy and England. Toledo was selected because

38

of its strategic position; situated on a rocky eminence in the centre of Castile, it dominates the surrounding plain. Already known in Roman times, Toledo and its Alcazar have played a heroic and famous role in our own day. Madrid was positioned on a fine site at the foot of the Sierra de Guaderrama, where a thousand feet up, Philip II was later to build the Escorial. The city was easy to defend and had the advantage of being in the centre of the country, at the junction of the most important roads leading from the coasts and frontiers of Spain.

Unlike Burgundy where there was always talk of crusades but never any action, in Spain, the *Cruzada* against the Moors was still an active force. Among the hidalgos and grandees there were still old men who had taken part in the siege of Granada, and the memory of the veterans and dead of the great campaign was still alive. Spanish chivalry, with its heroic and austere traditions was very different from that of the gay nobility of Burgundy. When the court of Spain adopted the ceremonial of Burgundy, it modified it little by little, finally transforming it into a solemn ritual. Brightly coloured stuffs – products of the inspired Flemish and Brabant weavers – were gradually replaced by more sombre materials until finally black was universally worn only relieved occasionally by cardinal red. These sombre hues were also predominant in the court of Vienna, until the Lorraines, in the time of Maria Theresa, and the rococo style added a gayer note to the austere ceremonial. Spain, although superficially altered by the Burgundian influence, remained basically unchanged.

After the dynastic marriages of the fifteenth and sixteenth centuries, the Habsburgs became, culturally and politically the most powerful integrating force in Europe.

Thanks to his Spanish tutors, Charles had learnt the language and customs of Spain and its people, but it was a far cry from this theoretical knowledge to a true appreciation of the national spirit which can only be acquired by personal contact with the country. Charles soon got to know the great Spanish families – the Manuels, Enriquez, Belascos, Manrique de Lana, de la Cueva, Hurtado de Mendoza, to mention just a few of the most famous. As well as these great nobles, the incumbents of the principal episcopal sees also played a leading role. And then a factor in Spanish politics not to be disregarded were the three orders of chivalry: Santiago, Alcantara and Calatrava, to which was soon added the Order of the Golden Fleece, whose statutes, embracing as they did the whole of Christianity, helped to establish it firmly on Spanish soil.

Finally, there were the cities. In Spain, as in France, and for a long time in Germany, the cities supported the crown against the feudal barons, but as experience proved, the citizens were not easy to govern. As soon as it was a question of their pockets, and once they had no more need of protection against the land-owning classes, they did not hesitate to use their economic and financial power to extort concessions from the king. Moreover in Spain they possessed two organisations which greatly increased their political influence: first, the *Cortès*, a representative corporation, in which citizens had a decisive vote. Secondly, the urban leagues – the *Santas Hermandades* – which were founded at the time of the *Reconquista*, and were similar to the city leagues of Germany, in particular the *Schwäbische Bund* or Swabian League, which together with the Hanseatic League, whose influence extended from Flanders to the Baltic, provided the Habsburgs, right up to the time of Charles v with valuable support. These German leagues, however, were economic rather than political blocs whereas in Spain, Charles was soon to realise the political power of the *Cortès* and the danger that the Spanish city leagues represented to him.

Public finance was dependent on the Crown's right to tax the church of Spain by consent of the Pope. This tax was known as the *Cruzada* because it was originally imposed to finance the *Reconquista*. After the expulsion of the Muslims from Spain, the war against the Barbary corsairs and the constant Turkish threat to Spanish possessions in southern Italy were considered ample reasons to continue with the imposition – an example that the law of economics, whereby a so-called provisional tax tends to become a permanent imposition, was in force long before our own century.

Since the reign of Isabella, Spain had been administered by a body of jurists appointed by the crown, known as *letrados*. This organisation, which by the standards of the time was exemplary, formed the backbone for the modernisation of Castile and paved the way for the government of Charles Quint.

Between the year 1504 when Isabella died, and the time when Charles, after many setbacks, eventually assumed the reins of government, there was a period of what was more or less an interregnum. The principal figure during this time was not Ferdinand, Isabella's husband and co-regent, but the Cardinal Archbishop of Toledo, Ximenes de

Cisneros, the strongest personality in Castile since the *Reconquista*. Although Ferdinand of Aragon was an able and ambitious politician and a master of tactics, nevertheless, in spite of all his efforts, his influence in Castile remained limited. Had he succeeded in participating in the government of Isabella, who during her life had always dominated her husband, he would have probably only damaged, in the long run, the union of the kingdom. It was Cardinal Ximenes who prevented this happening. Opinions concerning the Cardinal, both as a man and as a governor, differ according to one's point of view. In the light of what his policy achieved, he can be regarded as the saviour of the unity of the Kingdom, or again, as the instigator of the exile and annihilation of the Moors and Spanish Jews. Ximenes believed the latter to be necessary both in the interests of religious unity and for the maintenance of the authority of the state. At first his persecution was not directed so much against religious minorities and foreigners *per se*, as against what he called 'false Muslim Christians' and converted Jews. Because these conversions had been effected under political pressure, he maintained that they were insincere. Indeed, the most recent historical research shows that towards the end of the Middle Ages, collaboration, dissimulation and a purely superficial acceptance of the faith of the oppressor – whether Muslim or Christian – was a conscious tactical practice on the part of the Jews, and one which was even approved by the great Maimonides himself. It was against these false converts, the Marranes, who continued to practise their own religion in secret, that the persecution was originally directed; but as is nearly always the case, the persecution soon extended to include genuine converts and also those who courageously remained faithful to their ancient beliefs. During the great purge of 1492, it is estimated that thirty-six thousand people were expelled from the country.

It has been claimed that these measures were the main cause of the decline of the Spanish economy and her position as a world power, but this theory is open to doubt. The economic expansion of England and France for example was not hindered by their expulsion of the Jews – although there were fewer of them, it is true, than in Spain. Moreover, the decline of Spain dates only from the middle of the seventeenth century; its status as a world power disappearing as a result of the Treaty of Utrecht, that is to say, from five to eight generations after the expulsion of the Jews. These inhuman and barbarous persecutions certainly reflect no credit on those responsible; nevertheless, to take a

41

completely objective view, it must be appreciated that the standards of judgement were different from those of our day. Soon there were to be wars which would devastate all Europe, and for centuries Christians of one creed were to persecute mercilessly those of another, on the pretext of saving the souls of their victims!

Cardinal Ximenes successfully enforced the power of the crown in the cities by appointing civic representatives of the central authority. Certain writers have misrepresented the function of these representatives by comparing them to the *podestas* of Italian towns in the twelfth and thirteenth centuries. But these *podestas* – especially during the time of the Hohenstaufen – were partisan leaders or heads of armed groups, who often became local independent tyrants in their own right. No similar danger existed in Spain; the *corregidor* was a jurist and royal official, who could be recalled or dismissed at any time.

Ximenes jealously defended the interests of Castile against Aragon, but he was not afraid to ally himself with Ferdinand against the nobility. The king appointed the cardinal as his representative on the occasions when he was obliged to be absent in Italy. It was only in 1507, the year after the death of King Philip, that Ferdinand assumed personal control of his territories. The unity of the kingdom had been preserved.

One of Ximenes's most important political successes was the occupation of Navarre in 1512, the French bridgehead on the Iberian peninsula. Henceforth the passage of the Pyrenees to Spain was protected. The Cardinal was also the creator of the Castilian battle fleet. This fleet was later to give Charles an opportunity of carrying out operations in north Africa and to insure the defence of the Mediterranean against France, and finally made possible the crushing defeat of Islam at the Battle of Lepanto.

Shortly after Charles had been proclaimed king in Brussels, signs of discontent began to show themselves in Spain, though this disaffection was neither directed against the dynasty itself nor the young monarch, but rose from a fear of being ruled by a foreign régime controlled from Burgundy. If, as Ferdinand had wished, his younger grandson Ferdinand had inherited the crown, no doubt the transition would have been accomplished without trouble, but Charles refused to relinquish his rights. To divide Spain once again into two independent states – if, in fact, such an idea was ever seriously entertained – was rejected out of hand.

Confronted with this situation, it was a matter of urgency that

Charles should go to Spain. The young sovereign acted with circumspection and without undue haste, even at the risk of being accused of procrastination. For Burgundy and the Low Countries, Charles's accession to the throne of Spain presented above all fresh problems in their relations with France. Guillaume de Croy, the most influential supporter of a Franco-Burgundian entente, did his best to allay the suspicions of François I who was beginning to feel himself surrounded by Habsburgs. Once again there were negotiations for a Franco-Burgundian marriage – but this represented a gesture which was more symbolic than serious. It was proposed that Charles, aged sixteen, should marry Mme Louise, the daughter of François I, a baby of one, or alternatively her younger sister, as yet unborn. The Spaniards, on the other hand, were anxious that the future King of Spain should be free from any possibility of French claims on his Burgundian possessions.

But in spite of the tensions that were beginning to make themselves felt, the European situation on the whole was as favourable as it could be when Charles mounted the Spanish throne. The threat of Islam seemed to eclipse all internal problems and revive anew plans for a crusade. A feeling of euphoria, a new sense of unity, seemed to permeate Europe in this period just before Luther's appearance on the scene. At the festival of the Golden Fleece held at Brussels on 16 November 1516, the prevailing mood was one of optimism. François I was amongst the illustrious company and it seemed as if the great Christian enterprise to liberate Byzantium was at last to be realised.

Before leaving for Spain, Charles took another important family decision: he forbade the love match between his sister Eleanor and the Count Palatine Frederick and betrothed her instead to the King of Portugal. Already in Charles's mind, Spanish interests were more important than other considerations. On 6 September 1517, Charles put to sea with forty vessels, accompanied by his sister Eleanor and a numerous train of Burgundians. His arrival in Spain was heralded by unfavourable auspices. A storm scattered his fleet in the Bay of Biscay and the ships were blown off course. Charles was obliged to cast anchor in the little port of Villa Viciosa, on the coast not far from Ovieda. During his progress across north-west Spain, Charles avoided the large cities, having been informed that feelings there were unfavourable to him. Guillaume de Croy, obviously fearful of a meeting between the sovereign and the powerful Cardinal Ximenes, did everything in his power to postpone this meeting.

43

It was both perfectly understandable – and politically wise – that Charles should stop to visit Tordesillas to meet his mother whom he had not seen since his childhood. On the threshold of the sombre apartment inhabited by the queen, Charles dismissed his suite and retainers. It was suggested that lights should be brought, but he refused; he had no need of candles. No details have been left to us of the meeting between mother and son, with whom she shared – legally at least – the charge of the Catholic Kingdoms of Castile and Aragon. The two people involved confided in no one; the emperor certainly was very tight-lipped where personal matters or affairs of the heart were concerned. The sight of little Catherine, however, truly upset Charles and his suite. The child, now ten years of age, seemed timorous and neglected, and the company of her mentally deranged mother seemed already to have seriously affected her from a psychological point of view. On the other hand, there was a natural hesitancy about depriving the queen of her only consolation in her solitude, and so it was finally decided to provide the Infanta with her own little court to keep her company and for her distraction.

After visiting Tordesillas, the meeting between Charles and the man who, up to the time of his arrival, had been the most powerful figure in the kingdom, could no longer be postponed. Ximenes had already left to meet the king when he fell ill in the little town of Roa and before Charles could join him the old man died on 8 November 1517.

The subsequent meeting between the king and the young Ferdinand had already been planned. This took place under circumstances of great courtesy, even great formality. It was the first meeting between the two brothers, who later were to strive together for the glory of the House of Habsburg and the empire, for common ideals and the unity of Christendom. Their characters were in many respects dissimilar and their collaboration was fraught with some difficulties but these were the result of the different temperaments and not because of any basic differences of opinion on fundamental problems. In fact neither of them was ever led by envy or discontent to make common cause with the enemy of the other.

In the course of the conversations between the brothers and the members of their suites, the idea was put forward that Ferdinand should remain as viceroy, or even as king of Spain, while his brother returned to Burgundy to reassume the Austrian heritage. But such an idea was immediately rejected by the sovereign. Ferdinand accepted his brother's decision with dignity and it was he who left for the Low Countries. His aunt Marguerite welcomed him with open arms; he had no difficulty in winning her affection, especially as their characters were so similar, both having inherited many of the same traits from Maximilian. The latter, for his part, took an active interest in his grandson; indeed, in his opinion Ferdinand might well play a major role in settling relations between Hungary and Bohemia and in resolving the problem of the imperial succession.

In order to celebrate Charles's visit to Spain in a worthy manner, the court organised a great tournament in which the sovereign himself took part carrying a shield with the device *Nondum* ('Not Yet'). This tournament had a profound effect on the Spaniards, so greatly did the courage and bearing of the Burgundians arouse their admiration. Ten horses were killed in the lists, there were a quantity of broken bones and wounds, and knights fighting hand to hand had to be separated by main force. This determination to risk their lives, even in a tournament, pleased the soldiers of Castile and Aragon, themselves courageous warriors. Charles, on his side, quickly accustomed himself to the Spanish national pastime, the *Corrida*, and soon descended into the arena to fight the bulls. But if the pomp and virile displays of these fêtes earned the commendation of the Spanish, they asked themselves anxiously where the necessary money to finance such a glittering court was to be found. These minor pleasures and personal cares soon gave place to more serious matters. Charles, ill-advised by Guillaume de Croy, had been imprudent in his selection of nominees to the Spanish episcopal sees. The mission of Adrien of Utrecht had already aroused resentment. The appointment of other Burgundians to high ecclesiastical offices was regarded as a provocation, and jealousy and general ill-feeling turned into active opposition. It was at this time that Pedro Ruiz de Villena submitted his *Miroir des Princes* to the king; to all appearances it seemed to be a literary work, but it was in fact a political programme containing suggestions and advice, and even courteously worded criticisms. This work was similar in content to the petition consisting of eighty-eight points drawn up by the *Cortès*. To this last petition the king gave a friendly reply, without compromising himself too much. One can only assume that de Croy, as a highly intelligent statesman, had begun to understand the realities of the Spanish situation. Before becoming too involved with the demands of the *Cortès*, Charles went to Aragon in the spring of 1518. Here he acted with such prudence, that one of his biographers, Karl Brandi, delivered himself of the following appreciation: If prudence is one of the principal virtues of princes, this virtue was practised by Charles, perhaps under pressure of events for the betterment of his cause.

3

The Great Problems
of the Period

EMPIRE, STATE AND NATION

At the turn of the fifteenth and sixteenth centuries, opportunities for a revival of the concept of the Holy Roman Empire seemed more favourable in Burgundy than anywhere else in Europe. Its medial position between France and Germany caused Burgundy to seek a political and cultural ethos common to these two heirs of Charlemagne. This European mission was expressed in the art of the time by the Master of Nuremberg, the genius Albrecht Dürer, who as a superlative visionary painter, was one of the great men of his time. It is related that one day when he dropped his brush, Maximilian picked it up, remarking that Dürer, as master of the kingdom of the mind, was the equal of the emperor. In his painting of Charlemagne, Dürer represents him wearing the Crown of the Holy Empire and introduces shields bearing the lilies of France and the eagle of Germany, a reminder that the two European kingdoms both had the rights of succession to the tradition of a universal empire. It was in Burgundy that the heirs to this tradition met, and only here was it possible to forge the idea of a Franco-German Empire. Here there still existed a tradition dating back to the Carolingians, and Burgundian culture was saturated with historic memories. It was the only country where chivalry still remained unimpaired, a chivalry which during the golden age of medieval times, had provided the empire with its élite and principal support.

Burgundian chivalry alone had not degenerated. Under certain guises it might appear rather removed from practicalities, even somewhat fantastic; but, nevertheless, it had nothing in common with the image of the Spanish hidalgo of the end of the sixteenth century, immortalised in the tragi-comic figure of Don Quixote. It is true that in

47

France there was a whole series of men of noble and exemplary character such as Bayard, the *'chevalier sans peur et sans reproche'*, but they were not sufficiently numerous and they lacked influence in the councils of the king. In Germany, despite the fact that the crown needed the support of a powerful élite, the number of knights of the empire were visibly reduced. Furthermore, the last representatives of the Hohenstaufen tradition were lost in their small feudal holdings crushed between the growing power of the cities and that of the territorial princes. Characteristic of this moribund German chivalry was Franz von Sickingen, the ardent partisan of the young Emperor Charles, whose tragic fate reflected that of his class. Another such was Florian Geyer who served several masters including the king of France in a diplomatic capacity; later he took the side of the peasants and was killed on the field of battle fighting his peers. Yet another was Götz von Berlichingen, immortalised by Goethe, who courageously tried to re-establish the political power of the knights, but whose efforts were condemned to failure through lack of funds.

But in Burgundy knightly chivalry had developed concurrently with the times. Under Charles v in particular its members found themselves appointed to important military commands, and to posts as diplomatists and royal councillors. As governors of fiefs of the Dukes of Burgundy, certain of the great knightly families were eventually to become very influential indeed.

A young prince, educated in Burgundy, sharing in the life of such nobles and who also came in to contact with the great burghers of the commercial cities, was bound to grow up with a keen appreciation of the practical possibilities of implementing an imperial policy. In Burgundy he found men who shared his views and were equal to their tasks, men who were capable of following a policy conceived on the grand scale. The Burgundian knights were not nationalistic like the knights of France and Germany; they spoke French, but saw things in a European context. Their country had no natural frontiers and no ethnic unity, and this made them all the more receptive to new ideas, ready to launch themselves into what amounted to a spiritual struggle, that same struggle that was to engage Charles for his whole life.

The empire of the Middle Ages had never been a territorial entity in the sense of being a sovereign state, as the term was understood in the eighteenth and even the nineteenth centuries. Naturally for practical purposes the emperor had to have his own estates but his authority was not derived from such personal property, but from the transcendental, almost religious respect in which the crown was held, which endowed him with the temporal *imperium* of all Christendom. It was only at the close of the Middle Ages, when the empire was shaken by internal strife, that the emperor felt the need for more tangible support, for without a territorial base, that is without family domains, he ran the risk of becoming merely a puppet in the hands of the ambitious Prince-Electors. Already by Maximilian I's time the true import of the crown of Charlemagne was gradually being forgotten as two new concepts infected Europe – the idea of a territorial sovereign state and a growing sense of nationalism. Nevertheless, the title and dignity of emperor were still regarded as pre-eminent. Even during the time of its decline, when the empire was divested of almost all authority, powerful European monarchs such as Louis XIV still tried to secure for themselves what they considered to be the greatest title in Christendom.

But despite the general change in outlook, the concept of a united Europe, the *Orbis Europaeus Christianus*, received involuntary support in the fifteenth and sixteenth centuries from the growing power of Islam, since only by presenting a united front could the nations of the west establish an effective defence against the Turks.

Although it may seem paradoxical, it was logical that some of the great revolutionary movements of the period – in particular the peasant revolts – should have supported the empire. Reading the twelve articles summing up the demands of the German peasants and comparing them with the demands made by the Spanish peasants at almost the same time, gives one the feeling that there was an international agreement between them. Certainly their common viewpoint can be attributed to the fact that from one end of Europe to the other there existed, as in our day, identical social problems. As the rule of the territorial princes became ever more harsh and unjust, so the popular appeal of the emperor became proportionately stronger. The oppressed people hoped that an emperor who ruled without thought of personal or dynastic ambition, only to serve God, who believed in religious equality and the rights of man, would crush the despotism of their new masters. The overwhelming enthusiasm which greeted the candidature of the young prince to the imperial throne in 1502 – much to the surprise of the elector-princes – was an expression of these hopes. Charles V, as is testified by his writings, was well aware of the mood of his people.

Throughout his reign, the emperor worked towards the restoration of a Christian empire and for European unity. His efforts often seemed in vain in that they appeared to run directly against the course of history; but from a more general point of view we can see that Charles was clearly right, not only because of the demonstrable truth of his political ideals, but because in acting as he did he paved the way for future generations, a way which could lead to lasting peace. Indeed the idea of peace, based as much on the *Pax Romana* as on the *Pax Christi* of Christian philosophy, was closely linked with the concept of the empire. It implied an internal peace – the *Treuga Dei* – which had played an important part in the Middle Ages, and it also comprised the idea of a juridical order, since the *Imperator Pacificus*, the archetypal figure of the Middle Ages, was at one and the same time arbiter, judge and justiciar.

These ideas had a powerful influence on the character and life of Charles v. Many of his actions were regarded by his contemporaries as scarcely politic, and some of his historians have even found them incomprehensible, as, for example, his attitude towards his prisoner, François I. Doubtless, the emperor was unrealistic in placing Christian and chivalrous ideals above the needs of political expediency. But in so criticising him, one forgets his position as bearer of the Crown of the Holy Roman Empire, and it is essential to remember that this crown was not a symbol of power like the regalia of other kings; Charlemagne's crown signified that its wearer should serve the cause of justice and peace, and in consequence give proof of his confidence in his brother Christians and in his faith in the goodness of man. Charles always remained true to this ideal even after his confidence had many times been misplaced.

The House of Habsburg had been intimately connected with the Holy Empire ever since Rudolf's election to the throne of Charlemagne. We know how diligently Friedrich III preserved this ideal, even at the time when he lacked the material resources with which to impose his will. Maximilian too, however wayward his behaviour may have been at times, always based his policies on the idea of the Empire as a commonwealth of Christian nations. His scheme to make himself Pope would have been completely out of the question had he not regarded the imperial title as one that conferred on him a sacred duty. The decadence of the papacy towards the year 1500 often resulted in the ruling pontiffs assuming the mantle of political potentates, quite forgetful of their spiritual charge, and it was reaction to this worldly attitude which reinforced the religious aspect of the emperor's functions. In fact in his efforts to convene the Great Council to discuss the Reformation of the Church, Charles v often found himself in a position which recalls that of the anti-papists.

Historians of Charles and his age often speculate about the possible course of history had the emperor put himself at the head of the Reformation, and, breaking his ties with Rome, had used the new religious movement as an instrument to further his own political ends. But these are idle speculations, based as they are on unrealised possibilities. The fact, however, that such hypotheses were formulated, is proof in itself that his contemporaries and historians accepted the idea that the emperor was entitled to assume a religious function.

It was in a moral and spiritual sense that Charles understood his task. In addition to his high ideal of the role of the Holy Empire, Charles always maintained an unshakeable loyalty to the cause of religious unity in the west. Of course he was often in disagreement with the Curia, but as a Christian, a Habsburg and as Emperor, he was passionately opposed to anything that might lead to a split in the ranks of the Christian community of Europe. Because of his refusal to take up the cause of the German Reformation, historians have accused him of being 'mediaeval', and reactionary, but it is precisely the dreams of later generations of re-establishing a united church, the tragic consequences of the Schism, and the active interest shown in our own day in ecumenical ideas, which prove that Charles's vision extended beyond that of his own times. Had he adopted any other attitude than the one he did, he would have betrayed the imperial ideal.

As already mentioned, the strongest opposition to the concept of the empire came from the new idea of the Sovereign Territorial State. We see the beginnings of this new idea in the thirteenth century, and by the beginning of the fifteenth century, although territorial sovereignty was still far from its apogee (which was only reached four centuries later), it was a tangible reality in certain parts of Europe. Almost everywhere it influenced rulers and jurists. The old relationships of the Middle Ages, based on allegiances and blood ties, were replaced by purely national considerations and attachments to one's native soil. A criminal was no longer judged according to the laws of his clan but by the laws of the country where he had committed his misdeed. Between the thirteenth and sixteenth centuries Roman Law had been introduced, or re-established, in nearly every European country. The unique exception was England, hence the autonomous development of its social and public institutions.

The transitional period between the old order and the new, with its changed laws, caused most distress to the masses. Their lot was in no way improved, very much to the contrary, in fact, and this was one of the major causes of the great peasant risings in France and Germany, Italy and Scandinavia. In France, which economically was the most highly developed country of its time, and where Roman Law and a modern state had been established earlier than elsewhere, the Peasants' War, known as the *Jacquerie*, erupted well in advance of similar events in the German Empire. There, however, the rising of the peasants had been preceded at the very beginning of the fifteenth century by the Hussite war which had ravaged Bohemia and the surrounding German territories.

The idea of well-defined territorial boundaries and its corollary, the idea of the sovereignty of the state, did not, however, imply that the ruler was able to exercise an absolute prerogative. On the contrary, the end of the Middle Ages is marked by a complete lack of any clearly defined stable supreme authority. In the new sovereign realms a bitter struggle was waged between the ruler and his subjects. The new urban economy led logically to ever greater differences within the class structure. In addition to great landowners there was now added a class of burghers; at the same time, within the cities themselves, further class distinction became apparent, particularly between the oldest patrician families (often assimilated into the nobility) and the burghers engaged in trade, who often refused to agree to the privileges of the other. Furthermore, at the beginning of the fifteenth century, a proletarian society began to emerge. This was mainly composed of journeymen, who were virtually excluded from becoming mastercraftsmen and were forced to remain salaried employees for the whole of their lives. Sooner or later, in practically every country in Europe, these three urban groups were to clash violently, a struggle which was marked by bloody upheavals and exile or death for the vanquished. The brutality of these clashes can often be explained by the absence of any higher authority strong enough to act as arbitrator. While this political void and lack of any real legal power in the state was keenly resented by the minorities who were deprived of their rights, certain sections of the upper classes continued to fight tooth and nail to defend themselves against the empire which might attempt to curb such arbitrary jurisdiction on their part.

In the countryside also, legal relations between the great feudal lords and the peasants had changed with the introduction of a monetary economy and the re-establishment of Roman Law. Like the journeymen in the towns, the oppressed peasants also sought the support of the imperial authority to protect them from these fresh tyrannies to which they were subjected by some sections of the nobility and clergy. The latter, only too often, made a profit out of the new form of feudal dues.

There were to be continual resurgences of these social struggles which only ended in the seventeenth century with the advent of absolutism. The period of Charles v was one of transition. Already the first outlines of a modern régime could be described, whereby a ruler was able to crush the power of the nobles and establish his authority over all social classes. Though, on the other hand, there still survived a corporative system which in spite of its name was not representative of a harmonious whole, but was rather a multiplicity of estates within a state.

The drawbacks inherent in this old system are most strikingly apparent in the sphere of public finances. The reign of Charles v was distinguished by perpetual monetary difficulties, and many political projects were never brought to fruition through lack of funds. This is surprising in view of the fact that Charles ruled over many countries some of which, like the Duchy of Burgundy and Spain, mistress of the New World, had very considerable resources.

But this contradiction is explained by the lack of any regular fiscal system. The first attempts towards a proper organisation of the treasury were often merely improvisations made as occasion demanded. In this unstable and fluctuating situation, the sovereign, in order to meet the needs of his administration had no alternative but to ask the Estates for it, indeed to threaten them with physical violence on occasions.

The principal reason for this penurious situation was the exemption from taxation enjoyed by the nobility and clergy. A lack of funds was never so evident in countries where the ruling authority was sufficiently strong to induce the privileged classes to disburse regular contributions, nor in those states where the crown was rich in landed properties.

We must constantly remind ourselves of these facts in seeking the main reason for the power of the kings of France and for their frequent dominance over their rivals of the House of Habsburg. In France, the crown had long been assured of the control of ecclesiastical revenues. It had thus established an area of common interest between the temporal power and the clergy, especially the bishops. This partnership was in the long run of benefit to both. The crown was assured of regular revenues sufficient to cover its normal expenditure, and in return it interposed itself between the French prelacy and the Roman Curia. The king protected the bishops against Rome, and for some time in the fourteenth century he even had some control over the papacy when the sovereign pontiffs resided within the French sphere of influence at Avignon.

The Kingdom of France unlike that of Germany was thus in receipt of revenues which, if not quite adequate, were at least substantial. Louis XI, who crushed the power of the feudal barons, still further enriched the country by the establishment of a veritable public patrimony. What was most important in the political scheme of things was not so much the actual amount of the received revenues, but the knowledge that the payments would be regular, thus making it feasible to prepare some sort of budget. In fact, it did not become possible, in Spain at least, to mobilise effectively the great wealth of the country in the national interests until the reign of Charles's successor.

On the other hand, Charles v's councillors devoted infinite time and patience to putting his finances in order. The numerous wars and political enterprises which engaged the monarch's attention, his many journeys, and in particular the very great difference between the juridical statutes of his diverse possessions prevented the accomplishment of this task during his lifetime. Furthermore, the courtly and chivalrous style of living in Burgundy, the fêtes and tournaments, the upkeep of buildings, military pensions and the maintenance of the court, all absorbed considerable sums which far surpassed the modest revenues received.

The Habsburgs financed their wars by loans made against their various sources of wealth, such as the silver mines of the Tyrol, and later, after the union of the crowns of St Wenceslas of Bohemia and St Stephen of Austria, the Bohemian-Moravian mines as well as those of Upper Hungary. These passed into the hands of the great banking houses, in particular the Fuggers of Augsburg and the Welsers. The appearance of this new class of capitalist financiers, small in number but none the less influential for that, was a phenomenon not confined to the

Habsburg domains; in Italy, too, there arose a well developed banking system and in France, in the fifteenth century, the Farmers General played an important role, as witness the career of the famous Jacques Coeur.

The weakness of the financial system throughout many parts of Europe, hindered the establishment of a well organised administration, that is to say the establishment of a regularly paid body of officials. These conditions naturally extended to military affairs as well.

Over and above the financial advantages enjoyed by the French crown, the monarchy there also exercised great scientific and intellectual influence, thanks to its ties with the Sorbonne, the University of Paris. The great theologians and jurists who lectured there were highly regarded throughout Europe especially during the life of the Council of Constance, whose work they directed. These same scholars furnished the kings with the necessary arguments and documents in their embroilments with the papacy, the French episcopacy and nobles. When Charles iv founded the University of Prague in 1348, his overriding idea was to create an analogous instrument to that possessed by the King of France. He, too, wanted to benefit from the support of an intellectual élite, similar to the one he had known as a young man in France.

This historic event illustrates most strikingly the difference between France and Germany. From the very start the German princes hastened to compete with the emperor in the founding of universities; the grandson of Charles iv, Rudolf of Habsburg, known as The Founder, created the University of Vienna in 1365, only seventeen years after the foundation of Prague, and this initiative was taken up by others. It is significant that Wittenberg, the last of the great universities to be founded (1509) became the cradle and centre of the Lutheran faith. When a large number of German princes rallied to the cause of the Reformation by creating territorial churches and abrogating the power of the bishops, they relied for the greater part on the intellectual support of the universities and, in consequence, a whole new series of foundations were established. What was lacking, however, was an Imperial University and the wearer of the Imperial Crown was obliged to rely on the gratuitous co-operation of the institutions founded by the territorial princes for any historic documents or legal advice he might require in pursuance of his policies.

THE CHURCH

No event during the reign of Charles V so profoundly disrupted the life of states and individuals – in short, the whole of European society – as the Great Schism. Its effect was felt throughout all Charles's domains. Starting in Germany, the revolt against the old faith, and in particular against the Pope and the Church of Rome, spread with the violence of a hurricane throughout the whole Christian world. Its dynamism was not only derived from religious fervour; nationalist elements were also involved, together with demands for social rights.

This new conception of the nation as a common entity and through that the emergence of a national ethos was to have a profound effect on both men and events. During the preceding centuries there had of course been national and linguistic differences; there were even eruptions of chauvinism and xenophobia, principally involving peoples under foreign domination, but such occurrences had only been of a transitory nature. The political passions that were aroused in Europe at the beginning of the sixteenth century, on the other hand, already possessed a quality of permanence. A typical example of this new spirit was the Spanish reaction against the young king and his followers, when Charles, newly arrived in the country, had seemed to favour the Burgundians and Flemings over the Castilians. Similar sentiments prompted the risings of the German Protestants against Rome. Luther was prompted by genuine religious feelings with his verbal blasts against the Popish 'Whore of Babylon', a phrase which was to play such a major part in Protestant polemics over the centuries. Nevertheless, the dynamic forces behind the Reformation were far from being only spiritual and moral. Among many of the followers of the new creed – including perhaps Luther himself – the hatred of Latin and Italian, in short everything specifically Roman, was an important factor. It was a sentiment which ever since the Reformation has continued to exist in Germany, sometimes subconsciously, sometimes overtly, and at the beginning of the twentieth century there were still many Germans with a strong anti-Roman bias.

Apart from the nationalist factions, the Reformation in Germany was also motivated by economic and political considerations, particularly where the princes were concerned. In this there is nothing surprising; society cannot be arbitrarily separated into watertight compartments; there is always action and reaction and the faults are never all on one side. In part the Reformation can also be explained by certain un-deniable abuses perpetrated by Rome. Enormous sums of money had been transferred from Germany to the Eternal City, whose already abundant wealth had been further added to by the first Medici popes; the number of *années saintes* (holy years) and the sale of indulgences had increased in the most disgraceful fashion. Luther, who had visited Rome and had seen for himself the luxuries of the Renaissance, was to speak later of the German money used to build the marble palaces and magni-ficent churches which graced the home of the popes. Nor was Luther alone in condemning this dispersal of wealth for, in addition to a general feeling of indignation, the princes wished to appropriate for themselves the riches of the church and retain the monies which until then had been remitted to Rome.

It is significant that the immediate cause of the Great Schism was the controversy that raged over the infamous traffic in indulgences. Anyone with an historical sense must have been forcibly struck by the demands of the German prelates at the Ecumenical Council of 1965, when they vigorously insisted on a reform which would almost inevitably lead to the complete abolition of indulgences.

Nevertheless, these causes in themselves would not have sufficed if nationalism had not degenerated by a natural process into xenophobia.

Once these feelings were given free rein, it was an easy matter for many of those in authority to hide their cupidity and base political interests under a cloak of respectability, while, at the same time, keep-ing the masses in a state of suspense. No sooner had Charles received the Crown in Germany than the Elector Princes began to murmur of 'Spanish bondage' – a phrase that was to die hard. Once again their initial purpose was to conceal their political aims by posing as the defenders of the people against foreign domination. But these same Electors, while denouncing Spanish influence, had no hesitation in selling themselves to the king of France. They transferred the three bishoprics of Lorraine to him, justifying this political transaction by an argument which seen in historical perspective would have been incon-ceivable a couple of generations earlier. They argued quite simply that since the language of Metz, Toul and Verdun had been French for a long time past, these cities in consequence belonged legitimately to the French Crown. By accepting this new concept of international law, the Electors turned their backs on the idea of a supranational state founded on a Romano-Germanic Empire and on the federal principles of a

c*

Regnum Teutonicum. One might even go further, and claim that this date marks the official birth of German nationalism, which in the course of the nineteenth and twentieth centuries was to be the cause of so much suffering both for her inhabitants and those of the neighbouring states.

In France the concept of nationalism dates from the time of Joan of Arc and her victories over the English; the impetus given by the Maid of Orleans to the patriotic concept was bolstered and kept alive by the pretensions of the English kings to the French throne. The fact that this sense of patriotism was engendered by the saint and martyr of Domremy imbued it with an almost religious significance.

In Germany, on the other hand, the same movement sprang from the treacherous violation of the concept of the empire and betrayal of the secular mission of the eastern Franks, and thus had origins which were rather more sordid.

In addition to these general observations, the special position of the ecclesiastical establishment in France must be taken into account, for here the judiciary protected the clergy from domination by the Curia, and enabled the kings of France to impose strict limits on the transfer of funds beyond the Alps. Thus the jealousy of Rome which provided such an impetus to the Reform in Germany was lacking in France.

An additional factor favourable to the rise of nationalism was social 'reconstruction'. The influence of the bourgeoisie, who in everyday life and in their businesses used their mother tongue in lieu of Latin, had grown considerably. Already, even before Gutenberg, there were signs of such a revival in the literature of different European countries, for example Boccaccio in Italy, Chaucer in England, and, in the German-speaking world, the humanist poems of Ackermann of Bohemia. With the invention of printing, the masses began by degrees to buy and read more and more books. Literary works in German, English and Italian began to be widely circulated and because a flood of new works was in the financial interests of the publishers, the sale of Bibles in Latin and works by the writers of antiquity was being strictly limited. In this way the nationalist trend received a very considerable, if not decisive, impetus. The use of Latin, which for so long had been the common language of European peoples, was soon confined to a restricted circle of intellectuals. Moreover, the biting humanist critics who castigated the barbarous monkish 'dog-Latin' – as for example in the famous *Epistolae Virorum Obscurorum* – provided yet another reason for abandoning its use; anyone who could not speak it to classical perfection risked being held up to ridicule and hardly dared enter into a conversation for fear of revealing his ignorance. Moreover Latin had many strong opponents among a group of humanists who were keen supporters of Greek, a language which they had rediscovered. Their attacks were sometimes sly, but also often rabid, and their attitude was a curious combination of scientific amateurism and a subconscious resentment. If Luther, for example, turned to the Greek texts of the Scriptures and accused the Latin Vulgate of being a distortion of the Word of God, it was not necessarily just for religious reasons, but also perhaps because Latin was a language of Rome and the popes. Moreover there was an affinity between the Greek and German languages which inspired a profound sympathy to the linguistic genius of the father of the Reformation.

It is natural that all these factors should have played only a minor role in Roman Europe, and this explains why the religious schism led to a national split in Europe and divided the continent into a Germanic party and a Latin party. At the close of the Council of Trent, for example, only a few German bishops attended the sessions and Charles V himself recognised on several occasions that the attitude of the German ecclesiastical dignitaries towards the Council was just as hostile as that of the Electors; the Curia, for its part, took no interest in the proceedings until the sessions – thanks to the voluntary abstention on the part of the Germans – had become an almost entirely Latin concern.

The reformatory trends of the fourteenth century stemmed principally from the theologians. John Wyclif had more influence in Bohemia, thanks to his disciple John Huss, than in his native England. The passionate debates of the scholars at the great Council of Constance, and later at the ecclesiastical assemblies at Pisa and Basle, were of profound interest to a circle of princes, professors and bishops, but hardly affected the masses at all. The demand for a real reorganisation of the church was not a matter for popular concern until the sixteenth century, when the protagonists combined their religious demands with their nationalist fervour.

In a previous period, within limits which were still strictly regional, a similar phenomenon had already manifested itself around 1400, in the Hussite Movement which anticipated the Reformation by some hundred years. After the death of Huss at the stake, the reformer's teachings were widely disseminated, but the reasons for this were prompted as much by national hatred, vengeance and a desire for a new social order, as for their religious content.

It is worth noting that Huss's predecessors at Prague, and the doctors who gave his teachings their dogmatic form, were for the most part German. Huss himself had, on the other hand, begun his career at the university with a nationalist gesture, when he succeeded in persuading King Wenceslas to insure, by the edict of Kuttenberg, that the Czechs were given precedence over the other *nationes* of Bavarians, Saxons and Poles. A century later, the national idea, already very close to nationalism, had gained so much ground, that the spark kindled by Luther in his religious fervour against a too rigid dogma and circumscribed liturgy caused a conflagration which devoured, to everyone's surprise, many other things besides the church.

Of all Charles v's contemporaries, Martin Luther was undoubtedly the most remarkable. If one takes into account his role in history and the effects of his doctrine, one could also add that he was the sovereign's most dangerous rival, although during all his life he regarded the latter with sympathy and even respect. Seventeen years older than the monarch, Luther was a product of the middle classes – what we would today call middle-class intellectuals – who at that time played a very important role, similar to their twentieth-century successors the technocrats. His father was a miner, but we should not interpret the word in its modern sense. Miners were then a strictly organised class and enjoyed considerable status in society. Generally they were well educated men, for the distinction between engineer and workman was as yet unknown, and a miner was obliged to be a combination of the two. It was natural that a miner should consider himself a member of an élite, as indeed he was regarded by most people. His status it seems derived from some ancient pagan memories, when it was believed that the miner descended to the bowels of the earth to commune with the invisible forces who ruled there. Officially no Christian could still believe in such myths, but nevertheless, in the imagination of the people, these myths were very real, and were perpetuated in legend and oral traditions. This, however, did not prevent the fraternity of miners from being known for their firmly established religious views. Luther's background had thus already imbued him with a strong sense of the supernatural forces in life, a sense verging on that of the superstitious, which was to have a great effect on him, both as a young man and as a mature scholar. This goes far towards explaining why events such as the violent death of a friend, and the stroke of lightning from which he more or less miraculously escaped – according to him by the intervention of St Anne – had a profound influence on his spiritual and religious development. For years, too, we find Luther seeking an all-merciful God. And a fear of Hell and an awareness of his own shortcomings drove him to the study of the New Testament and interpretations of Holy Writ. We see his spiritual anxieties reflected in his teaching and in his actions.

Together with intense faith, the Master of Wittenberg was as we know inspired by nationalist sentiments. The origin of these feelings is attributable to the fact that he was born in the Eastern Marches, a region already under Slav influence; the inhabitants of frontier regions do generally have a greater tendency to assert themselves and behave aggressively than the inhabitants of the interior, who have no direct contact with other races or languages.

In Rome, the Augustinian monk, with his provincial outlook, was unable to comprehend the positive qualities of an intellectual and religious Power, the repository of fifteen centuries of history, which over the course of time had transformed and preserved for future generations the entire cultural heritage of antiquity. He could not appreciate the refinements of the Roman way of life, nor the exquisite taste and great artistic efforts which had produced works comparable, even superior, to those of classical times. The political manœuvres of the papal court he regarded as sheer trickery. In short, he condemned all the things which fired many of his contemporaries with such enthusiasm. Luther could only see around him decadence and moral depravity and what he considered to be a betrayal of the mission of the early church and of Christ's message. He lacked any sense of historical perspective. For him, Rome was a New Babylon, a den of vice, the haunt of the Beast of the Apocalypse, while the Pope appeared to him as the servant of a false god, the minion of the 'Great Whore'. Furthermore, he was convinced that all the splendid palaces, the resplendent vestments, the brilliant fêtes, the jewels of mistresses and the luxury which surrounded the cardinals, had been acquired with monies supplied by German Christians, who in all innocence had simply endeavoured to ensure their passage to heaven by contributing their offerings to the church. Luther returned from the capital of the world a German Nationalist, rebelling against the 'corruption' of all things Latin. Nietzsche speaks scathingly of the 'coarse little German monk', indifferent to the grandeurs of antiquity and the Renaissance. Without wanting to go so far, it is certainly true that Luther's reaction to Rome was that of a middle-class provincial patriot.

The decisive turning point in the life of the founder of protestantism was his meeting with the poet-knight, Ulrich von Hutten; Hutten, for his part, was left with an unforgettable impression of Luther. Hutten can probably be considered the first of the German nationalists, or at least the first to really inspire the people with his doctrine. His favourite theme of France as the hereditary enemy – of the traditional hostility between Gaul and German – was to poison German thought for years to come. But, objectively speaking, it must be admitted that these tendentious ideas would never have become firmly established had it not been for French policy under Richelieu, Louis XIV and Napoleon.

Hutten made Luther realise that his desire for religious reform and a German national movement were interdependent. From then on he no longer saw himself solely as a religious reformer but also as a political figure called upon to arouse and liberate his people from Italian oppression. Legendary memories of the struggles of the Germans against Caesar's legions were recalled by Luther who saw the glorious past revived again in the people's opposition to Spanish dominion. When we realise that such thoughts never entered the mind of Charles V, who probably would not even have understood them, we can understand how wide was the gulf separating these two great men. In spite of their mutual respect for each other, the conflict between them was inevitable. We have already remarked that the Latin peoples showed relatively little interest in the Reform, while it was a matter of deep concern to Germanic Europe. In the light of Luther's motivations, which were as sincere as they were complex, this phenomenon can also be explained irrespective of any nationalist factors. In the Mediterranean countries many classical pagan elements had been absorbed into Christianity, and these partly usurped the place of the Old Testament; this was the reason it never played an exclusive or even a major role in the historic tradition of the church. Humanism further reinforced this attitude by recalling the spirit of classical paganism. Thus we find the world of Olympus and the heroes of antiquity appearing side by side, almost in concord with choirs of angels and the glorious host of saints and the innumerable blessed who inhabit the kingdom of heaven.

In the Germanic countries, on the contrary, the old pagan gods had been metamorphosed into demons, and the conscience of many Christians was dictated by the God of Wrath of the Old Testament.

This was the God before whom Luther trembled, before whom he felt abandoned and helpless; it recalls the old Bavarian poem *Muspillii*, the epic description of the Last Judgement, where the human soul is all alone before the Great Judge, bereft of all support from the family and friends who surround one on earth. This gloomy dread was the very reverse of the comfort given by the priest who attended Charles v during his last moments, who told the emperor that St Mathias and St Matthew, his heavenly guardians at birth, would accompany him to the throne of God on his death.

Luther, despite his veneration for the Blessed Virgin and St Anne, did not believe that it was possible to be saved by the merits of others. It was in the middle of this period of spiritual torment that it was revealed to him, while reading the Epistle to the Romans, that man could be saved by faith and faith alone, by the grace of Christ crucified. Profoundly moved by this revelation he felt impelled to impart his creed to the theological students at Wittenberg. His views naturally caused him to explode with indignation at the sermons of Tetzel. The latter was the purveyor of indulgences, who, by a more than dubious interpretation of the teachings of the Church, promised the faithful an escape from purgatory if only they obtained a sufficient number of indulgences. Protestant propaganda has certainly exaggerated in claiming that Tetzel guaranteed paradise for the souls of those whose money 'clinked in the coffers' (*Wenn der Kreuzer im Kasten klingt, die Seele aus dem Feuer springt*). However, this exaggeration did have its origins in certain real and regrettable abuses and excesses which were to lead Luther, when still a young man filled with religious fervour, to quit the peaceful atmosphere of the lecture room and throw himself ino public life.

In spite of the decisions of councils and the various measures which the popes had decreed in the fifteenth century, many abuses continued to flourish. It is difficult to know whether these practices were worse in Germany than elsewhere in Christendom, but judging by Italian literature of the fifteenth and sixteenth centuries it would seem that they were universal. Nevertheless, in France, where the Church was largely subordinate to royal authority, reforms were more easily imposed than elsewhere. Bishops were not princes of the empire, and the Sorbonne kept a watchful eye on the purity of doctrinal beliefs. In Italy, on the other hand, the signs of decadence noted by writers, were not taken too seriously; witty and slightly cynical, Italians preferred to enjoy themselves, even finding certain advantages in the human failings of the clergy, since these weaknesses vouchsafed to the laity extenuating circumstances when they themselves came before the tribunal of God. The serious-minded Germans, only too often lacking in humour, and similarly the fanatical Slavs, reacted in quite a different way. They viewed the human weaknesses of the church with both sorrow and anger, and blamed above all the higher clergy, with whom, on a final analysis they felt, lay the responsibility for the predominant influence of Rome.

A large part of the responsibility for the crisis falls just as much on the humanists, who with their intellectual arrogance enjoyed pointing out the ignorance of theologians, and particularly their deficiency in Latin. These polemical discussions, however, scarcely touched the masses. In consequence, monks and clergy were accused of other faults, in particular, gluttony, drunkenness and violation of their vows of chastity. There is no doubt that there were many abuses of this nature. The sobriety of the *devotio moderna*, asceticism, was counter-balanced by an overflowing *joie de vivre*, which had nothing in common with the cardinal virtues preached by the church.

These difficulties were augmented by the economic structure of the period, which forced many members of the clergy to occupy themselves with worldly matters. For example, if a parish priest had a licence for an eating-place, on which the existence of his parish depended, it was difficult for him to preach sobriety; similarly if he had an inn, he more or less had to turn a blind eye to what was going on. One must therefore admit that on occasions certain priests must have directly profited from vice.

Nonetheless, it would be wrong to conclude from reading contemporary texts, that the dishonesty of which their authors speak was the general rule. A historian knows that the chronicler does not register the ordinary events every day, but carefully notes anomalies; he overlooks a hundred virtuous priests only to pick on one who sets a bad example to his parish. The polemical literature which proliferated at the beginning of the Reformation depicted, with manifest exaggeration, the moral condition of the old church as a 'heap of *ordure*'. Johannes Janssen's great, but never completed work, is the first of its kind to describe not only the negative side, but also the flourishing cultural side of life in Germany in the fifteenth century, the social institutions of the church and the remarkable achievements of the religious orders and of many branches of the church. Since the publication of this work, it is possible to form a more balanced opinion on the subject of a period which, like all others, had its moments of grandeur as well as misery.

To sum up: the mixture which detonated the explosive force that was the Reformation was composed of many different elements – humanism, nascent nationalism, political and religious criticism and the new pietism, the *devotio moderna*. Luther was the catalyst. The movement, however, to which he gave the impetus, was soon to surpass anything he had ever dreamed of – or ever wanted.

At the very beginning of the Reformation, the Emperor Maximilian had hoped to use the 'little monk of Wittenberg' as a tool against the pope, for he believed that the ethological disputes Luther had initiated might be directed and canalised to the benefit of his own temporal power. Only a little later, however, his successor, Charles, was to find himself faced with a situation which, although he at first regarded it as unimportant, was one he soon realised that he could not contain by himself; in fact to safeguard the unity and faith of the church, he would have to muster all the forces of the west. This was a task that seemed to him so important that he was ready to overlook all differences whether of a social, personal, or racial nature.

In pursuit of this praiseworthy aim, Charles v found some unexpected allies, among them Erasmus of Rotterdam. Unfortunately he also found relentless opposition on the part of the German princes and the Roman Curia, who were blindly and stubbornly resistant to all the emperor's efforts to convene a council to find a just compromise between the two extremes. Charles, as a pupil of Adrien of Utrecht and as a Netherlander, was open-minded on the question of reform. In the Provinces where he had been born, a revival of faith had already been manifest for some time. But this revivalist movement had made no attempt to change the political status quo, nor to proselytise; every man, it was believed, should act according to his own conscience. The Brothers of the Common Life maintained the heritage of the *devotio moderna*, which had had such a profound spiritual influence in the fourteenth century; the Beguines in Flanders also inspired similar sentiments. As we now know their movement initiated the development of a spiritual understanding between the Brothers of the Common Life – from the mouth of the Rhine and Holland – and the Augustinians of the convent of Erfurt, where Luther sought repose for his soul during the period of spiritual torment and doubt by which he had been so profoundly disturbed. From this same region, between the mouth of the Rhine and

Flanders, came the book, which up to the time of Pietism, was to have almost as great an influence on Christians as the Bible: *The Imitation of Christ*, attributed to Thomas à Kempis.

Life in the unpretentious palace of the Archduchess Marguerite at Malines proceeded calmly, dominated neither by the rigid dogmatism nor by the spiritual sterility which Luther found in the Rome of the Medicis. Charles had been brought up as a good Christian, and remained such throughout the vicissitudes of his life. What worried him most about the monk he was to meet at Worms was his fanaticism, which he suspected was not only a consequence of a religious reaction to the sale of indulgences and the primacy of the pope, but which he believed disguised other less worthy motives. The sovereign mistrusted Luther's egocentricity for he often gave the impression that he believed himself to be an infallible prophet, and by claiming to be the sole arbiter of his conscience, went so far as to deny the competence of the Council. Charles feared that Luther's doctrine, which pandered to the individual at the expense of the collective, might set fire to the communal house of the church, in which Christians had lived together for fifteen centuries. The emperor also feared that the Reformer might shake the confidence of every man in the doctrine that a *consensus omnium* in the church represented the voice of God. The sovereign unreservedly favoured a real reform and throughout his life demanded one. On the other hand he could not accept a refusal to recognise the authority of the Council, or the idea that several separate churches could coexist. His nature, education and faith forbade him to make concessions on this point: his universal religion was founded on the concept of one church and one pope.

In religious affairs, as in many matters during the course of his long political life, Charles V determinedly rose above party strife and even above the ethos of his times. In a brilliant study on the fundamental characteristics of the House of Habsburg, *Das Geschlecht Habsburg*, Erich von Kahler observes that one of the most distinctive features of this dynasty was its ability to think in advance of its times and independently of the moment, but to know when to beat a retreat when occasion demanded. A similar idea was put forward by Egon Fridel in his *History of Modern Civilization* (*Kulturgeschichte der Neuzeit*) and also by the poet Grillparzer, who has Rudolf the Second say that the House of Habsburg 'lives in the centre of a fixed axis awaiting the return of errant spirits'.

Because of his upbringing and because of his contacts with the most prominent personalities of his time, Charles belonged to the school of humanists. This side to his character is revealed by his knowledge of languages, his scientific curiosity, his appreciation of classical traditions and his humane attitude towards his fellow men. It is in this last quality that he differs from Henry VIII of England, who though no doubt an equally accomplished scholar was cruel and lacking in all compassion. The emperor's faith leaves no doubt that his humanism was clearly Christian in inspiration, his faith in which was never shaken. But Charles was also very much a man of the Renaissance as is evident by his love of classical forms, the style of his letters and other writings and by the kind of buildings he erected.

However, the emperor remained immune from the pride so characteristic of many of his contemporaries. He was the *uomo universale* in a very different sense from that of certain of his Renaissance contemporaries who corresponded rather more to the Machiavellian ideal. It would have been impossible to satirise him and his court in the way in which Rabelais satirised his great rival, François I.

Charles might rather be compared with Michelangelo, the greatest artist of his age. Michelangelo, great Renaissance artist though he was, remained fundamentally a man of the Christian Middle Ages in his complete devotion to his work, his humility, by the manner in which he reveals himself through his letters and poems and, above all, in his artistic creations. An example of this is seen in his gigantic picture of the Last Judgement, where he depicts himself among the last of the sinners.

One might imagine perhaps from the emperor's motto: *Plus ultra*, that he was an ambitious man, but his life story shows that he always respected the frontiers to which he had committed himself while he was still a young man, and *Non plus ultra* was his motto. When on the advice of the humanist Marliano he suppressed the word *non*, his action was prompted by the conviction that faithful to his mission as a Christian, as an emperor and as a son of the House of Habsburg-Burgundy, he would never cease to fight for his ideals.

A complex problem in the history of art and culture is whether the word Renaissance can properly be applied to the world which extended beyond the Alps. The notion of a re-birth, a *Rinascimento*, only fully applies to countries where classical culture once effectively existed. What we find therefore in Germany and the Low Countries, and even in the north of France, is something very different from the culture of the Mediterranean. It is in fact an autonomous development of Gothic, enriched by certain borrowings from Italian art; in particular, technical developments such as perspective. Moreover, one seldom finds in these northern lands the deep, passionate and vital love of pagan antiquity, the philosophy that makes man the master of his world, according him an almost God-like status which would place him above conventional notions of good and evil. In this context, it is only natural that Nietzsche should have so profoundly admired the Renaissance popes, who epitomised for him the incarnation of his ideal superman and of everything that a prince should be.

Just as it would be impossible to apply the term Renaissance to the painting of Matthias Grünewald in the sense it is applied to the works of Raphael and Leonardo da Vinci, so it would be equally inexact to define, in simple terms, Charles as a Renaissance man. Both emotionally and intellectually the Gothic Middle Ages and Christianity were still the vital factors in his life, which took precedence over the great revolutionary ideas of his time.

The extraordinary dichotomy of his nature and of his position in history arises from the fact that he found himself in the foreground of a humanist evolution, to which, by nature, he himself, could not subscribe. He carried on his shoulders an immense heritage which his contemporaries wished to destroy, but one which he was determined to preserve for the centuries to come. He lived between two epochs, outside his times, 'like a messenger from Eternity in an ephemeral world'. The monastic, eremitic character of his last earthly abode already presaged the Baroque, whose warmth and rapture he was not destined to savour, and to which he was not in any event attuned. Charles v presents to the world the exterior features of his epoch; but beneath the knightly armour and the patrician's costume he wears in the portraits by Titian in the Prado at Madrid, and in the *Pinakothek* at Munich, there hides a man to whom it was given to seek the essence of the imperial spirit beyond an ephemeral world, and who tried to realise his mission to the utmost of his ability.

THE ARMY AND THE NEW STRATEGIC WARFARE

Just as in politics, philosophy and the arts, the period of Charles v, from the military point of view, was a time of transition between the medieval system and the modern era. In reality there remained only a few traces of the military tactics of the Middle Ages, though, as yet, the new ideas had not been altogether assimilated. Modern principles of warfare, still in an embryonic stage, were scarcely formulated, hence the timidity of many commanders in the field to put them into practice. For almost two centuries now, chivalry had gradually been losing its military pre-eminence. In fact, it was the victory of the burghers of Bruges, allies of the Count of Flanders, over the armies of the King of France, and the famous Battle of the Spurs at Courtrai in 1302 which marked the beginning of a new epoch in military history. The crushing defeat of the Austrian and Swabian knights in the battles of Morgarten and Sempach was again the result of this new style of warfare. What had been started by the burghers was continued by the peasantry; in the Hussite campaigns, new tactical and strategic elements made their appearance. The wars of the Swiss Confederates against the Burgundians may be considered the culminating point of this evolution.

At the time of Charles v, military forces were not, as a general rule, nationalist in character, but were mainly composed of mercenaries. The military superiority, and almost inexhaustible army reserves, of the French kings was not so much because their armies were superior to those of their neighbours, but because their financial strength allowed them always to engage foreign mercenaries.

The mercenaries of the period were usually recruited from two regions where the military arts were traditionally practised: Switzerland and Upper Germany. Of course, in the sixteenth century not all soldiers were German, but with the exception of the Spanish, they were generally inferior to the *landsknechts*.

The main problem of the period was to combine the warlike merits of the knights with the military system of the mercenaries. We have already remarked that the emperor Maximilian had adopted the new tactics at the Battle of Guinegatte; but this was not so important from a tactical point of view as its effect on the morale of the troops. The real revolution had, in fact, been initiated by the same sovereign a short time earlier, when he made his entry into Brussels on foot at the head of his landsknechts. Up to this time the knight and his horse had been as one. The fact that a knight went to war mounted on a charger and clad in armour, while the landsknecht had to fight on foot, corresponded well with the social conceptions of the Middle Ages. The lord on his charger alone represented the true élite, the governing class.

The difference between the mounted knight and the foot-soldier affected the combative spirit of the latter.

Several times before, attempts had been made to use infantry without the support of cavalry. Often the result turned out ill; the foot-soldier was only at his best when immediately in the wake of a knight, or maybe when one or two foot-soldiers were stationed between two mounted men-at-arms. Without this support, the infantrymen often fled. This situation changed when the urban middle classes developed a sense of their own social dignity, a factor intimately connected with the liberty of the individual and when they acquired a sense of discipline from their work. In this way, troops levied the towns, although fighting on foot, were imbued with so much confidence that they could success-fully resist armies of knights. The weavers of Bruges, armed with long pikes known as *Goedendags*, and grouped under the orders of a captain of their own trade, Pieter de Koninck, together with the butchers, armed with axes and trained by Jan Breydel, formed a disciplined troop of matchless courage. Similarly, the Swiss Confederates were free men, who, armed with halberds and pikes, successfully resisted the charges of heavy cavalry.

However, as a general rule, this new peasant and bourgeois army served only in a defensive capacity. In particular, the burghers had no inclination to spend the night in open country after a battle, preferring to return home to their families. The Swiss, too, did not like to venture far from their base, while the armies of knights, on the other hand, were perfectly prepared to campaign far and wide.

In spite of this, the purely defensive attitude of the Swiss originated with mercenaries. In the time of Charles v there took place a decisive turning point in Swiss military history. Instead of entering the service of foreign lords, the Confederates organised themselves instead into an independent military force and left their native lands in search of con-quests abroad. They met with total disaster: at the Battle of Marignano, which lasted two days, they were crushed by the armies of the king of France, which comprised a minority of Frenchmen and a large number of German landsknechts. After this defeat the Swiss abandoned for good the idea of conducting offensive wars, and any man who wished to fight joined special units in the pay of foreign sovereigns.

One of the characteristics of this transitional period in the art of war was that neither Charles, nor his opponents, were ever able to achieve decisive victories. Even such an apparently complete triumph as that of

Pavia, only determined the immediate consequences of a campaign, or at best of a war; the permanent differences between the two states were not resolved even during a whole generation.

In the first half of the sixteenth century, a new conception of tactics developed in the Low Countries and in Spain, which in the course of years to come resulted in the formation of professional standing armies, and which influenced the strategy of Spaniards, Netherlanders, Swedes and French. The elaboration of this modern concept was due in a large part to Charles v's 'Gran Capitan', Gonzalvo de Cordoba, who during the war against Naples had undertaken the systematic training of his mercenary troops. In 1503 he was able to reap the benefits of his labours at Cerrignola. It is true that in 1512 the Spanish were defeated at Ravenna, but this defeat itself only enhanced their reputation as infantry. It is no coincidence, therefore, that the word 'infantry' derives from the Spanish fanteria.

In France, at the same time, the infantry were known as l'extraordinaire de la guerre, while the cavalry were known as ordinaire de la guerre. Such terms reflect the classic strategic idea that the cavalry was the principle arm. Both French and Spanish armies, however, had a problem in common, and a difficult one to resolve: how to protect themselves from enemy fire without a change of tactics. The latter had always been based on a compact phalanx of horsemen armed with lances, whose final thrust was regarded as the ultimate hammer blow, while the fire of sharpshooters was merely a preliminary means of weakening the enemy, of throwing confusion into their ranks, and of impeding their advance.

As we can see from his letters and his reports on technical subjects, Charles v was intensely interested in military questions. In this connection, it is interesting to read his study on the disposal of troops for the defence of Vienna in 1532. The efficiency of the system which he extols was difficult to prove in reality, as the Turks retreated without giving battle. To complete this memoir there is a letter from Ferdinand I to his sister, in which the King of Bohemia and Hungary gives a detailed description of the troops at his disposal and how his army was drawn up. The figures that he gives certainly seem nearer the truth than those of other chroniclers. An army of 80,000 infantry and 6,000 horse was drawn up in battle order. Schartlin von Burthenback speaks of 65,000 and 11,000 respectively. The pikemen formed three large squares with a front of 140 and depth of 150. Between these were posted the cavalry, in similar depth. The whole of this force was surrounded by sharp-shooters to a depth of five men, while the artillery was placed to the front, protected by Hungarian light horse. Hans Dellbruck, who made a scientific study of this plan, contends that it was drawn up more like a parade than an order of battle. Even if he is correct in this assumption, it remains nevertheless that this demonstration of force achieved its purpose, since the sultan, Suleiman, at the sight of the enemy, did not launch an attack, but ordered a retreat.

The writings of Charles also show that he attached great importance to military history. He paid particular attention to Caesar's battles, which he read and pondered in the *Commentaries*. He even sent a scientific commission to France to visit the Roman camps of the Gallic wars and to describe them in detail. As a result of their field work, the experts sent him no less than forty plans.

The emperor possessed great personal courage and never lost his self-possession in battle. He had a thorough understanding of tactical subtleties, together with an adequate knowledge of the overall strategy of major operations. His ability was proven beyond doubt in the campaign which ended in the triumphant battle of Mühlberg. Economic problems rendered him weaker, however, since for most of the time he was obliged to disband his mercenaries for lack of money, ready to enrol others when occasion demanded. This system forbade the execution of any long-term plan, a weakness disastrously apparent in his policies. It is also interesting to note that during the conquest of Tunis, he showed a remarkable knowledge of maritime strategy. If he failed before Algiers, his defeat was not due to errors of judgement but was mainly caused by the terrible weather which impeded the disembarkment of his troops.

We have already stressed that this period was very much one of transition. Similar periods had put the adaptability and clear-headedness of other rulers to the test. Charles was open-minded to the needs of the new era. Realistically, he forced himself to elaborate a fresh military system allowing the retention of certain chivalrous principles which, at the same time, he integrated into new technical developments, always taking into account changed social circumstances. A real revolution was caused by the introduction of the pistol, which considerably reinforced the cavalry, allowing them to fire on the enemy without dismounting. His battle formations – like the 'snail' or 'caracol', or again the 'chess-board', known under the name of the 'Spanish

Brigade' – may sometimes seem artificial, but his various experiments were to open the way to future developments.

The art of modern warfare as practised by the Spaniards, for which the emperor was partly responsible, was to serve as an example to all European states for more than a century, and assured the Iberian Infantry of a reputation for invincibility. Charles lived long enough to have the joy of seeing his son's generals, products of his school, applying the new principles which he had taught them to win the victory of St Quentin.

One of the great tragedies among the many which Charles had to face was the act of indiscipline perpetrated by his mercenaries, known as the Sack of Rome. As is shown by documents and writings of the time, the responsibility for this does not lie with Charles and his generals, despite the political advantages that he gained through it. This terrible event proved in the most striking manner possible how dangerous it was to recruit landsknechts and, through lack of funds, fail to pay them. What was needed was a permanent army, well trained and disciplined, which more by its quality than its numerical strength would be in a position to implement in a practical manner the strategies of the high command.

Compared with his famous contemporary, Nicolo Machiavelli, Charles was the more enlightened concerning military affairs. The scribe of Florence, the great political philosopher, organised in his native city a militia, which to begin with met with some outstanding successes, since it managed to subjugate Pisa. Nevertheless, this Florentine army was defeated in 1512 by the Spaniards in the Battle of Prato, and was practically annihilated in the retreat that followed. In fact the Florentines lacked discipline, a prerequisite for well-organised troops. Machiavelli, who in his theory of the state appears as the apologist for an unscrupulous and unlimited dictatorship, had committed the error of believing that in an army composed of the bourgeoisie, the right to command should be strictly limited. The ideal of Machiavelli's *Prince*, at this time, was almost exclusively represented by Charles's adversaries – men such as François I, Henry VIII of England, Maurice of Saxony, some of the popes of the period, certain diplomatic representatives of the Curia, the prince of Saxony and a number of other German princes. The emperor's tragedy was, perhaps, that unlike his enemies, he saw the state, politics and war through the eyes of a knight, an emperor and a Christian. But his reverses have themselves contributed an essential element to the great place he holds in history. The machiavellian princes, however, had not learnt their arts from the philosopher of Florence; rather it is the latter who interpreted the ideas of his times, of which the princes were representative.

4

The Emperor in Germany

THE IMPERIAL ELECTION

The immediate reason for Charles's departure from Spain was the death of the Emperor Maximilian, the news of which reached him at Lerida at the end of January, 1519.

At the Diet of Augsburg, the emperor, already at the point of death, had worked hard for the election of his grandson as King of the Romans. The negative attitude of the Electors showed him, however, that without sufficient money he would never achieve his purpose. Maximilian, generous by nature, was incapable of keeping anything of his own; no sooner was he in funds than they were spent. After having been short of money all his life, he was so completely impoverished by the end of his days that many bills of exchange which bore his signature were no longer accepted. The story goes that when he passed through Innsbruck on his last journey from Augsburg to Austria, the innkeepers refused to accommodate his suite unless he paid the debts incurred on preceding visits. This long journey in bad weather, with its many different stages by boat and carriage, no doubt hastened his end. Once arrived at Wels, he had no strength to continue, and he died there on 11 January 1519. He was not buried in the splendid tomb he had erected in the Hofkirche at Innsbruck, but in the Residency of Wiener Neustadt. His body lies under the altar, so that a priest celebrating the mass stands immediately above his heart. Maximilian had piously prepared himself for the next world, and during the last weeks of his life had withdrawn more and more from temporal affairs to devote himself to the salvation of his soul.

The scramble for his crown followed immediately on the emperor's death. If Charles wished seriously to aspire to his grandfather's throne, it was essential that he leave immediately for the Netherlands, so as to be in touch with events. For all that, a whole year was to pass before the fate of the empire was decided.

At the beginning, the attitude of the Spanish to the king's candidature for the imperial crown led to a further estrangement in relations with their sovereign. There was widespread disquiet and a renewal of disturbances, and the three conditions laid down by the *Cortès* as a *sine qua non* for their collaboration with the Court had a growing effect on public opinion. Their demands were that the king should not leave Spain, that he should not export gold or silver, and that he should not appoint any foreigner to public office. In order to arrive at some sort of agreement without accepting these terms, Charles convened the *Cortès*, but dismissed them whenever they refused him money only to reconvene them in another city of the kingdom.

Charles was well aware that it would be pointless to go to Germany without the several hundreds of thousands of ducats necessary to encourage the 'patriotism' of the Electors. In the meantime, the number of aspirants to the throne multiplied. François I of France was a much favoured candidate, and another interested party was Henry of England. To begin with the Roman Curia maintained a neutral attitude towards the election – their opposition to the House of Habsburg was usually of an underhand kind – but in the end, having failed to persuade Frederick the Wise, Elector of Saxony, to stand as a candidate, they came out in open support of the French King. Frederick was, in fact, the most respected of all the princes of the empire, his piety, tolerance, fair-mindedness and intellectual probity were well-known. Thus he protected Luther, a professor in his own university, because he considered it unjust to violate the liberty of conscience of an honourable man. On the other hand, the elector remained faithful all his life to the principal dogmas of the old faith, despite the fact that his country was the centre of the Reform. He was, even for those times, the greatest collector of holy relics, objects of a cult which the new creed regarded as idolatrous. He had acquired as many as eight thousand, most of which he had brought back from a pilgrimage to the Holy Land, and among which was the straw from Christ's crib. The Elector Frederick's decision to support the House of Habsburg was a decisive factor in the struggle for the imperial crown.

At Charles's request, the Archduchess Marguerite took a discreet part in the negotiations. Her remarkable talents as a diplomatist enabled her to enlist the aid of her vast network of personal friends on behalf of her nephew; however, she too pointed out to Charles that without large sums of money he could not hope to succeed.

Meanwhile, in Spain Charles had convened the *Cortès* for the last time. He chose Corunna, the port of Galicia, for the assembly so that as soon as he had obtained a satisfactory reply he could embark immediately for the Netherlands. His previous setbacks had taught him that it would be unwise for him to be represented at the *Cortès* by a foreigner such as de Croy or Gattinara, so he chose instead the Spanish bishop, Mota, his old teacher and one of his most respected advisers. The prelate, with close understanding of his compatriots, delivered his speech at the opening session of the Estates with consummate skill. He began by emphasising the greatness of Spain and its monarch, and then went on to an exposition of the honour that the election of their king to the imperial crown would bring to the country.

He stressed that hitherto this most exalted of all political offices had only been attained by the kings of the Franks and Germans; now, for the first time a Spaniard had a real chance of succeeding to the throne of Charlemagne. As emperor, he would be king of kings and his glory would reflect on all his compatriots. In a historical digression, Mota reminded the *Cortès* that their country had once been an important part of the Roman Empire, providing Rome with three of its most illustrious emperors, Trajan, Hadrian and Theodosius; now an occasion was offered, he pointed out, to renew this glorious tradition.

His eloquence worked wonders. The *Cortès* voted on the spot the funds demanded. More than 400,000 ducats were paid to the king's treasurer and, thus supplied with money, Charles was able to sail on 20 May 1520.

History provides frequent examples of the way in which both favourable and unfavourable events go in cycles, one example of which was that the attitude of Spain was reflected by a similar attitude in Germany. The Germans could be very obdurate, especially when anything concerning Rome was in question. The pope had ignored this fact in trying to fight the Habsburg claims by recommending the electors to vote for François I, but this intervention by the Curia had just the contrary effect. Probably for the first time in the history of Germany, public opinion manifested itself. This new phenomenon impressed the princes, who had never experienced a similar reaction from the populace. It was almost as if a wave of patriotism was

77

travelling from the North Sea to the Alps: everywhere the nobility, bourgeoisie and the masses were united in favour of the young Habsburg, who, from being completely unknown before, had suddenly developed into the great hope of the nation. This sudden acclaim was also probably due to the popularity enjoyed by Maximilian.

While the electors were still preparing to cast their decisive vote, the people had already dismissed all the other candidates. But as this change in public opinion only came about in the last stages of the election, it scarcely affected, one way or another, the promises which had already been made by the prospective candidate. Although it would have been extremely difficult for them to vote contrary to public opinion, the princes were thus still able to extract money from the Habsburgs. It is indicative of the mood of the country that Charles was elected unanimously. Only the Archbishop of Mainz, Albrecht of Brandenburg, who had already received too much in the way of money from the King of France to desert him entirely, expressed reservations in voting for Charles. He declared publicly that he supported the Habsburg out of fear rather than from the dictates of his conscience.

The cost of the election was finally assessed at about one million gold écus, half of which had been devoted to direct payments to the electors. Without the help of the Fugger banking house, Charles would never have been able to honour his promises, despite the generosity of the Spanish Cortès. Nevertheless these financial sacrifices, heavy as they were, were nothing in comparison with the political concessions which the princes obtained by their blackmail of the candidate.

In this way the election of 1520 marks an important stage in the constitutional history of Germany. The Empire openly assumed the aspect of a republic of princes, that is to say, a régime in which the Estates expected to have a decisive influence in government. It was anticipated, in fact, that during the emperor's absences – on which the princes counted because of the numerous engagements which occupied the sovereign's time – a federal republican government would be in effective control. Eugen Rosenstock rightly emphasises that it was from this moment that the expression 'Emperor and Empire' (Kaiser und Reich) became familiar. It signifies dualism and diarchy – government by two independent authorities – a constitution similar to that which prevailed in Rome at the time of Augustus. Another very important condition imposed by the princes was that the Habsburg should make a solemn promise never to lead Spanish troops into Germany.

But despite these concessions, subsequent events showed that Charles had in fact more power than any of his predecessors of the previous hundred and fifty years. The real influence of the emperor was not so much due to the territorial power of his family as, in the main, to his strong personality. Once again it must be stressed that constitutional government is dependent on the support of real authority, as opposed to that which exists only on paper.

At the time of the first meeting between the young emperor and the electors, we find contemporaries already remarking on a discreet change in personal relations. Maximilian had treated the princes as colleagues, who were thus accustomed to regard the emperor more or less as a *primus inter pares*, but Charles, to everyone's surprise, managed to create a sense of distance from the very beginning. In spite of the fact that this Habsburg was so much their junior in age, the princes accepted the new situation easily enough. The royal bearing of the young emperor inspired a profound respect in the princes, just as much as he himself was conscious of the importance of his new exalted position, which his grand chancellor energetically encouraged. Added to this was the fact that, owing to his international position, the Duke of Burgundy and the King of Spain was a very great lord in comparison with the German Electors; Charles was already beginning to build the empire 'on which the sun never set'.

On 22 October 1520, the new emperor made his entry into Aix-la-Chapelle. Like his former '*Joyeuse Entrée*' it was a very solemn occasion. This city which houses the tomb of Charlemagne lies so close to the Netherlands that one can easily imagine the kind of Burgundian-style ceremony that took place.

The pope was obliged to accept, although with very bad grace, this Habsburg triumph. In fact, only a short time before the elections he had persisted in sending a message by his nuncio Orsini to the assembly of princes at Oberwesel. Basing his case on the promise of Ferdinand of Aragon when he had obtained the Crown of Naples, the pontiff stressed that Charles, as sovereign of that kingdom, was ineligible for the imperial crown. Thus, in a new sixteenth-century form, the old problem of *Unio Regni ad Imperium*, the union of the Kingdom with the Empire, cropped up again after having already been the subject of so much litigation between the Hohenstaufens and the Curia, and which had led to the rupture between the Guelf Emperor Otho IV and Pope Innocent III. Rome in fact feared such a personal union which would encircle the papal states and endanger their independence, for if the King of Naples was at one and the same time King of the Germans, he would also be entitled to the iron crown of Lombardy and would thus automatically become the liege lord of the imperial fiefs in north and central Italy. Four centuries later, after the unification of Italy, this same strategic situation was to bring to an end the temporal rule of the Vatican.

During the negotiations which preceded the imperial election, Marguerite had suggested putting forward Ferdinand of Austria as a candidate, should the choice of his elder brother encounter insurmountable difficulties. Charles rejected the idea almost brusquely. He explained his point of view in detail, in the instructions he gave in a personal letter directed to the regent by the hand of Adrien de Croy, Seigneur de Borain, recently appointed a Knight of the Holy Fleece. Charles herein states his decision to have his brother elected King of the Romans, which clearly proves that he had no intention of permanently linking the imperial title with the Kingdom of Spain. In the meantime, however, it was essential that all the Habsburg territories should remain united in order to reinforce the influence of the imperial crown, since the preservation of the faith, and the defence of Christianity in the face of a common foe, were the principal objectives of the emperor's mission in Germany, as elsewhere.

The problem of the relationship between the two brothers and the necessity of assigning some function to Ferdinand became acute after the election of Charles. It would have been quite against prevailing notions for the brother of the emperor, and what is more, his heir presumptive, to live at the imperial court, without being given some important post, or being invested with some territorial authority. There was also the question of finding a constitutional formula to unite and govern the Austrian countries – the traditional base of Habsburg power. Charles had not, as yet, visited his Austrian possessions. Brandi in fact claims that these family estates were as foreign to him as the Americas, but this is rather an exaggeration. All the same, it is true that at this time Charles could not even speak the language of those of his possessions, which extended from the Porte de Bourgogne to the River Leitha. When obliged to address his Germanic subjects, he spoke the Flemish of his native country, and it was not until later that he learnt to speak German fluently.

The House of Habsburg's German possessions were of great importance. There was, in the first place, the County of Alsace, to which were added the territories which later passed to the Swiss. To the east of the Rhine lay Breisgau and the Swabian possessions, in particular the Marquisate of Burgau, Vorarlberg and Tyrol, whose government was established at Innsbruck. Beyond stretched the Austrian archduchies – Styria, Carinthia, Carniola and the Windische Mark, all administered from Wiener Neustadt. To the south, the Habsburg territories extended as far as the Adriatic to Frioul – Trieste after 1382 – on the foothills of the Alps, together with the bishoprics of Brixen and Trento, which commanded the Italian route and the passes leading to Milan. From here it was an easy matter to link up with the Spanish possessions in the Peninsula.

In 1521, at the Diet of Worms (which will be discussed further), the first agreement was reached between the two brothers concerning the division of the family domains in Germany. Ferdinand was invested with upper and lower Austria, Styria, Carinthia and Carniola. This last province suffered the loss of its lands between Pustertal and Istria, which Charles kept for himself because of their strategic importance in relation to Italy. Moreover, he also reserved for himself all west Austria, Vorderosterreich and the Tyrol. However, in 1522 a definitive agreement was signed in Brussels whereby Ferdinand was invested with the whole of Austria. A secret agreement added as a rider to the treaty, assured Ferdinand of all hereditary rights to Austria in the west, but stipulated that on his death, Pfirt, Alsace, and Haguenau should revert to Burgundy.

In 1520, the position of the Habsburgs in southern Germany, that is to say, between the Rhine and the Alps, was considerably strengthened by the acquisition of Württemberg, whose quarrelsome and restless duke, Ulrich, had been driven out of his country into exile. The Swabian League had made war against him, and on this account were claiming damages and reparations to the sum of 220,000 florins. As usual the Habsburg coffers were empty, but Burgundy stepped in and advanced the funds necessary to assure the dynasty's possession of this important territory. On 7 February 1522, Charles ceded the country to his brother, who in 1525 took the title of Duke of Württemberg.

The reign of Charles had started under auspicious circumstances; a visit to Canterbury had been a great success and the alliance with England was once more assured.

The main problem now was what attitude the Diet of Worms would take with regard to the Reformation of the Church. Rome had demanded that the situation should be resolved immediately. The Diet reassembled on 27 January 1521, and on 6 March of the same year, Charles called on the professor, Martin Luther, to appear before it in person. Already this gesture marked a big concession to the German ideas for a Reform; in fact the question should never have been discussed by an assembly of purely temporal dignitaries and should have been left exclusively to the competence of the ecclesiastical authorities.

THE REFORMATION IN GERMANY

The religious crisis that had erupted in Germany was much more than just a controversy between theologians, as both the emperor and the pope's special envoy, Girolomo Aleandro, were quick to recognise. Naturally, Charles was as yet unable to grasp the full historical significance of the event, but his political sense told him that this crisis could contribute decisively either to the success or the failure of his plans. The emergence of Luther with his attack on indulgences, and the haughty manner in which he confronted the pope, were not enough in themselves to give the new movement its revolutionary character; this stemmed rather from the passionate interest which a reform aroused in the Estates and in the German peoples.

It has already been indicated that the religious movements of the fifteenth and sixteenth centuries were to a large extent nationalist in character; there was a resurgence of primitive instincts, compared with which the weightiest theological arguments were nothing. Besides the reaction to the abuses of the Church, there were three principal causes which set in motion the religious revolutions, often giving them an irresistible impetus.

First, the humanists, who for a long time had been sapping the foundations of the church by their continual criticism of its structure. Most of their grievances were amply justified: the ignorance and lack of education in churchmen, their neglect of pastoral duties, the state of their religious life which was becoming increasingly devoid of spiritual content and thus remained confined to external forms. In a similar way, Erasmus of Rotterdam, prince of humanists, although he was a priest himself, lost all true sense of religion and for many years, as is well known, omitted to say mass altogether. Lortz, the Catholic historian, was able to say with justification, that he had debased the doctrines of the church by turning them into a purely moral philosophy; indeed, one might well wonder whether his Christianity was not just a form of theism in the eighteenth-century sense of the word. And if Erasmus remains the most imposing figure of humanism, his intellectual concepts are in fact those of two generations of humanists.

At the time of Luther's emergence on the scene, a violent controversy was raging round the person of the scholar Reuchlin and the *Epistolae Virorum Obscurorum* of Ulrich von Hutten, who expressed in very forthright terms the humanists' attitude towards the church. The humanists might have just tolerated the abuses which shocked lesser men – the accumulation of benefices, the immense wealth of the church, the pomp of the bishops, even the traffic in indulgences – all so remote from the spirit of poverty, charity, contrition, and piety, virtues particularly preached by the mendicant orders; but what was inexcusable in their eyes was the bad Latin spoken and written by the monks, which seemed to them a vulgar attack on the noblest of values – the tradition of classical antiquity.

Objectively speaking, these criticisms were not in fact always justified. For example, the Bible of St Jerome, the *Vulgate*, was attacked for misrepresenting the original texts. But some centuries later, Biblical studies were to show that the *Vulgate* was in fact much closer to the original Holy Writ than the Greek edition published under Erasmus's direction, which later served as the basis for Luther's (German) translation. Most recent research devoted to the reformer has proved that the errors contained in this work nearly all derive from the Greek text, and that his remarkable success in the linguistic sphere was, on the contrary, largely due to the *Vulgate*, of which he had so perfect a knowledge that he was able to write his German version in one stretch, in a surprisingly short space of time.

Charles v sympathised with the humanist criticism levelled at the meddling of the Curia, the organisation of the church and at the cultural standard of theologians and prebendaries. From 1516, Erasmus was nominated to the Imperial Council. It is true that in Spain, the Dominicans denounced the Master of Rotterdam as a heretic, but the emperor defended him personally and made no secret of the fact that he greatly admired his *Institutio Principis Christiani*; he even considered that the *Enchiridion Militis Christiani* was essential to the education of princes.

The second important factor contributing to the Reformation, and one which was also important to Luther himself, was on a different plane. Matters of conscience and religious doubts, such as those which assailed the young monk in the Monastery of St Anne at Erfurt, had almost nothing to do with humanism. These derived, above all, from the mysticism of the Middle Ages, the *Devotio moderna*. We have already emphasised the contacts which existed between the Low Countries and the Augustinians of Erfurt, and thus enabled the pious teachings of Adrien of Utrecht to establish a link between the emperor and Luther. The latter, however, went much further than the Brotherhood of the Common Life. It is impossible to understand either Luther or the explosive character of the movement which he had launched, if we judge him as a modern man or merely as a humanist. In fact he was much more rooted in the Middle Ages than most of his illustrious contemporaries. Erasmus, Zwingli, Calvin, and even perhaps Melanchthon, already belonged to a new epoch; Luther did not. This comes out most noticeably in the religious debates held at Marburg on the first and fifth of October 1529. Zwingli, true to himself, denied the actual presence of Christ in the bread and wine of the Eucharist, and maintained that God had neither the wish nor the right to demand that men should act irrationally. Luther, on the contrary, boldly held to the opinion that man must obey God in everything. In his rather crude way, he swore that he would even eat excrement if God so willed. His religious doubts, moreover, were irrational. During his monastic life, he was tortured by his belief that original sin and man's weakness and limitations were so deep-rooted that it was impossible to justify himself before the Almighty and would certainly therefore be damned. It was while he was suffering these spiritual torments that Luther discovered in Saint Paul's Epistle to the Romans the passage on justification by faith alone – *sola fide*. He clung literally to these words, on which he founded his whole doctrine of salvation and redemption, believing that he had at last found the all-merciful God his troubled soul so earnestly craved.

Luther was a sincere believer, but subordinated everything to what he considered to be the dictates of his conscience. He even went so far as to speak familiarly of 'the Lord Jesus Christ and myself'. This was a personal doctrinal concept which the humanists could not comprehend, and it was this that finally led to the rupture between Luther and Erasmus, and widened the gulf which, in spite of certain common sympathies, was to separate the reformer from the emperor. Luther

84

admired Charles and frequently voiced this admiration. Late in his life he was still praising the sovereign's taciturnity and reserve, comparing them favourably with his own loquacity; often he remarked that Charles said less in one year than he himself said in one day. With profound psychological insight, the reformer believed, as far as religion was concerned, that in him he had found a twin soul. Nevertheless, Luther does not seem to have realised that, to Charles's way of thinking, the idea that faith and religion could ever be incompatible was an impossibility and that he could never follow his own convictions if these ran counter to the traditions and doctrines of the Church.

It is to this medieval attitude – in fact an attitude which was profoundly reactionary – that the Reformation owed much of its success, especially in the first phases. The masses were only mildly interested in abstract ideologies, but on the other hand, such a simple concept as justification by faith met with a powerful response among a people, who because of the decadence of the established church had come to dream of a return to the simplicity of Christ's teachings and the poverty of the primitive church. Once awakened, these deep-rooted sentiments became allied to German nationalism – the third factor at the root of the nascent Reformation, and one which was to develop into an irresistible force.

This national struggle with conscience had been undergoing a period of gestation for some time. Henceforth, it would develop by natural progression into nationalism and then into xenophobia, that is to say, into a hatred of Rome, of the sovereign pontiff and everything Latin. The smouldering fires were stirred, particularly during the early years of the Reformation, by the attempts of the church to extort more and more money from Germany. In actual fact, though, it was less the popes in Rome than the German bishops themselves who, by their insensate financial demands, gave the final impetus to the Revolution. One of the most ominous of these bishops was the Archbishop Albrecht von Brandenburg, whose unprepossessing features have become familiar to us through Grünewald's great picture *Saint Erasmus and Saint Maurice*. The cardinal paid his enormous debts to Fugger with money received from the sale of indulgences; Fugger's agents were even allowed to accompany the preacher Tetzel on his rounds, and bank the contributions of the pious populace on the spot. Albrecht's actions derived from his insatiable greed to add to his jurisdiction by incorporating the archiepiscopal see of Magdeburg with that of Mainz.

The union of the two archdioceses had unfortunate results, the historian and jurist, Eugène Rosenstock being the first to draw attention to this very important fact. Until the Reform, cultural and political policies were within the competence of the church, as were affairs connected with marriages and their legal consequences. As by degrees society became more and more specialised, due to the continual expansion of the administration and the growing importance of internal affairs, so the temporal authorities grew increasingly irritated with their lack of influence in any of these matters. This quarrel came to a head when Albrecht von Brandenburg, by uniting the diocese of Magdeburg with Mainz, placed all the territories of the Elector of Saxony under his ecclesiastical authority. It was this, according to Rosenstock, that roused the Elector of Saxony's sympathies to the Reform.

This conflict of temporal and spiritual powers is highlighted by the writings of the period. In 1511, the humanist Wimpfeling published his *Gravmina der Deutschen Nation*, a protest against the export of German gold to Rome. This document is of particular interest as here we find for the first time a combination of religious, national and economic theses. Similarly, Ulrich von Hutten, who, as already mentioned, was one of the first German nationalists, both supported Luther and was in his turn a strong influence on him. Taking Luther's condemnation of the papacy as a pretext, the princes seized the goods of the church. Their religious enthusiasm thus served their personal and financial interests; this was particularly the case with those ecclesiastical princes who rallied to the Protestant cause, who, thanks to their position of authority and administrative power, transformed their spiritual rule into a temporal and hereditary government, founding dynasties and increasing the power of their houses with the acquisition of new territories. For example, Prussia, a province belonging to the order of Teutonic knights, was seized to the benefit of the Hohenzollerns and united with Brandenburg. It is hardly surprising that princes who had become enriched by these means should embrace the cause of Luther and bitterly oppose the Council, which they had every reason to believe would demand the restitution of ecclesiastical property and wealth. It is at once tragic and grotesque that in this negative attitude these princes should have been on the side of the pope against the emperor. It was this paradoxical grouping of disparate forces that eventually prevented a true ecclesiastical reform.

When Luther went to Worms in 1521, the new movement was

already well under way, and while the rebel monk was acclaimed everywhere, the papal legates were openly threatened and insulted. At the Diet, Luther seemed at first intimidated but soon his oratorical gifts prevailed. His declaration, 'Here I bide, I cannot do otherwise' (*hier stehe ich, ich kann nicht anders*), was greeted with unqualified approval by the Estates.

The emperor was not shaken. We know from the notes of his associates that he himself drew up the resolution which he wished put before the Diet. His argument here mapped the course that imperial religious policy was to take over the next thirty-five years.

With his desire to promote a reform of the Church and demonstrate his tolerance towards the innovators, the emperor regarded the council as vitally necessary; at the same time, however, he exerted himself to the utmost to preserve the unity of the church. The placing of Luther under the ban of the empire was the logical consequence of the emperor's message to the Diet, from the minute it was foreseen, that this edict would not be put into effect. The safe-conduct promised to Luther on 25 April 1521 guaranteed him a delay of three weeks and gave him time to find a safe asylum. The emperor did not sign the warrant for his arrest until 8 May, and one may presume that he wished to avoid having him arrested.

The Elector of Saxony, who remembered what had happened to John Huss after the Council of Constance, had little confidence in safe-conducts. He therefore organised what appeared to be an arrest, in order to get Luther to a place of safety, but as a way of appeasing his conscience, refused to be told where Luther was to reside. His emissaries took their 'captive' to the Castle of Wartburg, which had been one of the intellectual centres of Germany during the glittering reigns of the Counts of Thuringia. In the solitude of this exile, Luther underwent another serious crisis of conscience, reproaching himself bitterly for having sought safety and thus betrayed his mission to teach the German peoples the new road to Eternal Salvation. Frederick the Wise also had his own difficulties, since during the enforced absence of its leader events were precipitated and the Reformation took unpredictable turns.

At Wartburg, in the meanwhile, Luther translated the New Testament. This was first published in 1522 by Hans Luft at Wittenberg and reached an unprecedented number of editions. This book was to have significant repercussions, as much from a doctrinal as a linguistic point of view. In comparison with former translations of the Gospels, either in high or low German, and often in a heavy and incomprehensible style, the work of Luther positively glows with life and vigour. Written in a literary German, it imposed a common idiom, used in the Imperial Chancellory at Prague, which became a vital link between peoples of southern, central and lower Germany.

While Luther was struggling with the devil at Wartburg, believing he had actually seen him in person – another indication of the medieval quality of his mind – his university friends and colleagues at Wittenberg were not inactive. They had begun to change the life of the church – the mass was abolished, private confession and the Latin liturgy disappeared, divine service became a sermon accompanied by hymns sung in German. Bread *and* wine were served at Communion. Among the churchmen entrusted by the princes with the formation of the new church were to be found both moderates and radicals. Among the latter were Andreas Bodenstein (who adopted the surname of Karlstadt after his native town on the Main); he was the spiritual father of that group of fanatics who later were to cause Luther so much trouble and lead to such violent reactions.

Many years were still to pass before Luther and Melanchthon could establish the definitive form of their doctrine and rites. It was not until the end of the century that it became possible to draw a clear line between the old faith and the new. For quite a long time, the two religions existed side by side, a situation which resulted in many mixed forms. So it often happened that the same parish priest would say the Latin mass in one parish and in a neighbouring village give bread and wine at communion. This state of affairs gave rise in the sixteenth century to a number of things which historians have found difficult to explain, for example the 'secret Protestantism' of the Emperor Maximilian II, nephew of Charles v.

The fluid nature of the line of demarcation between the two religions explains why during the last years of his reign Charles hoped to be able to re-establish the unity of the church through a council. Most people usually ignored the existence of a schism, since the insurmountable differences which did exist between the old and new doctrines had not yet penetrated the consciousness of the faithful. Thus Communion *sub utraque specie* was acceptable to Catholics, since the Council of Basle had authorised this practice for the Bohemian *Utraquists*. The emperor for his part was quite prepared to make substantial concessions to the

Protestants on disciplinary questions such as the celibacy of the priest-hood, and the saying of sermons and prayers in German. But on the other hand the primacy of the pope remained an overwhelming obstacle, for Protestants not only denied the Bishop of Rome his prerogatives as head of the church, but were equally filled with unreasoning hatred against the whole institution of the papacy. During Luther's lifetime, that is until 1546, the latent antagonisms were not broached since the Reformer himself continued to venerate the Virgin and St Anne, to say his rosary and confess himself. After his death, however, Protestants began to term these practices as idolatrous by claiming that Catholics had deified Mary, and even violated her sanctuaries. The Catholics reacted vigorously to these attacks, and the Marian cult was taken up to an even greater degree than in the past. Profiting by this polarisation of sentiment, the doctrines of Zwingli and Calvin were able to take root in Lutheran countries. A quarter of a century later, a political factor, the war between the Catholic Emperor and the Protestant princes, was to introduce a further poisonous element into an already unhealthy situation.

While staying in Worms, Charles suffered a cruel loss: on 27 May 1521, Guillaume de Croy, Seigneur de Chièvres, died from a fever at the age of sixty-two. Doubts have been cast on the cause of his death, but, in fact, from the very detailed accounts of his last illness which have come down to us, it seems that this statesman, who was in daily atten-dance on the emperor and worked to the very last, died from consistent overwork. Of all Charles's teachers and advisers, this shrewd and discerning Burgundian diplomat was the closest to him. His death left a void which was never filled, and until the end of his reign, the emperor continued to lament the loss of this man. In consequence of de Croy's death, Gattinara's influence became stronger. The imperial concept, with all its ramifications, now assumed priority in the mind of Charles v.

THE REVOLUTION IN SPAIN

After Charles had embarked at Corunna in May 1520, Castile and the kingdom of Valencia, together with the Balearic Islands, became the scene of violent political upheavals, which are among the strangest phenomena of modern history. The revolution of the *Communeros* and *Germanias* between 1520 and 1522 offers certain similarities with other events at the end of the Middle Ages and at the beginning of modern

D*

times; it also anticipates by its motivations and violent and confused character, the more bloody and deeper-rooted revolutions which took place several centuries later, in England and France, and even in the Paris Commune of 1871.

To begin with, the risings in the cities were due mainly to a temporary convergence of the interests of the knights and the master craftsmen who, as elsewhere in Europe, were organised in guilds. The *hidalgos* or *caballeros*, that is the minor nobility, lived for the most part in the towns and occupied most of the municipal posts. Nevertheless, there were also master craftsmen in certain administrative positions. With the exception of Valencia, where events took on a different character from those in other parts of Spain, the line of demarcation between knights and the bourgeoisie was sufficiently fluid. But the minor nobility, however, often had contacts with the great feudal lords, who for their part were not always on the side of the government; they sometimes adopted an ambivalent attitude and some among them even conspired with the rebels.

The dangerous force, which gave to the *Communero* rising its truly revolutionary character, came from the more numerous and virulent semi-proletarian classes whom the original instigators of the movement – the minor nobility and the guilds, who remained relatively moderate in their attitude – had, either deliberately or unintentionally, reunited. Nevertheless, the factor which gave to all these divergent forces in Spain a common platform and allowed them to preserve a degree of unity for several months, was their united resistance to foreign interference – that is to say, the resurgence of nationalism.

The sovereign had made the great mistake of appointing a Burgundian as Regent. It is true that Adrien of Utrecht was not a foreigner in the same sense as Guillaume de Croy; he was after all the incumbent of a Spanish episcopal see and as such could be considered a citizen of Spain. His ecclesiastical status moreover, afforded him some protection and gave some sort of legitimacy to his office. Nevertheless, the fact that he was not entirely Spanish partially diminished his authority, and in any case, this pious bishop was scarcely qualified to act decisively and boldly in his exalted political position or, in such difficult times, to give strong support to his sovereign, far away in Flanders.

The ill-considered haste with which the *Cortès* had been dissolved at Corunna also had unfortunate consequences. It made obvious the fact that the government had been solely interested in raising money – what was termed the *servicio*; the sittings had been suspended even before the main points of the day were discussed. On a legal and constitutional level, the problems of the composition of the *Cortès* and the election of delegates remained unresolved; nor had the economic and basic financial problems of the country been settled. Moreover, the question of obtaining official recognition for the new government having its authority acknowledged as indisputable had been entirely ignored. Personal animosities poisoned the atmosphere, and as soon as it was known that the king was planning to leave Spain, the sense of uneasiness that had been aroused began to spread through the country, in an unprecedented way.

Heading the opposition were two leaders of real ability, Hernando d'Avalos and Juan Padilla. Having been issued with an official summons to appear before the Regency Council, they resorted to numerous subterfuges to evade the order, but when this proved no longer possible, they began to stir up the populace and provoke civil disorder.

It was in Toledo, where the leaders allowed themselves to be arrested and locked up in the Church of Saint Francis, that the rebellion first broke out. The crowd, by now fully roused, drove out the royal officers and went on to capture the Alcazar. Charles, who had not yet embarked for the Netherlands, wanted to postpone his departure, but was dissuaded from this by de Croy. Despite his superior intellectual gifts and his unswerving devotion to the sovereign, it was de Croy who was mainly responsible for the numerous errors of judgement committed by the young king during the period of his involvement with Spain. In fact the king's presence at Toledo would probably have had the effect of calming the people, and if the monarch personally had made a forceful but magnanimous gesture, he might well have prevented worse troubles to come. Unfortunately they abandoned at the same time the plan to surround the Regent with Castilian advisers. When the necessity for a reform of the electoral system was finally appreciated, the subsequent elections were carried out in such a slow and dilatory way that they indeed appeared to have been brought about solely by outside pressure, and any benefit that might have accrued from them was lost. Besides, it is open to doubt whether the persons elected – the Constable Inigo de Velazco and the Admiral of Castile, Don Fabrique Enriquez – were really the most suitable candidates for the tasks entrusted to them by their sovereign. At all events they showed little enthusiasm for their duties, an attitude which at the beginning was widespread among the great landowners who, fearful for their fortunes and their lives, adopted an ambivalent position, particularly after the revolutionaries had like all terrorists perpetrated several outrages to intimidate their adversaries.

Soon the rights of the regent were further curtailed when some of his functions were delegated to the governors of provinces – to Juan de Lanuza of Aragon, Diego de Mendoza of Catalonia, and, lastly, to the dowager queen, Germaine de Foix, who was governor of Valencia. Correspondence between Charles and the regent shows how weak and inadequate the latter felt himself to be. Adrien of Utrecht made concessions in the hope of appeasing the leaders of the revolutionary movement. But mistaken about the feeling of the country, and aware that a number of the rebels' demands were really justified, he committed the fatal political mistake of displaying weakness, and thus frittered away the authority which he needed in order to impose salutary reforms in the face of the resistance from the privileged classes.

At Toledo, where the rebellion had first erupted, it remained contained within certain limits, controlled by strong personalities like Pedro Laso de la Vega and Juan Padilla. Everywhere else, however, where the minor nobility and the master-craftsmen had been unable to find in their ranks an intelligent and forceful political leader, the agitation degenerated rapidly into anarchy. This was particularly true of Segovia, where the deputy to the *Cortès*, Rodrigo de Tordesillas, was hanged, his colleague, Jean Vazquez, escaping with his life only with great difficulty. Pillage and destruction spread rapidly from the city to the surrounding countryside, and Adrien of Utrecht was obliged to have recourse to force to prevent an expansion of the disorders. He sent a small military detachment against Segovia, but without intending it to be a punitive expedition; he thought it sufficient to impose a legal sentence, supported by this token force, to bring the rebels to heel. News of this march on Segovia, however, only led to a further increase of tension in the country. At Salamanca, the people led by a draper, Juan de Valloria, took over the town hall. At Burgos bloody riots broke out, which were only terminated by the grant of substantial concessions. The municipality decided to send a delegation to Charles himself.

As the tide of revolt swept forward, the towns, which up to then had acted independently of each other, felt the need to concentrate their forces. The appeal for unity came from Toledo. With a view to organising communal action, the municipalities decided to convene an assembly of delegates at Avila, on 1 August 1520. Soon the question was to arise: should this central Junta advise or govern; should it carry out the orders of the cities, or take it on itself to make the necessary decisions? Another major difficulty arose from the fact that urban juntas differed from one town to another, according to how far the revolutionary movement had developed. In certain communes, for example, the hidalgos were still the masters, while elsewhere the revolutionary masses were in control.

Ronquillo, a judge appointed by the crown, who had been ordered to restore order in Segovia, was unable to occupy the town, while in his turn the Captain-General, Antonio de Fonseca, arriving with reinforcements, failed to storm the city walls. The regent was therefore requested to send cannons in order to start a real siege. Ever since the time of the Catholic Monarchs, however, the artillery arsenal had been at Medina del Campo, a town which supported the *Communeros*, and consequently forcefully opposed the departure of the artillery to join the royal forces. Negotiations dragged on, until the situation became so fraught that once again violence ensued and Fonseca was killed in a hand-to-hand clash with the populace.

The cardinal-regent then decided that to cool matters down he would make further concessions. He promised to indemnify Medina del Campo for the destruction caused by the army and to disband the royal forces. As a result of this manifest show of weakness, the revolt gathered strength and even extended to the seat of government at Valladolid. On 23 August it had reached Tordesillas, where the town hall was taken by assault and the rebels demanded to see the queen. For a long time now there had been rumours that Queen Joanna, a prisoner of the foreigners, was not really mad, nor incapable of governing, but only suffering from extreme melancholia.

Most revolutions are characterised by such a need to insist on the legitimacy of actions carried out in their name and to use the most representative personalities to achieve their ends – for example, the Americans claimed for a long time that they were supporting George III against the House of Commons; in France, Louis XVI was regarded by the French as their protagonist against the aristocrats while the July revolution put the Orléans on the throne to maintain some semblance at least of historic continuity.

The people of Tordesillas were granted permission to send a delegation to the castle. When the doors were opened, the populace followed and soon hundreds of people filled the royal apartments. Wisely, in spite of her madness, or perhaps because of some atavistic instinct, Joanna refused to negotiate under these conditions but declared herself ready to discuss matters with a small delegation only, if and when the crowd left the premises. In the negotiations which followed, she made certain concessions, but refused to involve herself by giving her signature to the rebels. An identical situation took place in September, on the second occasion of a visit by the *Communeros* to Tordesillas.

In the meanwhile a situation developed which was as paradoxical as it was unforeseen. Now that the king's army had been disbanded, the *Communeros* found themselves with no definite objective to attack. While some resorted to pillage and occupied castles, their forces were so scattered that any organised action became impossible, and their units gradually began to disintegrate. Furthermore, in typically Spanish fashion, the masses now began to turn on their leaders, reproaching them bitterly for exploiting the queen's name to further their own ends. Because the dynastic image was so deeply rooted in the people, the rebel leaders had constantly to reassure and prove to their troops that they had nothing against the monarchy in itself, or against the august person of His Majesty, King Charles. The lack of confidence which characterised all the actions – or perhaps one should say the inertia – of the revolutionaries made the social differences between the *Communeros*, the incompatibility of the aristocratic, artisan and semi-proletarian elements more acute. There was also the attitude of the clergy to be taken into account. Most churchmen sided with the opposition because, after the nomination of Adrien of Utrecht, they were afraid that Burgundian favourites would deprive them of the better benefices. Although it does not admit of absolute proof, it also seems probable that German influence and the nascent Reformation, and ideas similar to those of Luther, also played a part in the revolt. Indeed, during the course of the *Communero* movement, some very strange events took place in the religious sphere; for example, when Antonio de Acuna, Bishop of Zamora, took the field against the royalists with a force of armed priests. This ecclesiastic was one of the most curious figures to emerge from the movement and in many ways reminds one of the religious fanatics who were later to appear in Germany – in particular the Anabaptists.

Despite the great distance which separated the Low Countries from Spain, the king followed with sustained attention the events in the Iberian peninsula. Contemporary observers report that he was slow to make up his mind, and certain people even had the erroneous impression that he paid little attention to current affairs. Actually, Charles, at this point simply needed plenty of time in which to make decisions, but once taken he then put them into practice. The crucial point, once again, was the question of money.

Despite the wealth of the Low Countries, Charles was unable to raise sufficient money to maintain an army; but by resorting to various expediencies he did succeed in raising a force of three thousand German mercenaries, which he put at the service of the Spanish Regency, with instructions that it should not be used for repressive measures unless such action was absolutely necessary. At the same time Charles authorised the regent to make important concessions to those towns which proved their loyalty to the crown. It was a realistic attitude, and one that shows the justice and humanity with which the monarch viewed the trends and methods which although alien to him he was able to recognise as being well-founded.

Thanks to the developments we have just outlined the troubled areas began to be contained and isolated. South of the Sierra Morena there were practically no revolutionary centres, and what few uprisings there were, were strictly localised and of short duration. The principal towns of the south, like Seville and Cordoba, in fact declared themselves ready to send help to suppress the rebels. Such an attitude was perhaps natural in a region which, only a generation or so earlier, had been the frontier of Christendom. Similarly, the extreme north, which having France as a neighbour made it also a frontier region, remained loyal to the government. The revolutionary movement was thus confined to Old and New Castile, the Province of Valencia and the royal cities. None of the smaller towns, which were not directly administered by the government but were still under the control of the great feudal lords, made any move – or at least not to begin with. The common denominator which linked the ill-assorted revolutionary forces was the aversion to foreign Burgundian rule and the demand for a return of the national government. Here this factor was scarcely present.

The urban junta which has already been mentioned and which by this time had taken the name of 'The Holy Junta' soon showed itself incapable, however, of uniting the insurrectionists. It was not even capable of regulating internal affairs and even less successful in determining its exact political aims. For example, should it continue to address petitions to the king, or should it be politically autonomous?

Now that Charles had granted most of the demands presented to him, there was no real reason to continue the revolution, and even less reason to dethrone him. Nor was there any suitable national candidate to replace Charles for the leaders were reluctant to side with those extremists who wished to proclaim Ferdinand of Austria as King of Spain. Nor had the use and abuse of Queen Joanna's name, which had been used as a cover for a *Communero* oligarchy, produced the anticipated results. True, the Holy Junta was received once more by the queen at Tordesillas on 24 September 1520, but once again, any agreements reached were purely oral, and no means could be found to extract Joanna's signature.

As a final measure, the Junta decided to usurp the rights of the *Cortès* by inviting the cities to retain all monies received from taxes and duties levied. But because the cities were unable to decide on the constitution of a central authority, or to recognise the Junta as representative of a national government, the results of this move were fruitless. An analogous situation occurred some centuries later, when the Paris Commune tried to turn France into a collection of semi-independent republics, but did not succeed in extending its authority any further than the capital.

It is perhaps idle to speculate on the consequences to the Spanish Revolution had the Holy Junta assumed the character of a revolutionary National Assembly, an idea which was by no means foreign to the times. Probably, the king and regent would have had greater difficulty in suppressing the *Communeros*, for they would have then been confronted with a centralised force with financial and military backing. But instead of directing its energies to these ends, the Junta lost time in discussions, protests, constant new demands and attempts to intimidate the royalist government, as, for example, when it ordered the government to assemble at Tordesillas to expedite current business there and to justify its past actions. When the regent and his council refused to comply, the *communidad* of Valladolid was ordered by the Junta to withdraw its allegiance to the regency and arrest the members of the council. But in order to implement such a serious decision, the Junta should have immediately created an opposition government. Instead, it did nothing; worse still, differences of opinion sprang up between the communes on the question of financial military commitments and the command of the army. On 27 September 1520, the Junta published a new manifesto, but was still unable to prevent the

1 Philip of Burgundy ('le beau'), son of the Emperor Maximilian I and father of Charles V, from a fifteenth-century painting of the Flemish School
2 Joanna the mad, mother of Charles V, by the Master of the Legend of St Madelaine
3 The Emperor Maximilian and his family. At the back (*from left to right*): the Emperor Maximilian, Philip, his son, the Empress Maria of Burgundy, Maximilian's wife. In the foreground: the Archduke Ferdinand, Charles V, Louis of Hungary and Bohemia who was betrothed to Charles's sister

4 A detail from a tapestry showing the battle of Pavia (1525). The sixteenth-century Flemish tapestry was designed by Barend van Orley

5 The entry of Charles V and Pope Clement VII into Bologna on the occasion of Charles's coronation (1530)

6 Martin Luther by Lucas Cranach

7 The sack of Tunis by the troops of Charles V in 1535. Cartoon by Jan Vermayen

8 The interior of the old Town Hall at Regensburg

9 Erasmus by Holbein

10 Pope Paul III by Titian

11 Charles V at the battle of Mühlberg by Titian

12 Charles V and his
brother Ferdinand
riding to the Diet of
Augsburg. Woodcut
by Jörg Brue

13 Philip II of Spain
by Antonio Mor

14 The Monastery of Yuste

15 The tomb of Charles V at the Escorial built by his son, Philip II

gradual disintegration of its forces. For the last time it addressed itself to the king. In earlier documents, complaints and demands had been entered in the *cuaderno de peticiones*, which is remarkably reminiscent of the famous *cahiers* of the French Estates-General of 1789 in which were noted the grievances of the peasants. This time the Junta set out every point it had raised, and all proposals for constitutional reform, in the *Capitulos del Reino*. The document was transmitted to the king accompanied by a peremptory invitation to sign it without argument. Charles felt himself personally affronted by this document and reacted strongly, as he always did when he believed legal authority to be endangered. Adrien of Utrecht attempted to regain his freedom of action in leaving Valladolid; when forestalled he fled in secret.

This event marked a decisive turning point, and the royalist forces were organised to liberate the mad queen Joanna. While the constable continued to hesitate, his son, the Count de Haro, was entrusted with the command of military operations. By a bold stroke, he captured Tordesillas and the position of the two parties was now reversed. The regent and his council were established at Tordesillas, while the Junta moved to Valladolid. At this point, the latter suddenly suffered a serious loss through the defection of its military commander, Giron, and the Junta found it necessary to recall Padilla, whom they had just relieved of his duties. Efforts to interest the pope and the King of Portugal in the cause of the National Revolution met with no success; on the contrary, Emmanuel of Portugal supported Charles and the regency.

Nevertheless, the vacillations of the regency council and the weakness displayed by the Admiral of Castile allowed the Junta to gain time and survive the winter. But in the meantime the rebel army, composed largely of master-craftsmen and artisans, was defeated in every encounter it had with the royalist forces. The constable was able to occupy Burgos, and at the same time granted important concessions to the city; one of the feudal partisans of the *Communeros*, Count Salvatierra, defected from the movement and the Bishop of Zamora's forces were annihilated. In the spring of 1521 the end for the Castilian *Communeros* was approaching, and on 24 April Padilla suffered a crushing defeat at Villalar.

At the same time a new revolt started in eastern Spain – in Valencia and in the Balearics. Here a controversy had arisen over the right of citizens to carry arms, a privilege granted to them so that they might defend themselves against the Moorish pirates. The spark which ignited this conflagration was typical of these revolutionary times, when the masses were only too easily transformed into bloodthirsty hordes. At Valencia a large crowd had gathered to witness the execution of criminals condemned to be burnt alive for sodomy; others accused of the same crime had been condemned to a less terrible fate. The populace revolted and demanded that all should receive the same sentence, and succeeded in getting their own way. This violation of the law, dictated by the rabble, unleashed the revolution.

The movement was better organised in Valencia than in Castile. It was sustained by better relations between the guilds, while the *caballeros* had no say at all in the direction of affairs. The outcome of the war remained uncertain; in the north of Valencia two units of *Germania* were defeated, on 30 June 1521 at Oropesa, and on 18 July 1521 at Almenara.

One of the leaders of the rebellion, Miguel Estelles, was captured and executed. In the south, on the other hand, the rebels achieved considerable success; but they abused their powers by their stupid and barbarous treatment of the survivors of the Moorish population whom they forcibly converted to Christianity. Nevertheless, the position of the rebels gradually worsened, and this enabled the government to find a compromise solution, for which the credit must be given to the Marquis de Zenete, the viceroy's brother, who was appointed Governor of Valencia and managed to re-establish peace.

Once Valencia had been pacified, it was only in the Balearics where they had established a violent and revolutionary régime that the rebels continued to hold out. But at last, in 1522, their leader, Joannot Colom, was captured and taken to the castle of Bellever, the scene of most of his misdeeds, where he was hanged, drawn and quartered. This marked the end of the great revolution, which at first seemed on the verge of rocking the very foundation of the Spanish monarchy and of bringing the country to a state of ruin. The revolt was crushed, not so much by any action on the part of the government, which throughout had remained feeble and indecisive, but because of the lack of unity and the anarchistic tendencies of the *Communeros*.

Towards the end of the Middle Ages, cities which sided with the crown and state against the nobility and the feudal system invariably prospered. The German Hanseatic towns owed their prosperity in the fourteenth century to the fact that in many respects they represented the authority of the crown in northern Germany. The Hanseatic League was a powerful confederation of cities which formed a separate oligarchy – republican without being democratic – and whose constitution resembled that of the empire, whereby the power of the crown was dependent on that of the elector-princes.

In Spain, at the time of the *Communero* rebellion, the towns in contrast allied themselves with a certain section of the nobility and, although not daring to come out into the open, were opposed to the monarchy. In some respects this political situation is reminiscent of what had happened in England, where first the barons deprived the throne of its most important prerogatives, and then the towns in turn deprived the barons of theirs. In England, however, neither of the two rebel parties ever questioned the validity of the state. In Spain, on the other hand, centuries of war against the Moors had meant that provinces, certain towns and even individual strongholds, had been forced by circumstances to organise themselves into what were virtually independent units and thus there had arisen a proliferation of *de facto* and *de jure* autonomous kingdoms.

At the time of Queen Isabella's death, the political division between Castile and Aragon had not yet entirely disappeared. The *Communero* movement therefore represented a serious threat, not only to the unity, but the very existence of a Spanish state. For the same reasons, revolutionary assemblies such as the Holy Junta were also quite incapable of establishing any central authority, even in the territories which had rallied to it.

When Charles, who had been crowned King of the Germans and was now emperor-elect, once again set foot on Spanish soil at Santander on 16 July 1522, the revolution had already been crushed and the rebels punished. Order had been re-established and the king could not therefore be held responsible for the punishment of the rebel leaders; he was in fact able to mitigate some of the harsher sentences, and thus effect a reconciliation between the opposing parties. Nevertheless, death sentences carried out in his name were to haunt Charles for the rest of his life, for as we know from his full and varied personal correspondence, he was a deeply religious man and one much given to meditation. As he grew older, the objective outlook he possessed and the dictates of his own conscience made him even more appreciative of the underlying causes of the rebellion. It is this that distinguishes him from the majority of his contemporaries, Renaissance princes who once invested with power only too often regarded themselves as above all considerations of good or evil, and showed no remorse in 'legally' taking a man's life or for slaughtering their enemies.

As a result of the events in Spain, Charles was not only personally but also politically the wiser. He decided to reorganise the administrative system of Castile – to rid it of its inherent weaknesses, and make it competent to deal with crisis situations. He succeeded in healing the breaches created by the rebellion and carried out reforms without much difficulty in a comparatively short time – none of which the *Communeros* had been able to effect. Although Spain was hardly yet in a financial position to undertake the task with which it was becoming increasingly burdened, the foundations were already being laid which, within half a century, were to transform it into the most powerful nation in the world. Political foresight alone would have been insufficient for Charles to succeed in his aims without his indomitable will and personal magnetism. The task whose successful completion could not even be effected by such a remarkable man as Adrien of Utrecht, nor by any other person among the nobility or clergy of Spain, was fulfilled by this young king, thanks to common sense and the dignity and long family tradition of authority which he had inherited.

With Spain debilitated by rebellion, the French considered it an opportune moment to invade Navarre in 1521. This move, however, was quickly scotched; the foreign troops were driven back beyond the Spanish frontiers and Spain's territorial rights were again re-established.

Shortly before the emperor's return to Spain, another event had taken place which was to have important international repercussions for the Habsburgs in central Europe. This was the double marriage of the Archduchess Maria to Ludwig II, King of Hungary and Bohemia, and of the latter's sister, Anne of Jagellon, to the Archduke Ferdinand. No one suspected at the time that this union, planned for so long, would mean that in a few years time a Habsburg would unite the crowns of St Stephen and St Wenceslas. But it was from this moment that the growing importance of Ferdinand's place on the political chess-board of eastern and central Europe became clear, and one which was all the more important with the Turkish menace drawing ever closer.

THE TRIUMPH OF CHARLES AT PAVIA

Between December 1521 and the spring of 1522, Charles engaged in his first love affair. It was only a brief interlude in his life, but its importance stems from the effect it had on the development of his character. It both brought him happiness and helped very much in giving him a sense of independence. The young man of twenty-two had just lost the counsellor and guardian of his youth, Guillaume de Croy, who in many ways had been a father to him. After such an unhappy event his need for human contact seems very natural; natural also, at his age, was the fact that he no longer regarded women in a purely platonic light. The young woman with whom he fell in love was a Netherlander, Jeanne van der Gheenst. She bore him a daughter, Marguerite, who was to inherit a considerable amount of the political acumen of Charles's aunt, whose name she was given, and by whom she was brought up. Known in history as Marguerite of Parma, Charles's daughter later played an important role at the side of her father and her half-brother Philip. She was also to succeed the older Marguerite as Regent of the Low Countries, where she defended the Habsburgs' Burgundian heritage under conditions far more difficult than any which her aunt had ever faced.

Despite all the adversities she encountered, Marguerite of Parma displayed an ability and energy which place her as one of the most remarkable women of her time. Her mother, Jeanne, was to disappear rapidly from the scene but whether this was Charles's wish or whether, as seems more likely, her departure was instituted by the Regent Marguerite and the imperial councillors, is not known.

The most important political change to take place at the end of 1521 was the death of Pope Leo x on 1 December. As his successor the cardinals elected Adrien of Utrecht, Charles's old tutor and Regent of Spain. This papal election, which for the last time in the history of the church elevated a subject of the empire to the Throne of St Peter, has been misconstrued over the years. Many writers, including some great historians, have seen it as a masterly stroke of political strategy on Charles's part – a triumph for the Habsburg faction among the cardinals. But historical data at our disposal today contradicts this hypothesis, though it seems to be the logical conclusion. The idea had obviously never been entertained by Charles – on the contrary he was extremely surprised by the result of the election and for a moment even saw the cardinals' decision as representing a loss for himself and for Spain. Far from rejoicing at the news he was dismayed that his representative, who had just begun to acquire valuable experience of the Iberian peninsula, should have to leave the country for Rome. Adrien himself was equally unprepared and did not regard his elevation to the papacy with any enthusiasm as, with his knowledge of papal affairs, he felt quite unequal to the task that awaited him there. Under the Borgias and Medici, the pontifical court had become a centre of intrigue and power politics, which this pious scholar from Louvain detested. He hesitated for months before leaving Spain, and only took ship on 2 July 1522, to arrive in Rome a few weeks later.

Once resigned to his exalted position, Adrien made up his mind to make the most of his opportunity to put into practice urgent church reforms and to bring to an end the most flagrant abuses. In Rome he led a monastic, indeed a most saintly existence – his interest centring on the salvation of souls. But this behaviour provoked the hostility of the cardinals, for the gulf separating the sovereign pontiff and his entourage was thus made all too clearly apparent. The emperor, once he had got over his first surprise, wanted to make the most of this unexpected windfall that the election had brought. His letters demonstrate his delight in the fact that the principal obstacles against his imperial coronation and the convocation of the council had now been removed. Furthermore, he hoped to find in the new pope a firm ally against France. On this point, however, Adrien felt obliged to disappoint the emperor; it is apparent from his letters to Charles that where this matter was concerned, his conscience was uneasy. While on the one hand he wanted to remain faithful to his sovereign and help him to the best of his ability, on the other he wanted to keep the church from becoming involved in wars and political intrigues in Italy, and restore to it its spiritual mission.

Had Adrien lived long enough to influence papal policy decisively, the emperor could have probably counted on his support on two definite points: his coronation and the council. However, time did not allow for his either helping or hindering his former pupil. On 14 September 1523, he died as the result of an illness, which his contemporaries, as usual, ascribed to poison. In the last months of his life, the pope was a broken, disappointed and politically isolated man, betrayed by the intrigues of his cardinals. It seems feasible that his death could have been caused by despair at seeing the path towards any spiritual renaissance of the church barred by forces against which he was powerless.

The pope, like the emperor, was profoundly disturbed by the resurgence of the offensive spirit of Islam. In 1521, the Turks had reconquered

Belgrade and Semlin, and a year later, Rhodes, the last bastion of Christianity in the Levant, had fallen. This famous fortress had been defended ever since the crusades by the knights of the Order of St John. Now their last representatives were obliged to retreat towards the west. While these events were taking place, the German princes, whether seriously or not, proposed to the Diet the absurd idea that the help of the King of France should be invoked against the Infidel; this suggestion was made at the precise moment when François I was preparing to give battle to the emperor in Italy. At such a proposal, Ferdinand of Austria lost his temper, and in a tone perhaps almost too violent refused to send such a message. For the first time the phrase 'Spanish domination' was hurled into the debate. Henceforth it was to become a favourite expression among the German princes to describe their pretended 'humiliation' as subjects of the King of Spain. These same princes, however, had no compunction in accepting bribes from the King of France or of promising him rights to imperial territories.

To the loss of Pope Hadrian (Adrien of Utrecht), and the disturbing news from Hungary and the Levant, there was added the news of the collapse of Christian II's throne in 1523. The King of Denmark, who was married to Isabella, one of Charles V's sisters, subsequently arrived as a refugee in the Low Countries with his wife and children. A brutal and impulsive man, his arbitrary and cruel acts, like the wholesale execution of bishops, had already lost him Sweden. And it was for this reason that Sweden had become an independent country, separated from the Catholic Church. After this, Christian had been unable to avoid quarrelling with the Estates of Denmark, who had then driven him from the Danish throne, and all his blundering efforts to regain the crown had been in vain.

From a Burgundian point of view, the Scandinavian marriage of the infanta Isabella was of particular economic importance. Indeed, where the Netherland sea lanes were concerned, it was essential to keep the passage of the Sound open, and thus allow the Low Countries to trade freely with the coastal regions of the Baltic, and especially with the Hanseatic towns. On hearing the news of the revolution in Denmark, most political factions in the Netherlands favoured some kind of military operation in conjunction with the deposed king, to overthrow the new government in Copenhagen. Marguerite, on the other hand, used all her influence to induce her ministers to use their common sense, and maintain the peace. She was in a strong position here thanks to the prestige which she had acquired as a result of two remarkable diplomatic successes, which seemed like the belated realisation of the great concept of Charles the Rash. After a dispute with Gelderland, she had managed to incorporate Overyssel, in the north-west, within her Burgundian territories in 1522, while in 1524 she had acquired Friesland, and thus 'rounded off' the Low Countries.

In the meanwhile, Charles had continued to woo the English with a view to obtaining an alliance against France, without however abandoning the hope that at the last minute he might come to a pacific solution with the latter. There was a variety of marriage plans, together with exchanges of territorial rights, all of which played an important part in these negotiations. Charles was even prepared to surrender his rights to the Duchy of Burgundy (although these were in fact merely theoretic) if France, for her part, would renounce Milan.

The policies pursued before 1525 often seem obscure and lacking in purpose, sometimes even irrational, but a closer examination reveals that this confusion was not just the result of Charles's procrastination, or François I's vain, whimsical and aggressive spirit. What, in fact, seems to have been at the root of this European confusion, was the unscrupulous policy of Cardinal Wolsey, the English Chancellor. This worldly, avaricious and corrupt bishop was his king's evil genius, and resembled nothing so much as the Renaissance man depicted by Machiavelli in *The Prince*. His diplomatic achievement was to set Charles against François and provoke crises and war; he sabotaged the aid which England had promised to her allies, negotiated secret treaties, and cheerfully perjured himself when his various oaths of fidelity became inconvenient to him. His complex dealings, however, were always to his own personal advantage. When, as a consequence of the most Machiavellian of political intrigues, France and England signed the Peace of Boor on 30 August 1525, Paris paid one million, seven hundred golden *écus* to England – and a bonus of a hundred and thirty thousand to Wolsey personally.

In the midst of this political chicanery, military action was slow to develop. The first decisive battle took place on the Italian front on 27 April 1522, and although this did not put an end to French domination in the Italian peninsula the balance of power thereafter no longer remained in France's favour. The French commander-in-chief, Lautrec, had drawn up his army of French and Swiss before Milan. Had he not been so rash as to attack the entrenched positions of the Spaniards and

German landsknechts near *La Bicoque*, it might well have proved impossible to dislodge him; instead he suffered a crushing defeat. Colonna and Pescara, the Spanish commanders, went on to capture Genoa and imprison the French commander, Pedro Navarro, and the doge, Fregoso; they then nominated Antonio Adorno in the name of the emperor as supreme commander of the city.

At the same time, that is to say still under the pontificate of Hadrian VI, another significant event occurred in Franco-Spanish relations. Cardinal Sodernini, mouthpiece for the French faction in the College of Cardinals, volunteered to undertake a diplomatic mission with a view to preserving peace. The dishonesty of the cardinal, who had done everything he could to prevent any mediation on the part of the pope, was discovered when his letters were intercepted and Adrien had him imprisoned in the Castle of St Angelo. François I reacted to news of the pope's action by publishing a pamphlet in which he threatened him with a fate similar to that of Pope Boniface VIII who, two centuries earlier, had been attacked and imprisoned by the French. Such an insult caused the pope to look towards the so-called Grand Alliance for support; this alliance, which had already been formed against François I, consisted of the emperor and the Archduke Ferdinand, together with England and the Venetian Republic. In order to finance their campaign, the allies came to an agreement with the Duke of Milan, the Medici Cardinal, the Genoese Republic, Sienna and Lucca, and the pope guaranteed a sum of fifteen thousand ducats a month.

But, even at this late hour, Charles had not altogether abandoned hopes of a reconciliation with France with a view to making a common cause against the Turks. Nor did he hasten to open hostilities. Moreover, allied plans were retarded because of the machinations of the Constable de Bourbon, whose behaviour admirably illustrates the political morality of the Renaissance, a time when politics were devoid of any ethical or legal principles and were used entirely for personal ends or to obtain imagined advantages of the most bizarre kind. De Bourbon, for example, opened negotiations with Spain and England – who made the mistake of overrating his character and influence – in the hope of obtaining the French crown for himself. The constable was generally regarded as a very able soldier and politician, quite capable of rocking the firmly established power of his suzerain, the King of France, and a secret treaty was signed by which de Bourbon was provided with large sums of money, without it being specified exactly what services he should render in return. This enterprise, however, never got much further than the discussion stage; indeed, the King of France, informed of the Constable's intentions, confiscated his possessions. But de Bourbon succeeded in escaping justice, leaving the allies with nothing but a financial deficit.

In Italy the political scene changed in November 1523 with the election of Clement VII, a member of the House of Medici, to the Throne of St Peter. The new pope immediately ranged himself on the side of the French, and the Republic of Venice also went over to them. The Grand Alliance had virtually ceased to exist.

In 1524, the imperialists invaded Provence against the advice of the Constable de Bourbon, who had wanted to make a direct attack on the enemy, march on Lyons and risk a battle in open country. Pescara tried in vain to capture Marseilles while the French were preparing a counter-offensive. François I in the meanwhile, taking advantage of the procrastination of the imperial leaders, crossed the Alps into Milanese territory, captured the city and by a master stroke took the enemy in the rear. The scope of this strategy and the boldness and precision with which it was executed aroused great admiration, even among the imperialists.

Towards the end of 1524 and the beginning of the following year, Charles's situation was distinctly bad. In Italy he was further than ever from the goal envisaged by Gattinara. Chances of peace were compromised and any idea of a joint alliance against the Turks seemed more and more remote. François I was in Lombardy, and the final battle for the possession of Italy – Naples included – could not be far off.

The town of Pavia was still occupied by four hundred Spaniards and five thousand German landsknechts under the command of Leyva. The French laid siege to the city and after the fashion of the time established an entrenched camp. Their position had been well chosen and seemed almost impregnable. One wing of the French force was encamped in a park, a vast estate surrounding the Charterhouse, which lay surrounded by a great wall which was particularly strong at the farmstead of Mirabello and by which the French generals considered their flank to be adequately protected. In the meanwhile, a fresh force of imperial landsknechts, under the command of Georg von Frundsberg, Max Sittich and Von Embs, had crossed the Alps to relieve Pavia. In spite of such seemingly unpropitious circumstances, they decided to attack the French camp. During the night three big breaches were made in the park walls by Spanish sappers equipped with battering rams, and as soon as the *vastadores* had accomplished their task, the landsknechts, advancing at daybreak in three columns, occupied the park. They had already penetrated far by the time that the French, alerted too late, counter-attacked. At the start of the ensuing battle the French cavalry overwhelmed that of the imperial forces but, a little later, the musketeers retrieved the situation and Charles's mounted forces counter-charged. With a force of twelve thousand landsknechts, Frundsberg and Embs surrounded and annihilated the famous fighting formation of five thousand mercenaries from lower Germany known as the 'Black Hand'. The Swiss, arriving on the scene too late, were attacked in the rear by the garrison of Pavia which had sortied forth. The destruction of the French was completed, when the Duke d'Alençon, in a moment of panic, ordered the bridge over the Tecino to be destroyed. By this manœuvre he managed to save the rearguard, but the majority of the French army was abandoned to its fate. François I himself was taken prisoner, and this news shocked all Europe. Charles and some of his loyal followers saw an act of God in this utterly unforeseen result to the battle, particularly as this day of victory, 24 February 1525, was also the twenty-fifth birthday of the emperor. His only regret was that he had not been in the midst of his troops when they achieved the greatest military victory of the century.

This military achievement was followed by a return to the former out-dated Burgundian policies which were to deprive the emperor, if not of all the fruits of victory, at least of all those he most desired.

5

From the Treaty of Madrid
to 'The Ladies Peace'

THE TREATY OF MADRID

For a long time after his victory at Pavia the emperor remained in doubt as to the best course to follow. The many problems under consideration included the fate of the imprisoned François, the diplomatic moves towards peace negotiations with France and the question as to what terms Charles should beforehand decide to try and impose on France. Moreover, the political situation in Italy remained confused. Gattinara, the Grand Chancellor, mistrusted Pescara; indeed, it is true that this victorious general found himself at one of those extraordinary cross roads of history – a situation described so effectively by the Swiss novelist Conrad Ferdinand Meyer in his fine novel, *The Temptation of Pescara*. Pescara, the victor of Pavia acclaimed everywhere by the crowd and admired by the army, could have seized this opportunity to make himself the sovereign unifier of Italy. It would perhaps even have been wise for Charles to appoint his vassal viceroy of the peninsula. However, it seems Pescara never considered seriously the possibilities of following the example of the Constable de Bourbon and betraying his master, despite the fact that he had a legitimate grievance in Charles's behaviour to him after his great victory; Charles had made no acknowledgement of him, nor shown him the slightest gratitude. This strange behaviour was probably due to Gattinara, who was perhaps obsessed with memories of the rebellions of the legions against the Caesars and the decline of Rome. But such suspicions were misplaced; not only was Pescara loyal but he was suffering from the effects of serious wounds which were soon to kill him. He died in fact on the night of the 2 December. His widow, the famous Vittoria Colonna, received a warm letter of personal condolence from the emperor, in which he expressed all the gratitude towards Pescara that the latter had waited for in vain until the hour of his death.

Meanwhile, Lannoy, the Imperial Viceroy in Naples, who had been appointed as François I's warder, was pressing for a decision on his royal prisoner. At last he was ordered to send him to Madrid, where he eventually arrived on 19 December 1525.

Negotiations for the concluding of a peace treaty dragged on indefinitely, with Charles adopting an equivocal position. On the one hand he stipulated conditions which France could neither accept nor respect without a situation being created which would sooner or later lead to another war; while on the other hand the emperor hesitated to exploit France's difficult position and continue his military offensive, for his Burgundian spirit and personal sense of honour made him shrink from the idea of taking advantage of the weakness of his enemy. Francois I, having declared himself incapable of ever accepting conditions which might prove disadvantageous to his own country, had charged his mother, Louise of Savoy, with the conduct of negotiations. This was an excellent choice on his part, for Louise was a brilliant diplomatist with a highly developed political sense. Time pressed, for François was now more worried by the manœuvres of the King of England than by anything that Charles might do. Immediately after the French defeat at Pavia, Henry VIII had once again revived former English ambitions with regard to the Crown of France and certain territories there. At the same time, England did not want the emperor to become too powerful and Wolsey began to demonstrate his powers of intrigue; having been informed that the marriage plans of Charles had now been settled once and for all by his betrothal to Isabella of Portugal, he tried to gain time by proposing another English candidate, the young Princess Mary, daughter of Henry VIII and of the emperor's aunt, Katherine of Aragon. This was the same Mary incidentally who was later to marry Charles's son, Philip, as yet unborn. At the same time, in order to embarrass Charles, Wolsey insisted on the emperor paying his old debts and recommended, in order to force the emperor's hand that the war be continued. Finally, the cardinal arranged the Treaty of Boor, from which he himself extracted so much profit.

Charles, for his part, needed peace, for the news from Germany, in this year of triumph at Pavia, was very disquieting. However, the situation was capable of being resolved providing only that Charles was free to visit Germany in person and direct government policy on the spot. In retrospect, we would be correct in supposing that by his procrastination, Charles missed important opportunities in central Europe.

This fatal loss of time was mostly due to the influence of Gattinara. The imperial policies followed by the chancellor are strikingly reminiscent of those of Friedrich II of Hohenstaufen who regarded Italy as the hub of the empire. With his similar viewpoint, Gattinara tried to relegate German affairs to second place and concentrate his emperor's attention on Italian problems.

In spite of the urgent need to reach a solution Charles dallied a long time before meeting his recent enemy. Such delay was a bitter disappointment for François I, who had great hopes of the effect that his own personal influence on the Habsburg monarch might achieve. In despair of ever attaining such a meeting, François finally resorted to a ruse and pretended to be gravely ill, or at least greatly exaggerated a minor complaint, in order to bring the emperor hurrying to his captive's death bed. Charles indeed arrived, but on discovering the trick played on him refused to enter into negotiations. The dowager Duchess d'Alençon, sister of the captive king, visited Spain a short while later, and was received by Charles in the most friendly manner, but any conversations between the two led to no further progress.

Negotiations were finally advanced by the arrival in Madrid of an important Burgundian official, one Nicolas Perronet, Seigneur de Granvelle, who was later to play an important role in imperial politics. He arrived charged with a mission from the Regent Marguerite, who as always insisted on behalf of her nephew on a compromise peace. Gattinara, on his side, now changed his mind and encouraged the conversations, in the hope of persuading his sovereign to leave then and there for Italy.

During this period, a project on a different political level was being mooted which, though unrealised at the time, was important from the insight it gives us into the attitudes of Charles and his grand chancellor. To resolve the continual financial problems which afflicted the imperial treasury, Gattinara proposed the formation of a special reserve, which would be fed by contributions from the church and from overseas territories. This fund, which would be put at the disposal of the emperor as circumstances demanded, would be administered by Alonso Gutierrez and Juan de Bozmediano, both reliable men. The fact that they were both Jewish shows that neither Gattinara nor Charles shared the same prejudices as their contemporaries; someone such as Cardinal Ximenes, for example, would have rejected such an idea with horror. The project, however, did not develop because of opposition from the Estates, who, on no account whatsoever would allow their control over public funds to be abandoned.

During the negotiations with France, there came the awkward moment when Charles presented his demand for the restitution of the Duchy of Burgundy. This demand could scarcely be regarded as reasonable from a political point of view; it was in fact a romantic throw-back to the Burgundian past, and represented an act of homage to the memory of one of the emperor's most revered of ancestors, Charles the Rash. It was one of those irrational sentimental acts which so often govern the policy of administrations – like the refusal of the Hohenzollerns to make the least concession over the glorious conquests of Frederick the Great, or again the obstinacy of India over the problem of Kashmir; or Great Britain's stand over the Gibraltar problem. But the question of Burgundy also had a judicial significance for Charles. He still regarded himself as the legitimate Duke of Burgundy, and wished to re-establish a right which, for a long time now, had been denied him. The French, for their part, neither could nor indeed wished to cede the territory which was of vital importance to them. In exchange, they offered to renounce their claims in Italy, which included Milan and Naples, and any rights to Flanders and the County of Artois, and, furthermore, to pay a ransom of three million gold écus. Although Charles found himself once again in a critical financial strait, he categorically refused the French offer. Such a disregard for the realities of political life was never to recur in his life after the diplomatic disaster which now approached.

In despair of his situation, François attempted to escape, but failed. This mishap rendered him impatient and towards the end of 1525 he declared himself ready to accept the imperial demands, on condition that he should be allowed to return to France to supervise the surrender of Burgundy. On this dubious basis, the negotiations continued, with François volunteering to render up his two sons as hostages. The times of the early Middle Ages were recalled when the Germanic kings sent their sons as warranty to the imperial court, or entrusted them to one of their peers as security for an agreement. As always at this period, matrimonial projects also entered into the scheme of things; Eleanore,

Charles's eldest sister and widow of the King of Portugal, was given in marriage to François I, himself a widower.

François signed the treaty of Madrid with no intention at all of keeping it. Already in the month of August 1525 he had had a formal declaration drawn up by a lawyer stating that if, having been so weakened by his captivity, he accepted terms contrary to his honour and duty, he would thus regard in advance any such agreement as null and void. The treaty, as much by reason of the king's intentions as by politically unacceptable conditions, was not worth the paper on which it was written. This document, which consisted of fifty clauses, ended with an oath made by both rulers to undertake a crusade together. Reading these texts, we are taken back to the Burgundy of the fifteenth century, to the chapter of the Order of the Golden Fleece, to those chivalrous fêtes, when (only too often) heroic legends were confused with *real-politik*. Gattinara, who before the end of the discussions had been summoned to the conference table, already saw the inherent danger which lay ahead, and opposed the project. To those who criticised him for his attitude, he replied that his knowledge of history and his sense of *real-politik* allowed him to forecast exactly the consequences of such a treaty. These were not merely the proud words of a humanist, Gattinara was to prove himself right. He remained faithful to his views and refused to affix the imperial seal to the document.

On 14 January 1526, François I signed and gave his oath to the treaty. What is more, he spontaneously gave his word as a gentleman to the viceroy, De Lannoy, that he would return to captivity if he found it impossible to keep his promise. This gesture, which was quite gratuitous, was to dishonour the king in the eyes of the world as only the previous day he had declared in the presence of three witnesses – his Ambassador, the Archbishop of Embrun, the Parliamentary President, De Selve, and the Constable, De Montmorency – that he would never honour the Treaty.

When Charles took leave of the King of France, he urged him again to keep his word and not to betray his sister, Eleanore, and once again François gave his solemn promise. On 17 March 1526, the King of France was set at liberty on the frontier of his country, and his two sons, hostages for their father, crossed on to Spanish soil. The first act of this drama of chivalry had come to an end, an affair which a century later was to inspire the Spanish Baroque Theatre.

Charles V, who had rather acted in the spirit of Charles the Rash, was heading for serious disappointments. From a historical point of view, perhaps such strokes of fate were necessary to gradually wean him from his old dreams of a restoration of the former Burgundy. A tradition as great as Burgundy's could not fail to move every human feeling, and even when it becomes necessary to sever the ties binding one to such traditions part of one always remains loyal to those beliefs. However, Charles, once this cruel trial had been gone through, was to become a wiser man, with a more objective view of life – that is to say, he was to become more of an Emperor.

German historians have severely condemned François I for his perjury at Madrid, which casts such a shadow over his image. There is no doubt, too, that he deserves such criticism, in particular for freely giving his word of honour to De Lannoy only to break his oath later. However, François did find himself in what seemed was an impossible situation; he had been obliged to conclude a peace treaty comprising a number of terms which were quite unacceptable without certain mental reservations on his part. The drama of Madrid, like the drama of the Germans at Versailles some centuries later, proved once again that for an agreement to be of value and for it to be conscientiously implemented, it must be both reasonable and freely assented to.

The year 1526, which had started with such chicanery on the political front, saw the beginning of great happiness in Charles's private life with his marriage to Isabella of Portugal. The princess, who was three years younger than her future husband, crossed the Spanish frontier in the springtime. Surrounded by the acclamation of the crowds, she entered the bedecked city of Seville a few days before the emperor. The marriage was solemnised on 10 March, after which the young couple left for Granada.

THE PEASANT WAR IN GERMANY

Since the middle of the fourteenth century there had been peasant revolts almost everywhere in Europe, and throughout events unfolded in what was almost invariably the same basic pattern. Troubles started with local disorders, usually provoked by some trivial reason, then passing beyond this initial stage developed into a veritable revolution. It was at this time that prophets, preachers and mystics, for the most part former churchmen – *Girovagues*, as they were called – made their appearance. The almost hypnotic influence they exercised over crowds led to larger and larger gatherings and finally to violence on the part of peasant hordes. Entire regions were thus devastated; there were real explosions of social hatred and countless atrocities occurred, particularly during the sieges and capture of the numerous fortified castles. Each campaign inevitably ended with the crushing of the inexperienced and poorly led peasant forces, and with the infliction of unnecessarily bloody reprisals by the victorious nobles on the unfortunate defeated.

Some of these revolts, like the Jacquerie of 1358 in France, seriously threatened the very existence of the state. In England in 1381, the country was disrupted by the Lollard rising, led by Wat Tyler and John Ball. In more respects than one the Hussite War in Bohemia was also a peasants' war, but with the difference that it was eventually the more moderate urban corporations which triumphed over the communistic sects. At the end of the fifteenth and beginning of the sixteenth century Germany witnessed other movements similar to the Lollard rising and the Jacquerie. A little later, the Reformation and agitations against the clergy and traditional beliefs again led to revolutionary uprisings among the German peasants. Among the reasons for the discontent of the agricultural populations were the many economic changes introduced. These involved pecuniary taxation in lieu of taxation in kind and the consequent implementation of a socage system calculated in terms of legal tender instead of working man-hours, or natural products which operated to the grave disadvantage of the peasantry. In addition to these disadvantages, the landed proprietors were to be found enjoying unlimited hunting privileges while the age-old rights of the peasants to the free use of timber, water and pasturage were almost all withdrawn. These material privations were further aggravated by the change from the old feudal ties peculiar to Germany, to contractual relations based on Roman Law. Finally, in addition to social grievances, the revolts were also inspired by a desire for political and religious reforms. The rural masses interpreted in their own way the theologians' ideas on ecclesiastical reform. They compared the 'rich man's Church' with the doctrine of Christian charity, the brotherhood of man and the poverty of the evangelists. Basing their philosophy on what were often in fact false premises, the questions that interested the people were often over-simplifications of the problem. The jingle, 'When Adam delved and Eve span, who was then the gentleman?' was repeated from one end of Europe to the other. This suggested a mythical Golden Age, a time of paradisial innocence which had been destroyed by a conspiracy on the part of the ruling classes. A new conception of the social structure and the rights of man began to spread among the underprivileged classes, partly as a result of the influence of humanism, and also due to the spread of the printed word. Before Gutenberg's invention it was only natural that the peasant should have been an illiterate and this often made him 'taillable et corvéable à merci', which, roughly translated, means that he could be mercilessly exploited. Now in each village there were people who knew how to read and thereby had access not only to the Bible but also to publications addressed specifically to the masses. Reformation pamphlets did not necessarily pass through the hands of the urban bourgeoisie or preachers, but were more and more frequently distributed directly among the peasants. A popular literary figure of the period was *Karst-Hans*. Walter Peter Fuchs has described him thus: 'the peasant who works his own land and is no longer the caricature of the brutalised man of old. Certainly, he is a common fellow, but simple, original and in every way normal in his outlook, which makes him superior in wit and virtue to doctors and clergy'.

Now the peasants began to show a growing interest in political affairs for, although the policies in dispute were not directly concerned with their own social problems, they hoped that a new order, better disposed to meet their demands, would eventually emerge. Most of the peasant revolts, therefore, were inspired by the people's desire for greater powers to be invested in the crown, so that the emperor might implement policies which would 'be pleasing to God and bring justice to the world'.

In 1514, even before Luther had appeared on the scene, one such rebellion broke out in southern Germany and in particular in Württemberg, which was called the 'Poor Konrad' rebellion. This revolt was directed against the oppressive measures of the feudal landlords and especially against the practice of devaluing money and arbitrarily changing standards of weights and measures, whereby the people were grossly cheated. The immediate cause of this rising was the scandalous administration of the Duchy of Württemberg by Duke Ulrich. In this revolt, as in others which were to occur later, former landsknechts who had returned to their homes played an active part. As trained soldiers, it was natural that they should be chosen as leaders; but even their experience and personal bravery could not compensate for the lack of discipline in the peasant armies when confronted with well drilled mercenary units. Events always followed the same pattern: once the first shots were fired, the mercenaries, following their well tried tactics, went into the attack; panic-stricken, the peasants would take to their heels and then there followed terrible massacres in which most of the rebel forces lost their lives. It was by such means that the great Württemberg rebellion was brought to an end within a year.

The great Peasant War started in June 1522 in regions to the south of the Black Forest. There are very apparent links between this peasant movement and the reforms preached by Zwingli, particularly as almost all Swabia had already been inspired with revolutionary ideas by the example of the Swiss Confederates. These revolutionary ideas were supported also by Ulrich von Württemberg who, exiled from his own country and placed under a ban by the emperor on 5 June 1521, had later made contact with the Swiss landsknechts and was supplied with money by France. Soon some of the towns and certain members of the knighthood also gave support to the movement and to the manifesto entitled 'the twelve articles of the Swabian peasants'. This document, which was drawn up by an apprentice furrier, one Sebastian Lotzer, was printed in Augsburg and had a wide circulation throughout all Swabia. It consisted of a summary of popular social and political demands, all justified by theological argument. Based on the Word of God and natural rights, it demanded a comprehensive reform of the empire, a reinforcement of the emperor's power and national unity. Influenced by the Swiss Reformation, it also demanded that parish priests should be elected by their parishioners.

From the very beginning of the insurrection, the Swabian League – primarily an urban confederation – decided to mobilise its military strength against the peasants, particularly after the rabble, which had now designated itself as the 'Christian League', had attacked the town of Waldshut in 1522. In accordance with a previously formulated plan, the peasants advanced in three large bands and set alight to monasteries, convents and castles. It is worth noting here that not only their revolutionary songs – in particular those of the Black Band of Florian Geyer – but also their whole ideology were to inspire the youth of Germany, in particular the Nazis five centuries later.

The Swabian League's well organised army, under the command of Georg Truchsess von Waldburg, was able to control the revolt without difficulty. Waldburg crushed one of the rebel armies near Leipheim and negotiated with another and much more powerful force from the south, which had come up from the neighbourhood of Lake Constance. Once their personal immunity had been guaranteed together with a promise that impartial judgement would be dispensed by the Archduke Ferdinand, whom they trusted, the peasants returned peacefully to their homes.

The revolt, however, was much more violent in Franconia, where social issues seemed to play a less important part than religious ideologies. The home of this revolution was in the valley of the Tauber, near Karlstadt, the homeland of the radical reformer Andreas Bodenstein. A second notable characteristic of the revolt in Franconia was the quality of the command. The leader of the rebel forces was Florian Geyer, a highly educated man of the world, who had served various princes in a diplomatic capacity, and who, like Franz von Sickingen, possessed to a high degree the knightly traditions of the empire which had been handed down from the times of the Hohenstaufens. Geyer was a natural leader of men, a quality even more important when commanding a revolutionary movement than when undertaking an ordinary military campaign. The Black Band, under his command, began systematically to capture and burn down all the strongholds of the Franconian nobility and within a short time sixty-three had been destroyed. True to their communistic religious tenets, the Band demanded from every noble who joined their cause that he give his consent to the destruction of his castle. Florian Geyer's own property was consigned to the flames, for all men were compelled to live by the same laws as those governing citizens and peasants.

In addition to the Black Band, there was also the Odenwalder Band, whose commander, after the occupation of Weinsberg on 16 April 1525, had ordered Ludwig von Helfenstein and all his followers to run the gauntlet of being flogged through the lines. This act of cruelty, which rumours circulating in patrician and aristocratic circles further exaggerated, stigmatised the peasants as torturers and murderers. And after the rebellion had been crushed it was this sort of atrocity that served as a pretext for reprisals which were no less abominable.

In Franconia, as has already been mentioned, a surprising number of knights joined with the peasants. Among the most notable was Götz von Berlichingen, though his contribution to the cause was, to say the least of it, dubious, and seems to have taken the form of a desire to place the nobility in charge of the movement. On 7 May 1525, together with Wilhelm, Bishop of Strasbourg, he signed the Treaty of Miltenberg, in which it was stipulated that the whole of the archdiocese of Mainz should be included in an alliance with the peasants and that all twelve articles of Lotzer's manifesto should be accepted. This, however, was an exceptional case; the Bishop of Wurzburg, for example, was regarded by the rebels as their arch-enemy.

In central Germany the campaign against the rebels was led by the landgrave, Philip von Hesse, the brutality of whose repressive measures ranks equally with that of the Bishop of Wurtzburg. The centre of the movement in this region was Mülhausen, a very important town, inhabited by a large number of journeymen workmen. Without any hope of ever becoming anything but wage slaves, these precursors of the nineteenth-century proletariat amounted, according to contemporary records, to forty-five per cent of the town's population. Unlike what was happening in southern Germany, the movement here soon took on a communist character and the idea of imperial reform ceased to be a decisive factor. The rebels of Mülhausen, united by a common ideology, met at Zwickau, where the presence of some religious fanatics, led by Nicholas Storch, had first been noticed around 1510. Storch was definitely influenced by both the Hussites and by the doctrines and activity of Karlstadt. However, the guiding spirit of the movement was Thomas Münzer, the lay-preacher from Stolberg, who had been personally recommended to Zwickau by Luther. Driven from the town, he went to Prague where he fell under the influence of Hussites. Back once again in Thuringia, he preached at Allstedt where he shortly founded the 'League of the Elect'. Unlike Luther, who called on the Word of God as his witness and frequently quoted from the Gospels, Münzer relied entirely on his own inspiration. He preached that one must live in God and that the Elect would one day, by the irresistible power granted to them by their faith in the Almighty, establish the Kingdom of Heaven on Earth. In this doctrine we find a distant echo of the teachings of the Taborites who preached of the 'Kingdom of God in Bohemia'. In 1525, Münzer was to be found in Mülhausen where he suppressed all the monasteries and confiscated their goods. His movement spread rapidly through the other towns of Thuringia where a flourishing textile industry had attracted a large number of proletariat workers. In the two principalities of Saxony, the authorities were unable to repress the revolt. Philip von Hesse, summoned to make war on the insurgents, crushed them at Grankenhausen. Münzer was captured and executed, and hostilities were ended by his death. In

Thuringia, as in Saxony, huge ransoms were imposed and the nobles took their revenge in an extremely bloodthirsty manner.

The Peasant Wars had a sequel in 1525 in certain parts of Austria. In the Tyrol, the movement was led by a miner, Michael Gaismair of Sterzing. He propounded a constitution which was manifestly more inspired by the Franconian peasants than by the extreme views of Münzer; in it he demanded the establishment of a peasant, democratic Christian republic. Gaismair was obliged to flee the country and was assassinated in Padua. In the Salzburg region, the farm people and miners rose against Matthias Lang, the prince-bishop, while in Styria the rebels inflicted a damaging defeat on the military governor (*Landeshauptmann*) at the battle of Schladming. Here, too, the movement did not last long and faded away without achieving the slightest result – on the contrary, as a result of the peasants' defeat, their social and economic position was aggravated.

While the rebels in south Germany were in close contact with Zwingli and the Swiss, in central Germany they placed their hopes on support from Luther. But the latter detested any sort of religious fanaticism and refused on principle to mix faith with politics, believing that all authority was vested in God, and that the Kingdom of Heaven would never be established on earth. Luther therefore considered the teachings of Münzer and the useless violence of a communist revolution as completely inimical to his own work. Probably he also felt a certain responsibility for events, and this conflict of conscience within himself caused him to lash out at the rebels and hurl abuse at them. His pamphlet, 'Against the Hordes of Peasant Bandits and Assassins' (*Wider die räuberischen und morderischen Rotten der Bauern*), made him an object of hatred to all revolutionaries for centuries to come and earned him the reputation of a paid lackey in the service of the princes. Such an idea is obviously erroneous but it is also undeniable that in his anger Luther lost all sense of proportion and self-control, as well as all trace of Christian charity; and he provided the nobles with justification for their bloody reprisals.

For a long time historians have made the mistake of believing that the Peasant War was simply a reaction to the miseries endured by the masses. Such an explanation is far too simple. A serious analysis, like Pierre Gaxotte's study of the origins of the French Revolution of 1789, and other historico-philosophical works on the phenomenon of revolution in general, show that this hypothesis is completely erroneous;

119

revolutions are nearly always instigated by a new rising social order seeking to achieve dominant control, and which attempts to resolve by violence the almost inevitable differences between its intellectual, economic and social position in society and its political influence.

In general, it is the new social order – and this is where the mistake is often made – which appeals to the poorest classes and uses them as the vanguard of a revolution.

This fact should hardly come as a surprise, since a man living on the lowest level of subsistence is entirely taken up with questions of food, clothing and keeping himself warm and has no time for other preoccupations. His interest in politics and social questions is only stimulated when his primary needs are satisfied. The moment of crisis in any collective society, therefore, can only occur when there has been perceptible economic improvement, that is to say when the idea of progress is no longer merely a dream, for it is only then that the people have more leisure to think of their condition. Improved conditions henceforth are regarded as part of their newly acquired rights and no longer as a gift.

During the relatively short time that these dramatic events were taking place in Germany, the emperor was in Spain, still hoping to obtain some advantage from his victory at Pavia and to form a Christian League of Nations.

THE 'LADIES PEACE'

Charles, whose experiences and disappointments at the Treaty of Madrid had left him a wiser man, was reaching one of the most crucial turning points in his political career. He was now ready to abandon for ever his dreams of reconquering Burgundy, the duchy which had inspired so many generations of knights and love for which de Croy had implanted in him. He renounced the ideas of de Croy in favour of those of Cardinal Mota, assumed the role of supreme arbiter of all his peoples and adopted a wider conception of imperial policy.

On 22 May 1526, while he was still enjoying the first days of family life, the League of Cognac was formed against him by the Pope, Francesco Sforza, Florence, Venice, and naturally François I. This was bound to lead, sooner or later, to another war with France. Another dangerous situation was also developing in Germany, where behind the scenes at the Diet of Speier, the princes were forming their own league. Brunswick, Mainz and Saxony joined together to form the alliance of

Dessau, while the Electors of Saxony and Hesse united with the Electors of Gotha, a league which was later to become a serious threat to the empire.

Even more serious was what was happening in the Danube basin. On 29 August 1526, the young King of Hungary, the emperor's brother-in-law, Ludwig II of Jagellon, was defeated and killed by the Turks in the battle of Mohacs. As Ludwig died leaving no heir, the treaty of succession which Maximilian had formerly concluded with the Jagellon dynasty should immediately have been implemented. It soon became obvious that the Crowns of Hungary and Bohemia would not revert automatically to the Habsburgs but that they would have to be won. That Ferdinand of Austria did succeed Ludwig as King of Bohemia was not as a result of the treaty (which the estates refused to recognise) but was the outcome of free elections to which the Habsburgs, Ferdinand, and the Duke of Bavaria submitted themselves as candidates. Ferdinand's victory was to have very serious consequences for a long time on Austro-Bavarian relations and was also of great significance during the German religious wars. The Habsburg claims to the throne of Hungary were opposed by a much more serious rival, John Zapolya, and it was only some time later, after an interregnum, that the Habsburg rights to the Crown of St Stephen were recognised. In the meanwhile, the political confusion had given the Turks an opportunity to exploit their victory and occupy nearly all the Magyar territory.

The emperor, who was in Madrid when the first news of the rout of Mohacs was received, immediately grasped the full significance of the event. From this time on he tried to conclude a lasting peace with France as quickly as possible and he endeavoured to reach an understanding with the pope in relation to his coronation in Rome. Gattinara's plan for the unification of Italy under the imperial crown and after this a resuscitation of the empire now seemed to have less and less chances of success. A papal brief, phrased in provocative terms, did not receive the imperial retort proposed by the grand chancellor, but was answered in a document drawn up by the emperor's secretary, Alonzo Valdez.

Events in Italy, however, suddenly took a wholly unpredictable turn, unforeseen by the pope and contrary to Charles's own wishes, with the sack of Rome in 1527.

Broadly speaking, this was an event which was to Charles's advantage because it gave much greater impetus to Gattinara's projects than the glorious victory of Pavia, the benefits of which had been thrown away by Charles's unrealistic policy. From a personal point of view, however, the Sack of Rome weighed heavily on the emperor's conscience; after this he became more sceptical and more inclined to passivity.

The causes of the march on Rome are fully explained in a detailed letter from Cesare Ferramosca to the emperor, and in a long report from the viceroy, Lannoy. It was not a premeditated action, and the facts were as follows: the landsknechts, who for a long time past had received no pay and who had been complaining of the poor quality of their rations, had gradually become more and more uncontrollable and the untimely death of Georg von Frunsberg had deprived the imperial command of one of the few officers with sufficient authority to maintain discipline among the mercenaries. There had already been a crisis before the battle of Pavia, which had only been averted when the veterans had yielded to the advice of their officers and waited patiently for several days, knowing that they would soon be marching towards the military glory that they sought. Now, however, all appeals and promises were useless, and the greater part of the army set out for the Eternal City. The geographical formation of the Italian peninsula, together with the magical appeal of the name of Rome and the legendary recollections of similar expeditions in the Middle Ages, drew the army onwards.

The assault on Rome began on 6 May 1527. The Constable of Bourbon was one of the first to be killed as he scaled the city walls, which was a courageous end to a wasted life. With his death, the last vestiges of discipline vanished, and the troops scattered throughout the town, plundering citizens and churches alike. The *sacco* was not a matter of a few days pillage, but lasted over several months of disorder and uncertainty, similar to the chaotic events which our century is pleased to call 're-education', 'liberation' or even 'decolonisation', as the case may be. These disorders broke all Clement VII's will to resist and also engendered an intense hatred of the Spanish and the emperor, despite the fact that he sincerely condemned the excesses of the unleashed army.

The imperialists continued to be dogged by fate, for on 29 September 1527, Lannoy, viceroy of Naples, one of the best qualified and most trusted of Charles's representatives in Italy, died. The danger from France was then aggravated when François I signed a treaty of alliance with England and thus upset the balance of power, which ever since the foundation of the State of Burgundy had remained more or less constant. To thwart the emperor's plans for resolving the religious crisis in Germany, France and England declared themselves to be opposed to a council. On 22 January 1528, a solemn declaration of war was conveyed to Charles. Everything was conducted as though this was in fact some great tournament. Charles, who was also imbued with the old traditions of chivalry, replied with a gesture which would have overjoyed his grandfather Maximilian. He offered to restrict the war to a personal duel in order to avoid useless bloodshed and to preserve the country from the ravages of war. His councillors firmly opposed such an idea; Diego Mendoza even put forward a theological argument, stating that it was not permitted to invoke the judgement of God by a duel, except where no other solution was possible because of some gap in the law.

In spite of the advance of the landsknechts which had resulted in the Sack of Rome, the French were once more at the gates of Naples. But suddenly the fortunes of war were reversed, as was so often to happen in Charles's life, and this confirmed his faith in his mission. On 21 June 1528, General Leyva defeated the French at Landriano, and a few days later, the pope concluded a peace treaty with the emperor at Barcelona. In December of the same year, the Doge of Genoa, Andrea Doria, who was blockading the port of Naples with his fleet, went over to the imperialists. In fact his contract to assist François I was due to expire with the New Year of 1529. The admiral stipulated that if he were to continue to serve him, François must recognise the independence and liberties of Genoa. But instead of making any concessions, the King of France ordered preparations for an attack on the Genoese fleet. On learning of this, Doria changed camps and thereafter became one of the most devoted vassals and closest personal friends of the emperor.

The war which had been declared in such a theatrical manner a year earlier stopped here. François I had learnt prudence from his defeats in Italy, while the King of England – always a somewhat dubious ally – showed no anxiety to undertake any operations which seemed to bring France more advantages than himself. Diplomacy therefore replaced military strength. It was then that the great ladies of the Courts of Burgundy and Paris took matters into their own hands. Thanks to their political experience and wisdom, Marguerite of Austria, the emperor's aunt, and Louise of Savoy, the mother of the King of France, were able to achieve what neither the two sovereigns nor their councillors had been able to do at Madrid – effect a reconciliation between the two rulers. Unfortunately this reconciliation would last only up to the moment when the restless and ambitious spirit of François I would once more overrule his political sense. But at least a reasonable armistice had been reached which at last gave the emperor the opportunity of visiting Italy, to be crowned by the pope.

On 3 August 1529 the Ladies Peace was signed at Cambrai. This same summer the Turks had advanced as far as Vienna and besieged the capital which was only weakly defended. With no army available to come to its relief, the fate of the city seemed sealed, when suddenly the Sultan Suleiman broke off the battle and withdrew his troops. Historians have never succeeded entirely in explaining the true reasons for this unexpected decision. Probably the main reason may be found in the commissariat difficulties experienced by the Turkish army. Anyway, Vienna seemed to have been saved by a miracle, although the hero of the defence, Count Nicholas Salm, died shortly afterwards from his wounds. Charles, still at war with François I, had been unable to come to the aid of his brother during this serious crisis.

Peace with France now provided the opportunity to prepare seriously for vigorous action against the Turks. Three years later, in 1532, a strong army under the personal command of the emperor was concentrated in the neighbourhood of Vienna. The troops of King Ferdinand were commanded by the famous mercenary captain Katziano, the imperial troops by the Count Palatine Friedrich, those of the Low Countries by the Duke of Nassau and the Seigneur de Roeulx; and finally the Italians and Spanish by General Leyva and the Marquis del Vasto. The Sultan, anxious to avoid a battle, raised the siege of Güns and ordered his army to retreat. Only his rearguard was engaged, and this was defeated by the Germans.

But to return again to 1529: the Ladies Peace had shown that the great Burgundian policy of an entente with her neighbours was a possibility, and that far from becoming lost in the pursuit of fantasies, as had happened at Madrid, a very complicated situation had been quickly unravelled, which moreover had clearly demonstrated that the peoples of western Europe had common interest.

This peace was the last of Marguerite's great political triumphs, her great moral victory and the crowning achievement of a life animated by a truly Christian and charitable spirit. Shortly before her death,

Marguerite, who had filled the place of a mother in Charles's life, was to have the satisfaction of knowing that her nephew had finally arrived at the goal which Maximilian had sought all his life – coronation by the pope.

6

The Mediterranean Empire

BOLOGNA AND AUGSBURG

At Cambrai the French promised to pay substantial indemnities; Charles as usual was in desperate financial straits the more so as it would have been impossible for him to make the journey to Italy with empty coffers. Europe's economic development between the fifteenth and sixteenth centuries was one of the causes for his predicament. The modern state, which was still in its embryo form, had had to assume new obligations and responsibilities involving financial demands on its exchequer far exceeding any that more primitive administrations had ever had to make. On a financial level, England and France were then far in advance of Spain and, what seems more extraordinary, of the Low Countries too, despite the latter's highly developed economics. There are many historical examples – financing of the Schmalkalden war in particular – which show that it was the church, with its immense privileges, which was responsible for exacting revenue from the Habsburg properties to meet the emperor's needs. In the papal states, which were territorially insignificant compared with the vast dominions of the emperor, the pope could without great difficulty raise funds, such as Charles was never able to realise throughout the whole of his reign. It is significant that an important part of the papal revenues were derived from Spain, while the Spanish king himself was unable to raise monies for the most obvious necessities from his own territories without permission of the Roman Curia. It is this that explains why anti-clericism was more rife in Catholic countries.

It was now that Mercurino Gattinara at last received the cardinal's hat which he so much coveted, and that Francesco Sforza was invested with the Duchy of Milan. Germany, in spite of her direct interest in the

126

coronation, was only represented by the young Count Palatine Philip, who held the orb during the imperial ceremonial investiture which took place on Charles's birthday, 24 February 1530. Two days earlier, on 22 February, Charles had been crowned with the iron crown of Lombardy. These were the culminating days in the career of Gattinara, who found in the ancient city of Bologna, which at the time of the Renaissance was embellished with many magnificent palaces, the reminders of classic antiquity and of the Roman Empire, which were so dear to his heart. Naturally he would have preferred the coronation to have taken place in Rome. However, even at Bologna it was possible to realise one of the principal tenets of the imperial policy: the German King and King of Spain, Duke of Burgundy, King of Naples and Sicily, monarch of realms beyond the seas, now wore the Crown of Charlemagne which, for Gattinara, was equivalent to that of Constantine and the diadem of Caesars.

At his moment of triumph, Charles could not appreciate the full historical significance of this event, which, in fact, was the last ceremony of its kind, and one which brought to a conclusion a long tradition initiated by Charlemagne. Charles was in fact the last *Imperator electus* to be crowned by a pope. Only one man after him, Napoleon, was to have the honour of receiving the crown at the hands of the supreme pontiff himself.

But in 1530 Charles could reasonably expect not only to consolidate the empire by the coronation, but also to insure the succession of the House of Habsburg. Nevertheless one fact was already decided: it would not be his son Philip, born 21 March 1527, who would eventually succeed him to the imperial title, but his brother Ferdinand and the latter's descendants.

While the emperor and pope were together in Bologna, a drama was being enacted on a secondary front – in Florence – which was to have repercussions long after the principal actors had vanished from the scene. Following the advice which François I lavished on them the Florentines had already driven out the Medicis and adopted a policy hostile to the emperor and to the pope. While the remainder of Italy had now rallied to the imperial cause, Florence was still playing for time, and when eventually she did send her ambassadors to Charles it was too late. The emperor refused to negotiate, advising them to come to terms with the papacy. The Florentines found the pontiff full of amiable sentiments, but obdurate where essentials were concerned. He declared he was quite prepared to grant concessions to his native city once the Medicis had been re-established there and the existing 'popular' government, which he described as a 'system of universal slavery', had been abolished.

While these discussions were pursued, the imperial army, commanded by Philibert, Seigneur of Chalon and Orange, was advancing slowly on Florence; the Florentines, dissatisfied with the results of the Bolognese negotiations, determined to resist. Their strong walls were reinforced and new defences constructed under the direction of Michelangelo. The siege of the city lasted six months. Finally, thanks to continual reinforcements received by the imperial army, lack of food and an outbreak of plague, the city was forced to capitulate on 12 August 1530 after being betrayed by its commander Malatesta di Baglioni. On 20 August, a new *Balia* composed of twelve leading citizens recalled the Medicis. It was the Florentines who, to save face, themselves elected Alessandro de Medici as head of the government; on 21 May 1531 he and his male heirs were officially recognised by the emperor as 'Lord Protectors' of the Republic.

During the siege Philibert d'Orange, the commander of the imperial troops, was killed. From a political point of view, this was to be the most important event arising from the battle; Philibert's heir was his nephew René, son of his sister Claude de Chalon-Arlay and Henry of Nassau. In this way the title and great historical name of Orange passed to the House of Nassau, which until the time of the eighteenth century was to play a leading role in opposing the interests of the House of Habsburg.

Towards the end of his visit to Bologna, the emperor received pressing appeals for help from his brother Ferdinand, who feared a Turkish advance on Vienna. Charles, however, made no haste to act. Contemporary sources give us reason to suppose that he was kept well informed by his intelligence service, which contradicted the understandably alarmist views of the Austrians. In this they were correct. Charles, therefore, did not proceed from Bologna to Vienna by way of Frione, the quicker route, but followed the old imperial road over the Brenner Pass to Innsbruck.

The coronation ceremony at Bologna was Cardinal Mercurino Gattinara's last great public appearance. On 5 June 1530, the High Chancellor died at Innsbruck, leaving Charles politically and personally more isolated than ever before. True, the emperor was surrounded by a staff carefully chosen from the immense reserves of manpower of his numerous domains. He had at his disposal diplomats, soldiers, jurists, economists and theologians, to whom he assigned various posts and with whom he took council.

Nevertheless, none of these could ever exercise the same influence as such men as de Croy, Gattinara, Adrien of Utrecht or Cardinal Mota. The emperor, while still retaining his entourage, now began to make his own decisions. Between the deaths of Guillaume de Croy in 1521 and that of Gattinara, Charles had considerably matured. He held very much to his own opinions and had determined on his own personal imperial policy; it was he who decided the general outline, and on the action to be followed within this framework. Charles who so often had seemed to be ready to listen to others, now showed more and more initiative. At the beginning of his reign he was still much influenced by the Burgundian ideology of de Croy or by the humanist ideals of Gattinara. Now the sovereign was himself obliged to meet the needs of a new epoch, even though the policies he pursued often seemed remote from his personal inclinations. The policy that he was to follow corresponded to an attitude of mind, a rational view of the requirements of the times, although the dictates of his heart were often pulling him in another direction. It is this apparent ambivalence in the sovereign's character that many of his contemporaries as well as a number of historians were unable to understand. Only in our own times, so similar to the great melting pot of the sixteenth century, has it been possible to make a correct historical assessment and a satisfactory interpretation of the most important events of Charles's career.

After the death of Gattinara the post of Grand Chancellor remained vacant. On the recommendation of his confessor Loaysa, Charles appointed Cobos as his financial adviser, while he relied more and more on the Seigneur de Granvelle as his principal counsellor on foreign affairs.

The religious problems in Germany, to which Charles now had to pay special attention, became more and more complicated as Diet succeeded Diet. The Protestants – the name they had assumed at the Diet of Speier when they had protested against the edicts of Worms – were unable to reach agreement among themselves. The efforts by the landgrave of Hesse to unite the parties, especially Luther and Zwingli, ended in 1529 in a long religious discussion between the two men at the Castle of Harburg. Although they agreed on a number of points, a gulf separated the German and Swiss reformers on the question of the Eucharist. As a wholehearted rationalist, Zwingli taught that the sacramental wine and bread were only symbolic, and that communion, for him, was no more than a reminder of the Passion of Christ. This teaching was based on the nominalist doctrines which had gained considerable favour in universities at the end of the Middle Ages to the detriment of scholastic realism. St Thomas Aquinas had already foreseen that by forsaking the truth of universalities (that is to say, by denying the effective existence of general notions or ideas) a mortal blow would be aimed at the doctrine of Transubstantiation; whoever admits that things are no more than what our senses tell us they are, will never be able to believe that the Eucharistic bread and wine can be transformed into the body and blood of Christ. In our own day, the very considerable importance of this problem has once more been appreciated. Erich Heller, the literary historian, in a brilliant essay on the Marburg controversy, recognises in these discussions the first signs of the soul-searching doubts which find expression in contemporary literature. Zwingli's doctrines, which were later to gain such influence thanks to Calvin, were not only to shake the foundations of religious belief, but at the same time to 'deprive poetry of its life force' (*sic*).

According to Heller, Existentialism, the philosophy of so many contemporary writers, owes its origin to the destruction of mythological beliefs by Nominalist and Calvinist teachings.

Probably the contemporaries of Luther and Zwingli did not foresee all the consequences which would arise from this problem. A phrase of Charles v's sums up the attitude of the time. The emperor when bitterly reproaching the defenders of the old faith, whose too rigid attitude, he maintained, made it difficult if not impossible ever to reach an understanding, described their line of reasoning as 'so much theological and semantic quibbling, far less productive than any of the problems set by the doctrine of transubstantiation, and which, in any case, could only be understood by an infinitesimal minority'.

In the same year as his coronation, the emperor suffered another grave loss. Following on the death of Gattinara, the Archduchess Marguerite died on 11 October 1530. By her death Charles lost the woman who had directed, and later supported and advised him from his earliest childhood, a woman who combined manly courage with essentially feminine, not to say maternal, instincts. In her last message to her imperial nephew, she once again warmly advocated the basic principle of his public career – the maintenance of peace with the Kings of England and France. It is true that Charles might have aptly replied to her in a phrase that twice occurs in his personal correspondence: 'It is impossible to keep peace without the consent of one's neighbours.' The emperor had at hand a worthy successor to Marguerite, and he appointed his sister Marie of Hungary, a widow since 1526, as the new Governor of the Low Countries. In Spain, he was theoretically represented by the Empress Isabella, though to all intents and purposes, his regent was Juan de Travera.

From a political point of view the emperor had made real progress at the Diet of Augsburg. On 1 January 1531 the Archduke Ferdinand, King of Bohemia, was elected King of the Romans at Cologne, and was crowned at Aix-la-Chapelle on 11 January of the same year. The most violent opposition he experienced at the Diet came from Bavaria, although the sovereigns of that country did not in fact hold the title of imperial electors. The Wittelsbachs allied themselves with the Protestant House of Hesse, and in the following years were to become the most dangerous adversaries of imperial policy, seeing clearly that resistance on the part of Munich prevented the union of the Catholic forces. The election of Ferdinand marks a date in the history of German institutions, in as much as it broke with an old tradition – whereby during the lifetime of an emperor, only his son (not his brother or nephew) might be chosen to assure the continuity of the imperial family line.

The Protestant cause suffered a severe blow with the death of Zwingli. Driven by fanaticism and ambition, Zwingli had over-estimated his own strength, and was killed on 11 October 1531, at the battle of Kappl fighting against the Cantons which still remained Catholic, and on which he had tried to impose his *Credo* by force. Habsburg policy, however, was unable to take advantage of this situation because of the gradual disintegration of the Swabian League. The Habsburgs' rights to Württemberg were also soon open to question, and in 1535 Charles lost this earlier territorial acquisition.

The Diet of Augsburg had scarcely come to an end when the emperor was once again obliged to ask for new subsidies for a war against the Turks. The Estates replied by presenting politico-religious demands; the Elector of Saxony in particular tried to obtain legal recognition of all his ecclesiastical spoils and the right to propagate publicly the teachings of Luther, besides demanding the annulment of the election of

Ferdinand as King of the Romans. The question of a German Council, tantamount to the recognition of a German national church, was once again raised. The emperor's difficulties were further increased by the equivocal attitude, to put it mildly, of the Catholic Estates; Bavaria in particular now maintained relations with France, and the Voivode of Transylvania which were clearly hostile to the empire. It was only thanks to his own-determination and ability that Charles was able to mobilise a large army against the Turks and force the Turkish command to break off its offensive and withdraw its forces.

Two major successes in German internal affairs mark the start of the third decade of the century. First, there was the edict of 1531, which contained important social and economic measures; then, in 1532, the unification of the penal code into one law, known as the *Majestas Carolina*, was enacted. The most important preparatory work on this law was due to the Court Chancellor of Bamberg, Johann von Schwarzenberg, the author of the Bamberg penal code of 1507; but as he died in 1528 he did not live to see the application of his crowning work as a jurist.

As far as purely religious questions were concerned, Charles V depended increasingly on the advice of Erasmus of Rotterdam, the man Gattinara had hoped one day would be the final arbiter between the different professions of faith. The Protestants, however, who regarded Erasmus as a traitor to their cause after his differences of opinion with Luther, would never have accepted him as an intermediary. Nevertheless, the idea had originally not been without merit. Walter Peter Fuchs remarks, that 'for intellectuals, at least to begin with, the Lutheran movement was no more than a continuation of Erasmus's thought'. But in the meanwhile, however, the evangelical profession of faith had become something very different from the dream of a small circle of erudite humanists. The point of rupture between the partisans of Erasmus and the followers of Luther was not only on a theological level, or more particularly on the question of freedom of will, but because of fundamental political differences between the concept of imperial authority and the ambitions of the territorial princes. However, public opinion was still widely divided between the nationalist and anti-Roman propaganda of the Protestants, and the western humanist doctrines. The humanists under no circumstances wished to break with Rome, particularly as they always saw beneath the façade of the city of the popes, the capital of the Caesars and of classical antiquity.

In spite of the fact that Luther had publicly repudiated Thomas Münzer and the rebel peasants, the revolution which he had fomented continued to engender fanatical outbreaks. This is not surprising, because as historical example shows any destruction of traditional barriers and legal authority tends to liberate forces which later are difficult, even often impossible, to contain. It is this which explains the progressive radical tendencies, which came to a culmination with the Anabaptist revolution. The extremism of this movement had already been foreshadowed. For example, the Moravian brotherhood, or Hutterites (*Hutterische Brüder*), although quasi-communist was as yet a non-violent organisation, well controlled and practising Christian charity. They were to continue to exist for more than a century. The Bohemian brotherhood, which lived according to the doctrines of Peter Chelczizki, was a similar formation. Their fraternity exists today, and constitutes a real religion whose small communities have retained their Christian and peaceful code.

MEDITERRANEAN POLICY

At the close of the Middle Ages and the beginning of our modern era, the political situation of the Iberian peninsula had changed radically. No other region of Europe had ever acquired world-wide influence and obligations of such magnitude. Profound changes in its constitutional structure were necessarily bound to follow.

The first step was the unification of Spain into a single kingdom. During the lifetime of the Catholic monarchs the link between Castile and Aragon was of a purely personal nature, while after the death of Isabella all that linked the two countries was the family tie. Philip I was King of Castile only, and indeed, his father-in-law, Ferdinand, exerted every effort until his death in 1516 to maintain the independence of Aragon, an objective in which he would have succeeded had Germaine de Foix presented him with an heir. Only after his death were the two countries constitutionally united under Charles V, though the king continued to acknowledge Aragon's special rights as well as Castile's. The unity of the Iberian peninsula was further strengthened by the marriage of Charles to Isabella of Portugal, with the friendly relations that this created transforming earlier resentments between the two nations into real solidarity. Thus, in spite of linguistic, cultural and political barriers, the Iberian peninsula combined to form a bloc and become a very important factor in European power politics; moreover, because of its natural sea and mountain frontiers, the peninsula possessed an internal cohesion greater than that of France or of the British Isles.

Other unforeseeable events like the premature death of the Infante Juan and Joanna's descent into madness, which obliged her sons to assume the mantle of power very early, and the consequent tension between Castile and Aragon resulting from such incidents in the royal house, brought Spain into closer contact with the rest of Europe. The Pyrenees had lost their political significance and despite the achievements of Magellan, Cortez and Pizarro, the real importance of Spain lay in the fact that she was now the southern arm of the giant Habsburg grip on the Kingdom of the Valois.

The fate of the Crown of St Stephen which had reverted to the House of Habsburg and the Turkish threat to the heart of their dynastic possessions in the east had similar consequences. Spanish territorial possessions in Italy, which had already been united with Aragon, now, at one stroke, became additionally important as the southern flank of the German kingdom and as the bridgehead to Rome, particularly as French aspirations to Milan threatened the traditional imperial route. The future of Milan also affected vital interests of the House of Burgundy, because if the Valois were once established in the capital city of northern Italy, not only the Duchy itself but Franche-Comté would be threatened from the rear.

With the rising significance of Italy's role in European politics, the importance of Sardinia, Sicily and Naples was also naturally enhanced. Here we find ourselves at the very heart of the great Mediterranean political design of Ferdinand of Aragon and his ancestors. Ever since the thirteenth century, when a branch of the Hohenstaufens was transplanted to Aragon, they had already recognised the strategic importance of Sicily.

Of course, during the whole period of the *Reconquista*, the Aragonese had always defended the flank of neighbouring Castile, for they too had a major interest in the expulsion of Islam, but, in seaports on either side of the Ebro, nothing could deter them from following the same course as this river, which flows towards the Balearics, Sardinia, Sicily and southern Italy, in the direction of the old Hohenstaufen and Norman heritage which had been wrested from the Angevins. Adequate protection for their maritime trade routes, which still followed the same traditional sea lanes of the Romans, was an essential. In pursuance of this aim, Aragon reinforced her position as a Mediterranean naval power by her union with Castile, which now protected her rear. Her only ostensible rivals were France and Genoa, though in fact the real enemy was the Turk and his vanguard – the corsairs of the western Mediterranean.

Under Charles v an important development took place when Andrea Doria, the Doge of Genoa, went over to the side of the emperor and became grand admiral of the imperial navy. At the same time, the Turks appointed the pirate Khair-ed-din Barbarossa as pro-consul of the Ottoman Empire in the western Mediterranean. France, which was too weak to play the role of a Mediterranean power alone, had the choice of either allying herself with Genoa and Spain or with the Turks; she chose the latter.

This decision was to increase the tension between the emperor and His Most Christian Majesty, François I. Charles's great plan was for an alliance of all the European states against Islam, not only to check any further advance by the Turks, but to drive the Infidel out of Europe itself. The first stage would be the reconquest of Hungary, and finally the re-establishment of Christianity in the Peloponnese, for which he depended on the co-operation of the maritime powers already mentioned, together with the Venetian Republic.

Before the Spanish had ever set foot in north Africa, Portugal had already conquered footholds in the western part, later known as the Barbary Coast. The search for a sea route to the Orient, which had become almost a national duty for the Portuguese, naturally focused their attention on the west coast of Morocco. With admirable persistence they had advanced in three generations towards the southern point of Africa. To dispel the fears roused by the old tales of Herodotus which told of lands south of the tropics so hot that no man could live, the ancient legend of Prester John, the Christian ruler who lived somewhere between Africa and Asia, believed by some to be Emperor of Ethiopia, was revived in order to give fresh heart to the mariners from the Algarve and Lisbon. The choice of name places such as Cap Nun shows that often these intrepid explorers believed that they had reached the farthest limits of this world, while the change of name from Cape Storm to Cape of Good Hope shows what confidence the Portuguese princes had in God. They continued to investigate the possibilities of endless new discoveries without ever losing heart in the undertaking.

The reason why such an enterprising nation as Portugal should have rejected Christopher Columbus's proposition and allowed him to turn to the Spanish will for ever remain mysterious. Some authors claim that the Genoese mariner had had certain legal difficulties with the Portuguese authorities and had been forced to leave the country. Intriguing as it may be, this theory is not very satisfactory. More logical would be the assumption that having pushed so far to the east, Lisbon did not wish to venture on a western route, which had been much less studied and explored. Another explanation corresponds much more to the general line of Portuguese thought; the Lusitanian explorers were trained in the foremost school of navigation and most famous astronomical centre in the world, which had been established at Sagres in the Algarve by Henry the Navigator (1395–1460), son of John I and grand master of the Order of Christ. Not only were the Portuguese exceptionally brave pioneers, but they were also remarkable technicians and never undertook a journey without first making careful preparations with a view to limiting the inevitable risks which such ventures entailed. At the moment when Christopher Columbus presented himself in Lisbon, the Portuguese were on the point of establishing contact with India by the eastern sea route. When therefore Columbus submitted his plans to the Portuguese princes, the latter's advisers knew that he had greatly underestimated distances. The Portuguese, unaware of the existence of a continent between India and Europe, were persuaded that Columbus's project could only meet with disaster, but not wishing to reveal their own calculations to a foreigner of whose loyalties they were uncertain, they merely refused his services. Moreover, as far as the East Indies was concerned, the Portuguese were correct, for in 1487 Bartolomeo Diaz successfully circumnavigated Africa, by the south.

In the course of their progress down the African coast line, the Portuguese had methodically established bases. In 1415 they had captured Ceuta after a bitter struggle, in which the Infante Dom Enrique had greatly distinguished himself. In 1471, Portugal occupied Tangiers, after a preliminary unsuccessful siege. By 1531, in the course of one century, Portugal had taken possession of all the most important towns of western Morocco.

Always impelled by the idea of a Christian people's union, Spain had avoided competition with the Portuguese, to whom she thus left the Atlantic coast line, while she herself concentrated on the Mediterranean African littoral. Apart from those places already mentioned, Spain occupied Oran in 1508. This victory had one major repercussion in particular. Following it, several north African potentates recognised the suzerainty of the King of Spain and paid him tribute and among them was Selim Entems, the Bey of Algiers. By a stroke of fate the Bey lost his throne and his life in a conflict with the pirate leader, Horuch Barbarossa, whom he had imprudently invited to Algiers and by whom he was assassinated in 1515. The son of the Bey managed to escape and took refuge in the citadel of Peñon de los Velez, which was occupied by the Spanish. Horuch blockaded and besieged the citadel while his adversaries were occupied elsewhere by a revolution in Sicily and the threat of revolt in Naples. At last in August 1516, Diego de Vera arrived at Cartagena with thirteen galleys and from there sailed to relieve the Citadel of Algiers. He was able to secure the mountain fortress, but imprudently went on to attack the town itself. The Spaniards fell into an ambush and suffered a serious defeat and only the artillery in Peñon de los Vera saved them from complete annihilation. Finally, on their way home in November, the fleet was struck by a storm and suffered the loss of several vessels.

This enterprise, however, gave Spain a moral victory which was to have strategic results. Although the position of Christians in north Africa was not much improved, the presence of the Spanish Kingdom on African soil was reaffirmed and it gained in importance in the following year, 1517, when Barbarossa met his death in a skirmish with the garrison of the citadel of Algiers.

The war against France and the threat that this brought to Naples prevented a systematic continuation of fighting in north Africa. For some years, nothing of further importance took place there. Tension was again increased when the Knights of the Order of Saint John of Jerusalem took refuge in Malta in 1530, and when in 1531, Alvaro de Bazan succeeded in occupying the important post of Tlemçen. The Turks took a growing interest in Tunisian affairs and allied themselves with Khair-ed-din Barbarossa, an unscrupulous but courageous pirate. Sooner or later Spain would be forced to make a display of force particularly since Charles, by being crowned emperor in 1530, had assumed responsibility for the protection of Christendom. The threat to Vienna finally decided him to open a new front and take the offensive in the Mediterranean.

It has often been asked why the Emperor did not use the forces which he sent to conquer the Americas for the pacification and Spanish colonisation of north Africa. Salvador de Madariaga, one of the most outstanding of contemporary Spanish historians, has written a highly interesting study on the subject. He has stressed the world power that Charles might have attained if, instead of wasting time in Mexico and Peru, he had conquered Morocco, Algeria and Tunisia, introduced Spanish colonists into these regions, converted the native populations to Christianity, and thus created a Mediterranean Empire to form a bloc with the mother country. By this means, according to the advocates of a Greater Spanish Africa, he would have been able to maintain, without too much difficulty, maritime predominance in the Mediterranean and unite Italy even more strongly with Spain.

This historical viewpoint, grandiose and attractive as it may seem, lacks a certain realism, and in fact, overlooks the true relations of power that existed at the time.

In those territories which are still called the West Indies, the Spanish explorers and conquistadores were dealing with peoples who were much less developed than the African tribes and their Ottoman suzerains. Cortez and Pizarro were able to overcome vast empires with extremely weak forces. The profound impression made on the natives by firearms was even exceeded by their 'terrifying horses' and their riders, which seemed to the Indians like some sort of antediluvian monsters or centaurs. Compared with the primitive islanders whom the Spanish first met, the peoples of central and southern America were certainly the products of a very ancient culture, but they had to some extent degenerated and were ready to submit to a stronger will.

Spain's adversaries in Africa on the other hand, were practising Muslims, that is to say, a people faithful to a warrior creed who believed they were called upon to conquer the world in the name of the Prophet.

An offensive to conquer north Africa besides would have entailed immense bloodshed, even if all the available troops had been employed, a fact which history has demonstrated. The recovery of the former Christian territories between the Danube and the Aegean lasted for centuries, despite the fact that the population here wished to be liberated from Turkish domination and as soon as the occasion allowed rose in revolt against their oppressors.

In the first half of the sixteenth century the Ottoman armies were still intact. It was not until the Battle of St Gothard in 1664, some hundred and thirty years later, that the first signs of weakness began to be apparent. The historic turning point finally took place before the walls of Vienna in 1683, and from then onwards, the might of Turkish power in Europe began to disintegrate more and more, but even in the midst of their decline, the Ottomans invariably fought courageously and continued to win important battles.

In the period in which we are interested, the superiority of the Turkish army lay above all in its discipline and in its admiration. The financial situation of the Turks was sound. They imposed a tax on their Christian subjects calculated per head of inhabitants and furthermore, they exacted tribute throughout the length of their immense frontiers, where conquered peoples and less powerful neighbours were obliged to pay tribute as the price of peace. The stability of their revenue made it possible for the Turkish military commanders to pay their soldiers regularly and insure that the troops received regular and abundant rations. It is interesting to note that not so long ago, military titles in the Turkish forces still corresponded with those of administrative officers, thus recalling the structure of the old Turkish army. In this army, the smallest unit consisted of about ten men who between them shared one tent, one cooking pot, and one packhorse. Eight to ten such 'tent' units comprised a company known as an *Oda* (room) or *Orta*, (oven), the commander of which was known as *Tchorbadchi Bachi*, that is to say 'soup distributor', and their officers were known by the title, or rank, of 'cook-in-chief', 'billeting officer', and so forth.

One must understand these conditions of naval combat in order to appreciate Charles's courage in defying the Turks by twice sending large fleets to disembark on the coasts of north Africa. By his Mediterranean strategy, he forced the Turkish command to act cautiously on the European mainland, and obliged the Sultans to keep a watchful eye on all their coast lines and islands to protect them from attack by sea. In such conditions one can quite understand why the Emperor did not contemplate abandoning his transatlantic conquests in return for the doubtful possibility of a successful occupation of north Africa, linking it with the mother country Spain.

Together with these practical considerations one must take into account the psychological conditions that humanism and the effect of the great discoveries created at this time. The educated classes were filled with an insatiable desire for novelty and constantly sought to enlarge the horizons of their knowledge. Men willingly accepted the risks of voyages such as those made by Magellan or Columbus, but refused when it became a question of risks in the pursuit of objectives closer to home and better known. Also they were inflamed by the quest for gold and silver – *auri sacra fames* – a quest by which man was once again obsessed. Willingly they sacrificed their lives, even their hopes of salvation, once the precious metals were within their grasp. Voyages to the Orient and the search for legendary countries like India or Japan were encouraged by fantastic tales, which painted in glowing colours the riches of unknown empires beyond the seas. In north Africa, it is true there were also fine conquests to be made, but the Maghreb was too near home for it to become a source of exaggerated legends and for facts to become embellished, as was the case with distant lands. Charles had brought back from Tunisia in their tens of thousands, Christians who had been captured by Khair-ed-din and had been collected there for sale in the slave markets of the Orient. They were set free and allowed to live once again like human beings, but as there was no material gain to be made from these unfortunate victims, their fate was of little interest to adventurers. The emperor and most of his advisers, together with the monks who battled heroically against certain methods employed by the conquistadores in the Americas, thought differently.

But despite the lack of means with which to conquer the Maghreb, the control of the Mediterranean still represented an important goal in the eyes of Charles. For a number of military and economic reasons, Spain, as we have seen, was obliged to protect the sea lanes which, via the islands on the west coast of Italy and Malta (since 1530 in the hands of the Knights of St John) and the Straits of Messina united her with the Gulf of Taranto and the Adriatic. This route linked up with those of Venice which led to the Ionian Sea and to the Republic's possessions in the Aegean.

In addition to these considerations, there was added in the second decade of the sixteenth century, the idea of a combined operation against Turkey. It was obvious that if the Turkish command could be diverted from the Mediterranean littoral and driven out of the western basin and its power shaken in the Levant, Constantinople would lose much of its essential revenues and thus the Turkish position in the Danube basin would be weakened.

Charles took a broad view of things. Although his negotiations with the Shah of Persia for a combined operation against the Turks came to nothing, the fact alone that there had been talks of this nature, which one day might result in an alliance, made a profound impression on the Pasha's court. A similar result was obtained by co-ordinated operations over enormous distances. The front which extended from Pressburg

to Tunis stretched for about nine hundred and thirty miles; the distance
from Burgundy to Austro-Hungary was six hundred and twenty-five;
Barcelona and Genoa, the main imperial naval bases, were a similar
distance to the rear of the Tunisian front. It is true that the axis which
joined Burgundy with Spain was intercepted by France, which was in
alliance with Turkey, but at the same time this axis was part of the
overall strategic plan, even if it was only of negative value. Never had
any other ruler, from the time of Henry VI of Hohenstaufen to
Napoleon, operated on such a vast field of battle and evolved plans on a
similar scale.

The hope of a crusade fostered by Charles was not just a Utopian
dream. Ten years of calm in the empire and a similar period of peace
with France, would have been sufficient to put into effect the great
project of taking the Turks in an immense pincer movement and
forcing them back out of Europe; but the realisation of Charles V's
master plan was thwarted by the German princes and the King of
France.

In 1534, a diversionary offensive against the Turks at last took shape.
The various contributory factors to this decision have been stated above
– Spanish interests, the emperor's own sense of responsibility as
Defender of Christendom, the urgent need to bring to an end the exac-
tions of the pirate Khair-ed-din Barbarossa and finally, the urgent
appeals for help made by Ferdinand of Austria. Preparations were made
in the greatest secrecy and the attack came as a total surprise. The
emperor, who was in Barcelona at the time, pretended that for once he
wished to rest and amuse himself. Reports from ambassadors tell of
nothing but hunting parties, tournaments and festivities. But at this
very time ships were already assembling in the ports, while Charles,
who in appearance seemed to be leading a carefree life, was actually
concentrating on work of the highest importance. This great conception of the enterprise and hoped-for victory against the Turks recalled
for him the fact that all earthly things are transitory and he therefore
redrafted his will and took measures to insure the government during
his absence. The empress would act as regent, assisted by Counts
Miranda and Osorno.

On 21 February, the ambassador of King Ferdinand of Bohemia
still knew nothing for certain, and it was not until the arrival of the
fleets that foreign observers were invited to a veritable 'curtain raising'
when Charles announced that he himself would take an active part in

the operations for which he had assumed full responsibility. The greatest European enterprise of this kind ever to have been undertaken was about to begin.

The history of the Crusades reveals some curious coincidences. At every climax in the struggle against Islam we find the families of Burgundian knights or princes at the head of the Christian armies. In the eighth century, when the Arabs had penetrated to the very heart of the Frankish Empire, it was a Carolingian, Charles Martel, who shattered their advance at Tours and Poitiers in 732. It was his grandson, Charlemagne, who created the Spanish March on the Ebro, from where the Catalan people were to derive their heritage. The Carolingians were from Heristal and thus Burgundian by origin. In the eleventh and twelfth centuries, when the Crusaders conquered the Holy Land in a great counter-offensive, their leaders were also of Burgundian stock, notably Godefroy de Bouillon, the defender of the Holy Sepulchre. In the sixteenth century the House of Austria and Burgundy reassumed this heritage. Charles V, born in Ghent, was admiral of the fleet that carried a Christian army across the Mediterranean to the coast of Africa, where he hoped to continue the Spanish *Reconquista* and drive out the Turks from the furthest posts still held by them within the confines of the empire. Charles's battlefield was thus the same historic ground where Scipio had once fought the Carthaginians. After the death of the Emperor, the House of Habsburg was to continue in the same tradition. The fourth encounter with the Turks which decisively put an end to Ottoman supremacy on the high seas, is forever linked with the name of the brilliant young admiral Don John of Austria, in whose veins ran the blood of the Emperor Charles. On land, the Turkish attack was crushed before the walls of Vienna where the relieving force was commanded conjointly by King Sobieski and Charles, Duke of Lorraine, a descendant of Godefroy de Bouillon. The emperor who ruled during the glorious war of 1717–18 against the Turks also bore the same name as his predecessor, Charles, Emperor and King of Spain, who had conquered Tunis and united his Spanish possessions in Burgundy and Italy with the Habsburg territories in the Danube basin. Whosoever comprehends history, not as a fortuitous sequence of events, but 'as a mirror of destiny which one must read before understanding', as Friedrich Meinecke put it, cannot fail to be struck by such a series of coincidences.

THE CRUSADE

The immediate cause of the Tunisian offensive was the increasing gravity of the situation in the western Mediterranean, which was endangering Spanish interests and the security of the Italian coasts. Khair-ed-din Barbarossa, by agreement with the Sultan of Turkey, governed a large part of north Africa as the latter's vassal; he accepted political and military directives from Constantinople, as well as receiving Turkish arms and equipment and – most important of all – ships. During the campaign, the imperialist forces found the pirate possessed of French equipment with which he had either been furnished directly or through the intermediary of the Turks. Sure of his military superiority, Barbarossa had attacked and devastated coastal districts of Spain, Naples and the Papal States, pillaged seaports and deported entire Christian populations whom he sold in the slave markets of Africa and the Levant. It was said that he specialised in hunting down beautiful and aristocratic women whom he sent as a tribute to the harem of the sultan. His movements were notoriously unpredictable; selecting an objective he would suddenly pounce on it without warning, only to disappear again within the space of a few hours. It being an impossibility to defend all the shores of the Mediterranean at one and the same time; the only solution Barbarossa's adversaries would find was a retaliatory counter-attack on Tunis, his centre of operations. Once this plan had been formulated, the emperor was able to act relatively quickly. Such swiftness was due to the fact that for once he had the complete support of Rome, for the Papal States themselves had similarly been the victims of Barbarossa's depredations. Once the necessary funds were raised, he was able to concentrate a navy at Barcelona, from where he sailed on 29 May 1535, while the army was assembling near Cagliari in Sicily. The fleet was composed of Spanish and Portuguese vessels, to which were added the Genoese ships of Andrea Doria – about one hundred warships in all.

Although he personally headed the expeditionary force, the emperor left the naval command to the Doge, while land operations were entrusted into the able hands of the Marquis de Vasto. With three hundred transports available to carry the army across the Sicilian Straits, they embarked on 14 June. Only twenty-four hours later the fleet hove to in front of the ruins of ancient Carthage at the entrance of a bay formed by two long sand spits, guarded by the fortress of La

143

Goulette. This they immediately laid siege to with every means known to the period, Alvaro de Bazan, the most highly qualified siege expert of the day, being charged with the technical operations. Then, with only a month's preparation, an assault was ordered for 14 July. The emperor himself took part in the battle, fighting in the ranks of the artillery.

The action was a complete success. Valuable prizes were captured including eighty-two vessels – practically the whole of Khair-ed-din's fleet – and French cannon, recognisable by the stamp of the royal lilies. Several of the emperor's advisers recommended that the campaign should be cut short after this victory; this moral and military success seemed to be sufficient for them. Charles, however, decided to continue in spite of what seemed almost insurmountable difficulties.

Once the situation had been rectified, the march on Tunis continued. Even before the Christian army had reached the city walls, a general rising had broken out on 20 July among prisoners and Christian slaves in the town, who were successful in occupying the city, thus greatly facilitating the imperial operations. But, at the last moment, as if by a miracle, Khair-ed-din succeeded in escaping and fleeing to Algiers. Any hope for a permanent pacification of north Africa were thus dispelled. In spite of this, the capture of Tunis was a most important triumph. For the first time a Christian counteroffensive had succeeded in gaining a victory both on land and sea. According to contemporary witnesses seventy thousand prisoners were set free.

To immortalise the great deeds of his 'Crusaders' the emperor had brought with him on this campaign the poet Garcilaso de la Vega and the Dutch painter Vermeyen. The latter made sketches which were to serve as cartoons for the magnificent tapestries woven in the Low Countries which can still be admired today. But as the historian Brandi has pointed out, these beautiful hangings idealise the campaign. They tell us nothing of the appalling privations suffered by the troops, of the thirst and unaccustomed heat; nor of the lack of draught animals which obliged the men themselves to manhandle their guns across the desert.

The extraordinary success of the operation made a great impression on contemporaries and many picturesque details were invented concerning the campaign, while the scope of the victory was exaggerated. The emperor who had personally prepared and directed the whole plan of action, had proved himself to be a prudent and clear-headed commander, with the ability to delegate authority to his best officers. Indeed, the battle of Tunis as conceived by him is a classic example of the true art of warfare because of the remarkable co-ordination and concentration of troops in an amphibious operation. The fact that the emperor was fighting alongside his troops, had greatly impressed his soldiers, who spread the fame of the new crusader throughout Europe. The emperor was received with delirious enthusiasm on his return to Sicily, and Messina' greeted him in a manner befitting a great victor. A scarcely less warm welcome was accorded him by the city of Naples and when, in the following year, he made his appearance in Rome, unpleasant memories of the Sacco seemed to have been forgotten, and the people of the pontifical city hailed him as their emperor.

Shortly after his triumph at Tunis an event took place which, as Charles rightly foresaw, was to mark the end of the Ladies Peace. On 1 November 1535, Francesco Sforza died and Milan once again became a free fief of the empire. Shortly before his death, the old duke had married the daughter of King Christian II of Denmark. She had been only twelve years old at the time and had had no heir from this unnatural union. This marriage had caused an exchange of acrimonious letters between Queen Marie and her brother. The regent protested vehemently – and rightly – against the considerable risk to which this child, her own niece, was subjected by such a marriage and stressed in particular the danger of a possible pregnancy.

Charles, who was normally very willing to listen to humane and Christian arguments, drily answered that all members of the House of Habsburg were obliged to make any sacrifice for the sake of the common cause. In this he was expressing the fundamental tradition of his family.

No sooner was the news of Sforza's death announced than, as the emperor had anticipated, France laid claim to Milan. To avert a fresh outbreak of hostilities, Charles now had to give serious consideration to how he might best compensate the French king. The emperor's position however, was now slightly improved. On 25 September 1535 Pope Clement VII died and in the following October the cardinals elected Paul III, of the House of Farnese, as his successor – a pope who was to be less consistently hostile to the emperor than his predecessor.

During his visit to Rome, Charles took the opportunity of having detailed discussions on all current problems with the new pontiff. Paul III, a stronger character than Clement, seemed considerably more understanding of the emperor's views in general. But what Charles does not seem to have appreciated, was the force that nepotism played in the life of this new sovereign pontiff. At the time of the Medicis Florence had played a decisive political role, and Clement VII as a member of the Medici family had put his concern for the interests of his native city above the interests of Rome and the Empire. Paul III, for his part, had his eye on the duchies of Parma and Piacenza and his greatest wish was to endow his numerous relatives and descendants – for he had several illegitimate children – with rich benefices and seigniories. Charles's diplomatic advisers strongly recommended that he should first satisfy the pope's personal and family ambitions before entering into discussions with him on major world problems and ecclesiastical policies. But despite his previous experiences with his contemporaries and with the Curia, Charles could not bring himself to agree – he could not believe that the principle interest of the head of his church could be in fact the enrichment of his children and nephews. Once again, the emperor appears in the guise of a rather romantic and chivalrous knight of the Middle Ages, lost in an alien world, and face to face with a Rome which had not only acquired the grandeur, but with it all the moral turpitude of the Renaissance. By appointing a group of young cardinals, Pope Clement VII had shown that his attitude towards church reform was both conciliatory and understanding. The most remarkable, from a political point of view, and the most moderate of these newly elected princes of the church was Gaspara Contarini, who had formerly served Venice, and who was later to be the papal legate on whom the emperor most depended. Unfortunately, there were too few of these young cardinals, and the majority of the Curia was too indifferent to ecclesiastical reforms for there to be any opportunity of immediately rescuing the church from the sordid political intrigues which were besetting Italy.

In the meanwhile, Granvelle had prepared a plan whereby the Milanese dispute might be resolved without recourse to war. He proposed that the third son of François I, Charles, Duke of Angoulême, should be invested with the duchy provided that the succession would revert to his direct descendants and not to any other member of the French royal family. The emperor, with better judgement than his counsellor, feared that such a step would only lead to innumerable intrigues and fresh disputes at a later date.

While Charles was still negotiating, seeking for some acceptable solution to the situation, François I decided, in the February of 1536, on a surprise move. Contrary to what might have been expected, he did not make a direct attack on Milan, but instead launched an offensive against the Duchy of Savoy, occupied Turin and from there threatened Lombardy. The Duke of Savoy fled and placed himself under the protection of the emperor, who, in consequence, was now obliged to include the alpine duchy in his plans, since its stategic importance was immediately apparent.

An unpredictable event came to Charles's aid during this critical period: his aunt, Catherine of Aragon, discarded wife of Henry VIII, died on 8 January 1536. With her death one bone of contention in his personal quarrel with the King of England was removed. There now only remained Charles's moral obligation to make sure that his cousin Mary, the daughter of Henry and Catherine, obtained her rights.

In order to pursuade the pope, who was still hesitating, to reach a decision on the French issue, Charles now initiated a very original plan, indicative of his fertile imagination and self-assurance and of his personal conviction in the justice of his cause. On Easter Monday, 17 April 1536, he invited the ambassadors of his enemies, France and Venice, to join him on a visit to the sovereign pontiff. They were received by the latter, surrounded by his cardinals, in the *Sala di Paramenti* of the Vatican. Here Charles took his place beside the pope and proceeded to state his principal arguments in a speech delivered in Spanish, which, contrary to usual practice, he did not read. Herein, Charles invited Paul III to support the party which he (the pope) believed to be in the right. When the pope interrupted, Charles listened with respect to his objections, only to resume his speech once again and insist that the highest spiritual authority in Christendom should pronounce a definite decision. He promised that if the pope were to favour the French cause, he, Charles, would abide by his ruling; if on the other hand the decision should be in his own favour, he demanded honest and effective support from the papacy. The Curia, finding itself in an awkward position, hastily found fresh diplomatic pretexts to avoid giving a definite reply.

Charles, in consequence, was left with no alternative but to open hostilities against France in defence of Savoy. He ordered his troops in the Low Countries to advance on Paris, while other corps marched along the coast from Genoa to Marseilles. The French tried to halt the Spaniards' advance by what we call today 'scorched earth tactics', but which were hardly known at that time. They destroyed all stores and set fire to many villages in order to starve out the enemy troops.

The emperor, with his predilection for amphibious operations, had made plans for his army to be provisioned by sea. But such an operation was not always feasible, since in the days of sail it only needed a storm (as the emperor was to learn at Algiers) to prevent ships putting to sea, or disperse them and preclude them from making port where planned. After about six weeks therefore, the Spanish army was forced to beat a retreat. General Leyva, one of the emperor's most able commanders, died during the campaign.

Operations in the north-west also took an unfavourable turn for Charles. In 1537 the French launched violent attacks against the Low Countries, and while the Regent Marie was still attempting to negotiate an armistice, they reoccupied Turin, which they had been forced to evacuate. The Spaniards, in their turn, tried to mount a counter-offensive by advancing from Roussillon towards Narbonne.

These encircling movements and the general plan of this campaign explain France's natural anxiety and consequent political line; France was in fact surrounded by the Habsburgs. Nevertheless, her position was extenuated by two considerations: Charles's penurious situation which prevented him from maintaining a well organised standing army, and the deficiencies of the imperial lines of communication. Although they were generally well planned, it was impossible in practice to co-ordinate operations on such widely separated fronts. Many decisions had to be left to chance, and since many offensives on one front or another were held up by some fortress or walled city, the ultimate objectives of a campaign were seldom attained. In a war of this sort, the possession of internal lines of communication gave François I an inestimable advantage.

In 1538 the pope finally decided to take the initiative and re-establish peace. He met the emperor and the King of France at Nice, where they stayed from 2 May until 18 June 1538. The negotiations however, were never three-sided; all conversations were bilateral. There was therefore never any possibility of reaching an agreement for a peace treaty, and instead, it was only decided to sign an armistice of ten years' duration.

7
German Affairs

THEOLOGY AND THE EMPIRE

After signing the truce of Nice and thus being relieved of his most pressing worries on the imperial frontiers, Charles now hoped that he would have necessary time to resume his policy of reconciliation in Germany. He was confident that he could find the means to bring about an understanding between the two faiths – at least on the question of convening a council – so that afterwards he could devote himself to a war against the Turks.

In 1536, Erasmus of Rotterdam, one of his principal advisers on religious matters, died suddenly at Basle. The emperor had probably over-estimated the influence of this 'Prince of Humanists'; the generation which had regarded Erasmus as an absolute authority had vanished; the princes and theologians of the period now looked on his humanism merely as a revered tradition, but one which carried little weight. Moreover, among the new generations there were a great many very original minds, although none, not even Sebastian Franck, nor the doctor-philosopher and naturalist, Paracelsus von Hohenheim, was as brilliant as any of their predecessors such as Erasmus, Reuchlui, Ulrich von Hutten, or even Luther himself. Even if in his old age, the 'anti-pope of Wittenberg' had become coarse and vulgar in his disputations, he still remained the mouthpiece and representative of the soul of Germany, as much for the princes as for the Reformers.

Throughout these crucial years the emperor had at his disposal the services of a group of legal and ecclesiastical advisers experienced in the ticklish problems of theological debate. Among them was Cornelius Schepper, a Netherlander, and Johann von Weeze, a German, usually referred to by the name of his archiepiscopal diocese of Land. A third,

149

Matthias Held, from Luxembourg, despite his great learning and good intentions, played a disastrous part in the negotiations with the imperial estates. Instead of seeking the compromise desired by the emperor, he obstinately maintained such a stubborn attitude over purely secondary issues that he only succeeded in hardening the opposition.

One of the major obstacles in the path of reconciliation was Bavaria, whose policy, inspired by Leonard von Eck, a staunch protagonist of the old faith and one of the most bitter opponents of the Habsburgs, was as contradictory as it was unpredictable. In 1538, Ferdinand of Austria succeeded in establishing a Catholic League to counter-balance the growing influence of the Protestants, who had organised themselves into the Schmalkalden League, so named after the Thuringian town where it was founded. The emperor had little faith in the efficacy of his brother's Catholic organisation, although Ferdinand was convinced that it provided a solution to the more and more complicated problems besetting Germany.

In addition to Charles's difficulties in Germany, he also had to contend with the problem of Denmark which had been infecting international relations ever since Christian II was exiled. In an ill-prepared and badly executed attempt to regain his throne, the deposed king had fallen into the hands of his enemies, with whom he remained a prisoner until his death in 1559. Frederick I of Holstein was elected as his successor, but died in 1533. Violent struggles for the throne followed, in which all the neighbouring states were involved. The Habsburgs had an interest in maintaining relations with Denmark because they needed free access through the Danish straits to the Baltic cities, which (as mentioned in a previous chapter) were of major importance to the Flemish merchants. Charles who was always interested in maintaining good relations with England, thought at one time of offering the Danish crown to Henry VIII. Had he done so, he would have recreated the vast North Sea Empire of King Canute of Denmark, with the only difference that its centre would now have been on the opposite shores. Queen Marie, who had no confidence whatsoever in Henry and was fearful of future tensions between Burgundy and England, actively opposed the idea, which in fact died of its own accord even before negotiations had been started.

On 1 May, 1539, Charles suffered the loss of his wife Isabella who, having been in bad health for a long time, died of a miscarriage on that day. The Infante Philip, who was only twelve years old, was obliged to accompany his mother's remains to the family vault in Granada. In accordance with the ceremonial custom of the period, it was he who, for the last time, was called upon to open the coffin at the gates of the city and identify the dead woman. Contemporary sources tell of the profound shock experienced by the child, who fainted on seeing the decomposed features of his mother.

A short while after the death of the empress, Charles had once again to leave Spain. He met François I at Aigues-Mortes, where in the true tradition of the House of Habsburg-Burgundy, various marriage plans were discussed. It was hoped that by a matrimonial alliance it would be possible to effect an exchange of disputed territories and reach some legal agreement, without either of the two great European powers losing face.

But the principal reason for Charles's departure from Spain was the critical situation which was developing in the Low Countries. The influence of the Anabaptists and other fanatical German religious sects was spreading throughout Flanders. The already permanently strained relations between patrician burgesses and master-craftsmen had become further aggravated by a rapid increase of the proletariat population.

These poor and rootless masses were beginning to react to their condition with an explosive combination of religious zeal and social awareness, similar to that which had fired the industrial textile centres of Saxony and Thuringia with violence and unrest.

Although Ghent possessed one of the most democratic constitutions of the age, it was here that the rebellion broke out with the greatest violence. An extremist dictatorship however, soon transformed the situation into a reign of terror, and despite the intervention of the regent, leading citizens were summarily tried and executed by their new masters. Once in the Netherlands, Charles lost no time in gathering troops to occupy his native city and crush the revolt. He took very severe measures against the guilty parties, and to set an example – which impressed the whole country – removed from Ghent the great Bell of Peace, declaring that a city which had violated the laws of the kingdom was unworthy to be its custodian.

Once more, peace was restored to the Netherlands. Without further delay Charles now gave all his attention to the assemblies which were being organised in Germany with a view to settling religious differences. After numerous delays, sessions were opened at Ratisbon in the spring of 1541. On the eve of his birthday, 23 February, Charles made his solemn entry into the city on the Danube. On this occasion he no longer sported the brilliant costume we see him wearing in early portraits painted at the beginning of the century, but was instead attired in a black suit similar to the one he wears in the Titian portrait in the Pinakothek in Munich. This almost funerary black can be seen not only as mourning for the deceased empress, but also as reflecting the gravity of this man who was prematurely aged at forty-one. It was the outward symbol of the evolution that his character had undergone. Later on, Charles was to tell how he had acquired his first white hairs during the Tunisian campaign, when he was only thirty-five.

The emperor had personally nominated the three representatives from each of the religious groups who were to sit together in committee during the negotiations. For the Catholic party he chose Gropper, Pflug and Eck; for the Evangelicals (Protestants), Melanchthon, Bucer and Pisterius. The sovereign himself often took part in the discussions, which sometimes departed from the realm of dogma to that of politics. Problems concerning divine rights and natural rights played an important part in these debates, and were later often to be in the cause of irremediable differences.

Cardinal Contarini proved himself an able mediator at Ratisbon; Melanchthon was courteous in manner, but fundamentally unresponsive in his attitude. Some of the princes honestly regretted that Luther himself had not been invited, for despite his verbal extravagances it was generally agreed that none was more competent than he to bring about a settlement and unite the church. It was thought that only he had sufficient authority and courage to make a truly magnanimous gesture and allay the often ignoble suspicions of the theologians. Soon it had to be recognised that the chances of ever obtaining any positive results from these sessions were growing more remote, and that the Diet was manifestly incapable of resolving the whole theological question. Differences between the Catholic and Protestant princes were gradually departing from the religious sphere and becoming political in tone and in consequence of the growing sterility of the debates – which in fact, were doing more harm than good – it was decided to dissolve the Diet on 29 July 1541.

It was probably during these long months of fruitless discussions at Ratisbon that Charles first conceived (and on good grounds) the idea of resolving the German problem by force – an idea which he was to put into practice five years later, but which up to then he had always rejected. Referring to the Emperor's state of mind during the summer of 1541, Karl Brandi writes:–

The peace negotiations with France, from which he had expected positive results, had foundered at Nice, just as the family discussion at Aigues-Mortes had come to nothing. The arduous work of many months to obtain a pacific settlement in Germany had proved to be completely useless. He left the Empire in sorrow and profoundly distressed.

On looking back over the history of Charles v, we are constantly led to seek the fundamental reason, that despite all his magnanimity, his unquestionably high-minded aims, his indefatigable exertions to which he selflessly applied all his physical and intellectual abilities, the emperor's plans, on a final analysis, led to nothing. Was it caused by some weakness in his character, or perhaps the superiority of his opponents, or was it in fact due to material factors beyond anyone's control?

Naturally there were certain problems of government which were practically insoluble in view of the contradictions typical of the period. For example while engaged in the conquest of an immense empire in America, where each territory was larger than all the emperor's European possessions put together, at the same time, in the old world, Charles was involved in interminable wars over some plot of land, a town, or the rights of some insignificant ruler. Such disproportion inevitably led to confusion which was aggravated by lack of communications. Reports from distant provinces took too long to reach the sovereign, and when decisions were eventually relayed from the Low Countries to Spain or Italy, much might have happened in the meanwhile to invalidate the emperor's orders.

In addition to these difficulties, there was yet another element to which historians have not paid sufficient attention. Charlemagne's Empire, like that of his immediate successors, was essentially one of the mainland. The danger which threatened the Franks came from the sea – from the Vikings in the north and the Saracens in the south. Within the Frankish Empire itself, however, communications were firmly in the hands of the monarch. Charlemagne's armies were able to undertake remarkable marches, precisely because they could repair without difficulty from the Ebro to the Weser, from Brittany to the plains of Hungary, from the Rhine to the Carigliano. It was possible to establish an efficient news service and the sovereign and his suite were able to travel easily to survey bishoprics, monasteries and landgravates. The

Empire of Charles v on the contrary, possessed none of these advantages. The sea route which linked Spain with Italy, although protected by the Mediterranean fleet (the only one of any consequence the emperor possessed), was always threatened by pirates in the pay of the Turks. Communication between the Asturias and the Low Countries depended on England's goodwill, for the imperialists did not control the shipping routes of the North Sea or the Baltic, although, as later events were to show, Holland was capable of providing a solid base for a maritime power. On land, the main imperial lines of communication were intersected by French territories separating the Low Countries from Spain, Spain from Italy, and both these countries from Franche-Comté and the Germanic Empire. Hence the hazardous conditions under which the emperor made his numerous journeys on land and sea – to which he himself referred in his great speech to the Estates of Burgundy in Brussels.

We can therefore appreciate how extremely difficult it was to make contact between different parts of Europe even in peace time, not to mention the obstacles that had to be overcome in the movement of troops during military campaigns.

The partitioning of the empire in the ninth century, which was to lead to the foundation of a French national state and to the rise of German nationalism in the sixteenth century, was increasingly revealed as a disaster for western Europe. Moreover, despite family ties, it was becoming difficult to maintain any rapport between Spain and central Europe. Towards the end of Charles's reign, the German princes – the champions of Nationalism – rebelled against what they termed 'their Spanish bondage'; at the same time they considerably modified their hostile attitude towards France which had still been so virulent in the time of Ulrich von Hutten, and even began to regard France as a possible ally. On the other hand, Spain and Portugal, thanks to free access to the newly discovered lands overseas, were unhindered from creating a new world empire and were turning their backs more and more on Europe.

As already mentioned more than once, Charles's greatest weakness – the Achilles' heel of all his policies – was his financial situation. Numerous efforts were made to remedy this, but these did not come to fruition until after the emperor's death. Under Philip II, revenues from possessions overseas made Spain a rich country, but Charles did not live long enough to see these changes. The economic potential of the

Netherlands only became apparent during the long war between the Seven Provinces and Spain, when burgesses and nobles joined forces unconditionally and the church placed its wealth at the disposal of the government of the province to finance a campaign which was to last ten years.

When one considers all the tremendous difficulties which stood in Charles's way, one finally comes to the conclusion that his tragedy was that he was fighting against the current of his times at a crucial turning point in history. From his lonely eminence, he appeared to his contemporaries as the representative of out-dated, or even medieval, ideas, although in fact his ideas contained many principles which were to be applied in the future.

The incredible multiplicity of problems with which Charles was confronted is reflected in the diversity of his activities. For example, while still in Germany, he was already planning a new expedition to Africa and while still occupied with theological discussions, he was sending his sister in Brussels detailed instructions for the manufacture of cannon. In this respect, he showed himself to be perfectly versed in technical detail and gave directions for the materials to be used in making these guns, some of which were to be cast in ordnance foundries in Augsburg, some in the Low Countries. Such precise instructions are all the more remarkable since Charles did not know to what use these weapons would be put – whether against Khair-ed-din Barbarossa (as was his intention), or to carry the war into Gelderland, or to defend a fresh attack from France, or whether he would have to rush them to the support of his brother Ferdinand, threatened by a Turkish invasion. Today historians have at last recognised that behind Charles's many and widely dispersed activities, there existed a comprehensive and great European strategy, with particular emphasis on the interdependence between the Danubian front and naval operations in the Mediterranean. Although it is impossible to state definitely the precise moment when the tide was turned, it is more than probable that the Turkish advance was checked for good on the day when La Goulette fell to Spanish arms.

THE HOURS OF ANGUISH

At the end of his life, Charles, in a massive correspondence, endeavoured to refute the accusation that he had lost precious time by

uselessly prolonging the Diet of Ratisbon and had thus caused the failure
of the Algerian campaign. He maintained in his own defence, that it had
been necessary to wait until the end of the summer before undertaking
any military operation in Africa. No doubt he remembered what hard-
ships the troops had suffered from heat during the attack on Tunis. But
in fact, the emperor's postponement of the African campaign until the
following year, 1542, was due to political and purely technical reasons.
In a letter to his sister he mentions among other matters, that he is
unable to leave Italy for Spain without a naval escort because of the
permanent danger of interception by the Turks or the French. One
might also get the impression from this remark that the attack on
Algiers was a manner of speaking, merely 'by the way'. However, this
is not the case; once again, Charles had carefully studied the African
enterprise, and if it failed it was certainly not due to any lack of
preparation.

On his way to join his army, the emperor met the pope at Lucca, but
their conversations were fruitless – the Farnese had become perhaps an
even more difficult partner, and even more cunning than his predecessor
the Medici.

The fleet this time was concentrated at Majorca. Andrea Doria was
once again appointed admiral, and the land forces were commanded
by Ferrante Gonzaga. The Spanish galleys were under the orders of
the Duke of Alva, in whom the emperor had an ever-growing confidence and whom he considered one of his best military advisers. As
soon as the fleet put to sea the weather changed and the more experienced veterans advised against continuing with the expedition. On 21
and 22 October violent storms blew up. However moorings were found
on the African coast, but with the attendant disadvantage that the troops
had to wade a long way through shallow water carrying all their
equipment on their backs. After disembarking, the prospects for an
attack on Algiers at first appeared to be favourable, as Hassan Aga,
Barbarossa's representative, seemed prepared to negotiate, and for a
time it looked as though the city might be won without a fight. But in
the end, Hassan finally decided to remain loyal to his master, perhaps
because he foresaw the difficulties the attackers would encounter. On
the night of 24 October, one hundred and fifty ships were lost in a
terrible tempest. In order to save themselves, a number of vessels
jettisoned supplies and cannon; others, to save their guns cut down their
masts; the main body of the fleet was dispersed. At the right psycholo-

gical moment the Muslims launched a counter attack, which took the already demoralised imperial force by surprise. The Italians fled and the enemy advanced as far as the immediate approaches to the emperor's tent. Rallying his Germans, Charles succeeded in restoring the situation, but foresaw that the siege might have to be abandoned.

Among the Spanish troops, together with veterans of many battles, was Fernando Cortez, the conqueror of Mexico. With his taste for danger, he strongly advised the emperor to give orders for Algiers to be assaulted; Charles, however, gave orders to retreat. Considered objectively, it must be conceded that his was the right decision. The lack of siege equipment, insufficient supplies and the loss of contact with the fleet justified his conviction that it would be tempting providence to engage in a pitched battle under such conditions. Besides, one cannot compare a conquistador like Cortez, separated by an ocean from his native country, alone in the midst of a strange world, who was prepared to win all or die a glorious death on the throw of the dice, with an Emperor of Christendom who, at a critical moment of a major campaign, decides that wisdom lies rather in being prudent than in courting danger.

The ships were re-assembled – or at least a sufficient number of them – to re-embark the troops and take them back to Europe. On 2 November 1541, Charles wrote a long letter to his brother Ferdinand in which he explained this disastrous operation. As always, he expressed himself in this document in a straightforward realistic truthful and simple manner, without any attempt to conceal the mistakes that had been made. At the beginning of December, the emperor disembarked at Cartagena, where once again he found himself faced with a formidable number of problems to be resolved.

Among those demanding his immediate attention was what action should be taken regarding the American Indians in view of the bitter complaints that had been submitted by the indefatigable Las Casas. In addition, there were all the usual problems – the Franco-Turkish alliance, the equivocal, not to say deceitful behaviour of the pope, the danger from Gelderland, the dissension over religion in Germany, and Turkish pressure on Hungary.

The succession in Gelderland had been a source of anxiety, not only to the emperor, but to all Germany and Europe ever since 1538, that is to say, since the death of Charles d'Egmont and the accession of William of Julich-Cleve-Berg. By this family alliance between two important rulers, a new power had arisen in north Germany and was a direct threat to the flank of the Low Countries. Furthermore, William was related to Johann-Friedrich of Saxony and to Henry VIII of England. In this way, a Protestant coalition might eventually be formed which would extend from England to the Elbe.

Shortly after the Diet of Ratisbon, Charles had signed a secret treaty with Philip von Hesse by which he hoped to break up the Schmalkalden alliance and paralyse the political activities of the Protestant princes. The fact that Philip attached himself to the emperor in this way says much for the prestige of the latter, the authority that the imperial crown still possessed and the importance attached to the imperial constitution in Germany. Philip's action in fact was prompted by fear of the punitive measures he anticipated from his bigamous marriage and licentious life. It is true that this bigamous marriage had been sanctioned by the theologians of Wittenberg and by the leaders of the Reformation, despite their usually strict attitude to questions of morality. In this particular case Melanchthon and Luther had salved their consciences by finding an alibi which allowed them to depart from their Christian principles. It is symptomatic of the period that they justified their sudden display of liberalism by moral theological argument. Because the landgrave – so they argued – was exceptionally sensual and incapable of controlling his passions, it was the lesser evil to allow him to canalise his desires by taking a second wife, than that he should satisfy the excessive virility with which God had endowed him by indulging in numerous liaisons. Of course, behind this hypocritical casuistry lay the Wittenberg doctors' interests in retaining on their side the military power and political influence of Hesse. But if the Protestant theologians and moralists appeared satisfied, there was still always the imperial penal code and the supreme court, the *Reichskammergericht*, to be taken into account. This court had been for many years an object of recrimination for the Reformers, who maintained that it had been biased in the suit concerning the secularisation of church property. Philip feared, no doubt, that in a trial for bigamy the court, even if not influenced by moral considerations, would be bound to apply the law rigorously and find him guilty. The landgrave therefore promised to remain neutral in any conflict with Gelderland, on condition that the emperor turned a blind eye to his private life; furthermore, he promised his political co-operation provided the religious freedom of the Protestant princes was respected.

While the emperor was preparing to resolve the Gelderland question, François I had once again succeeded in forming a strong anti-Habsburg coalition, consisting of the Turks, Danes, Swedes and Scots, and of course the Duke of Cleves. In July 1542, this coalition launched simultaneous attacks on several fronts at once. The French invaded Navarre, Rousillon and Lorraine and Marshal Martin van Rossem of Gelderland entered the Low Countries, burning and destroying everything before him in a veritable orgy of violence. He pushed forward to join up with the armies of François I which were attacking the Burgundian fortresses from Flanders to Luxembourg. Khair-ed-din Barbarossa, for his part, occupied Nice, where only four years earlier Paul III, François I and the emperor had signed a ten-year truce. Queen Marie, attacked on all sides, sought the help of Henry VIII, who entered the war in February 1534. England's participation on the side of the emperor provided the pope with a good excuse to express his indignation, although he had invariably refused to condemn the Franco-Turkish alliance.

As if the situation was not already dangerous enough, a fresh Protestant rebellion now broke out, most seriously in northern Germany. The imperial monasteries of Münster, Osnabrück, Minden and Paderborn abandoned Catholicism, and the Archbishop of Cologne, Eberhard von Wied, transferred his allegiance to the new faith, although deterred by scruples at the last moment did not dare turn his ecclesiastical territories into a temporal principality. In 1542, the Duchy of Saxony, under the young prince Maurice, declared itself officially Protestant. In southern Germany, Pfalz-Neuberg had joined the Reformers and in the Palatinate itself the Evangelical movement was making great strides; even the Archbishop of Mainz was hesitating as to which side to choose.

In the midst of these anxieties, Charles gave his consent to the marriage of his son Philip with the Infanta Maria of Portugal, a decision not only prompted by the desire to see the two Iberian nations united one day, but more immediately by his need of the princess's dowry to finance his campaign against the Duke of Cleves and the war against all his adversaries.

Furnished with the necessary funds, Charles decided to give priority to the Gelderland question. As usual, once he had decided on a course of action, military operations progressed rapidly. After a relatively short campaign, the Duke of Cleves was defeated and submitted to the emperor in the latter's camp at Venlo on 7 September 1543, where on bended knees he asked to be pardoned. He was obliged to cede Gelderland and to abolish the Reformed Church in Cleves.

In order to break up the Protestant League, Charles's Chancellor, Granvelle, had entered into negotiations with Maurice of Saxony. Intelligent, ambitious and unscrupulous, this ruler was probably the most typical example of the Renaissance prince as defined by Machiavelli. Maurice avidly swallowed the bait cast to him by the chancellor, who led him to understand that one day his master might be inclined to dispose of the electoral dignity of Saxony, now held by the Ernestine, or elder, branch of the House of Witten, in favour of the junior Albertine branch, to which Maurice himself belonged. This was the opening gambit in the proceedings which a little later, in 1546, resulted in Maurice being invested with the title of Elector of Saxony.

The Schmalkalden League was seriously weakened on another score, In 1542, the members of the alliance had attacked Duke Henry of Brunswick, who had remained faithful to the Catholic cause, and had driven him out of his lands, on which they imposed the new religion by force. This action which at first seemed to constitute a success soon revealed itself as a major error on the part of the League. Legally and constitutionally this act of aggression gave the emperor jurisdiction to intervene without running the risk of being accused of an infringement of religious liberty; in addition, the aggressors had alienated themselves from the powerful House of Brandenburg, to which the dispossessed duke was related.

The successful issue to the Gelderland campaign and the growing differences between the German Protestants considerably improved the imperial prospects. It now only remained to contend with France. The princes, who had been shocked by the Franco-Turkish alliance, exhibited greater understanding on this occasion than during previous crises.

Although the Diet of Speier, in 1544, only succeeded in reaching provisional agreement between Catholics and Protestants, it neverthe-less afforded an opportunity to prolong the religious peace. Once again, negotiations with the Catholic faction had proved more difficult than with the Protestants. It might almost be said that there had been a reversal of German political allegiances, with the Evangelical party seemingly siding with the emperor, while the Catholics remained un-decided, if not actually hostile. The pope, exasperated by Charles's concessions, and even more irritated because the emperor refused to understand the importance he attached to obtaining sinecures for his numerous relatives, released a papal brief in which he declared himself entirely in favour of French aspirations and predicted that Charles's end would be similar to that of the Hohenstaufens for rebelling against the head of the Church. Charles received support not from his co-religionists, but from a most unexpected quarter, for once again, Luther intervened in the battle and defended his sovereign in a pamphlet entitled *Against the Papacy of Rome founded by the Devil* (*Wider das Pabsttum zu Rom, vom Teufel gestiftet*).

Thanks to the co-operation of the princes of the empire, Charles was able to mount an offensive against the French in 1544, with an army of forty thousand men. While the English besieged Boulogne, Charles advanced cautiously along the Marne in the direction of Paris, masking fortified positions on his way, but resisting all temptation to engage in major siege operations. For the first time, it seemed as though a decisive battle would now be fought, an encounter which François i would be unable to avoid as he had done the preceding autumn. The people of Paris were filled with anxiety, but the French king, too weak physically to take the field – a severe disappointment to such a courageous knight – tried at least to maintain the morale of his subjects by showing himself everywhere in public; to show that he himself was unafraid and had no intention of abandoning his capital. But at the same time his diplo-matic advisers were busily negotiating with the imperialists, and on 19 September a peace was conducted at Crépy.

France hereby surrendered all claims to conquered territory and con-firmed afresh the fundamental principles of the Treaties of Madrid and Cambrai. Furthermore, François i promised to provide the emperor with military support against the Turks in the form of ten thousand infantrymen and six hundred mounted men-at-arms. Here was some-thing novel in the way of agreement and what was at least a moral victory for Charles. In a secret codicil, François also promised the emperor help in re-establishing a united church and to support his demand for the convocation of a council. Naturally, the two monarchs also discussed marriage alliances. A matrimonial choice was offered to the Duke of Orléans; by marrying with Anne of Austria, aged sixteen, he would receive the Duchy of Milan in the following year; by marry-ing the Infanta Maria, he would inherit the Netherlands after the death of the emperor. The emperor, however, still wished to consult Prince Philip and King Ferdinand before coming to a final decision.

Once the treaty had been signed, fresh problems arose. At the Diet of Worms it had been decided that religious negotiations should be continued in Germany. At last the council so long awaited opened at Trent.

The church had selected Trent because, as the emperor had already recommended to the pope several years earlier, being an Italian town under the jurisdiction of the Empire, it would be acceptable to the German princes. Unfortunately though, when the council met, few Protestants and German Catholics genuinely interested in church reform attended it. The Roman Curia, therefore, were able to dominate the proceedings and fix an agenda which was completely at variance to the emperor's wishes. For example, the main subject of discussion was not the elimination of abuses, which Charles considered the most important item and which would confirm that Rome was prepared to adopt a benevolent attitude to apostates, but, on the contrary, the council put forward a series of proposals which unconditionally rejected any Protestant opinions on questions still under discussion and closed the door on all Catholics seeking a compromise. This premature decision effectively prevented Charles from accomplishing the real purpose behind his plans for military action against the dissident Protestants in northern Germany, because once having had recourse to force, any success against the Schmalkalden League would be invalidated unless he was morally sure that major reforms had been decided by the council, and once victory was won, if he could not prove that the Catholics were honestly prepared to come to some agreement based on tangible concessions.

The council maintained, on the contrary, that the first obligation of the church was to decide those doctrinal points which still lacked definition – an opinion certainly held by the majority of the ecclesiastical councillors. In retrospect it can only be regretted that they did not accept the emperor's wise advice.

While preparations were being made for the Council of Trent – in which Charles put his last hopes for a peaceful settlement – he was at the same time making ready to attack the Elector of Saxony and the Landgrave of Hesse in the event of another impasse. Since their act of aggression against Brunswick, these two princes were considered to have violated the law and were declared enemies of the empire. The pope strongly supported the emperor in his plans and placed twelve thousand five hundred troops and two hundred thousand ducats at his disposal; furthermore, he granted him, for a period of six months, the revenues of the Spanish Church and five hundred thousand ducats received from Spanish monastic sources.

At the same time, Charles was also devoting attention to Bavaria which, because of Leonard Eck's incessant anti-Habsburg campaign, was the most vulnerable of the Catholic States. He was finally successful in signing a treaty with the Wittelsbachs confirming the marriage of Albrecht, the Bavarian heir apparent, with Anne of Bohemia and Hungary. This agreement marked the beginning of a major change in south German dynastic policy and was to lead an alliance between Bavaria and Austria which was to last for more than a century. In another agreement, Charles promised Maurice of Saxony the protectorates of Magdeburg and Halberstadt in return for his neutrality.

Although the members of the Schmalkalden League were well aware of Charles's preparations, they were still rash enough to acquire further enemies by a quite unjustifiable act of aggression, when, by imprisoning Henry of Brunswick on his attempt to return to his country, they incurred the anger of the Protestant House of Brandenburg. Moreover they further weakened their cause by their inability to decide among themselves on a commander-in-chief to be in sole control of the war which they saw to be imminent.

The emperor attended the festivities held in Brussels in honour of the visit of Queen Eleanore of France and the Duke of Orléans, and then, after a short delay, left for Trent to visit the papal legate, Cardinal Farnese. Here his enthusiastic reception by the Curia made him ill at ease, for their enthusiasm was not aroused by his plans for a war against the Turks, but on the contrary for one against the Protestants. Later, Charles was to complain that the pope had prematurely disclosed the details of the plot that was being hatched round the Schmalkalden League. Against all expectations, both parties in Germany still seemed to be hoping for a formula whereby their differences would be settled. 'Concord' was the almost magic word with which both parties sought to gain time.

The difficulties of following particular political designs in the sixteenth century were made even more complicated by sudden and unpredictable changes in dynastic family relationships, which were all the more important since nearly all state agreements and all peace treaties were based on matrimonial alliances. In 1545, Philip of Spain, who was eighteen, had a son, whom he called Carlos after his grandfather. This young man was destined to become a tragic figure of history and literature, although he was never to exercise political power. His mother, the Infanta, had died at his birth, and henceforth the House of Habsburg applied itself intensely to finding a second wife for Philip. At the very beginning, Marguerite of Navarre was suggested as the future queen. But a more delicate question was raised when the Duke of Orléans, who since the Treaty of Crépy in the preceding year had become a key figure in European politics, died on 9 September 1545. The emperor was to state in his memoirs that this was, for him, a gift from God for it freed him in fact from the necessity of making a choice between what the majority of his advisers agreed were two evils: whether to cede the Netherlands to the House of Angoulême, or to give up Milan. Either choice would have been equally disastrous for the House of Austria and Burgundy.

In the meanwhile, the princes of the Schmalkalden League continued with their discussions on religious affairs and territorial problems and plans for a change in the Federal Constitution. Their politico-military position, moreover, seemed once again to be improved. On 17 January 1546, the Elector Palatine received both bread *and* wine at Holy Communion, which could be interpreted to mean that he had rallied to the Protestant cause.

Towards the New Year, the emperor was in the Low Countries again where, on 15 January 1546, he attended a meeting of the Chapter of the Order of the Golden Fleece in Utrecht. On his departure, he promised his sister Marie that he would do everything possible to resolve the German question without recourse to war; but he pointed out, however, that it was essential to put an end to abortive discussions and re-establish order within the empire and the German Church. As his letters indicate, the emperor believed that the situation of Europe was favourable to a final reckoning. France and England were both, by mutual consent neutral, and the Turks too, for once, were peaceful.

Before leaving for Germany, Charles received a delegation of princes demanding that he should not bring foreign troops on to German soil. He also had a personal conversation with the Landgrave Philip von Hesse, still in the hope of reaching a compromise. Philip, however, remained intransigent. During this meeting, while the Landgrave was attempting to define the meaning of the empire, the Chancellor, Granvelle, growing exasperated, uttered the famous words which have become part of history: '*Pas un sou, rien que des ennuis et des soucis*' (Not a penny, nothing but sorrow and care). Philip von Hesse was then presumptuous enough to advise the emperor to devote more time to the Gospels and to reading Holy Writ. Charles had need of all his self-control to prevent himself from making a cutting retort to this man whose life was anything but Christian.

THE BATTLE OF MÜHLBERG

On 10 April 1546, the emperor made his entrance into Ratisbon. The members of the Schmalkalden League, openly lacking in respect, arrived well after the appointed date, thus holding up the debates and obliging the sovereign to await their convenience. No further theological discussions were held in his presence – the Protestants had put an end to them in a scarcely diplomatic manner. Besides, throughout these discussions the imminent possibility of war could no longer be disregarded by anyone. The debates continued in an atmosphere of irritability. The prince's demands to know against whom the emperor was arming, received only evasive answers, the emperor confining himself to the statement that it was his prerogative to impose his authority on recalcitrant states. A new crisis broke out when the imperialists forced the City of Ravensburg (which had joined the Schmalkalden League) to re-adopt the old faith.

But the carefree life of Ratisbon, which had been evident in former years, continued through the spring of 1546, and although the political barometer pointed to storm, many of the younger generation still continued a life of pleasure. Charles too, after following a cure for gout (which had been very successful), was in good spirits and in much better physical shape than in the past years. Before arriving in Ratisbon he had had some particularly severe attacks of gout and had suffered moments of extreme mental depression. His political testament of 1543 seems to have been written in the expectation of a not far distant death. Now all was changed. He joined in the gay life of his diplomats and other officers, whose pleasures were not only confined to the medicinal public baths but who also indulged in numerous amorous adventures with the maidens of Ratisbon!

Charles's liaison with Barbara Blomberg, a young bourgeoise, seemed to have been of much shorter duration than his love affair with Maria van de Gheenst a quarter of a century earlier. But it nevertheless had a happy sequel, both from a historical and family point of view; for the issue of this love affair was Don John of Austria, a son whose welfare Charles always had close to his heart, and whom he introduced, a few years later, into his immediate entourage. Don John was brought up with all the honours which according to the custom of the times were accorded to royal bastards of reigning families. After the death of his father, his half-brother Philip, treated him as a loyal paladin, very close to the throne. From his youth, Don John was to cover himself with glory, by his brilliant victory at Lepanto and later through his activities in the Low Countries. He is buried in the Escorial, not in the royal vault itself constructed *more geometrico*, but right beside it, in a large chapel. He lies in a sarcophagus ornamented with a high relief, which faithfully reproduces the features of this great soldier and diplomatist.

The mother of Don John was given a maintenance allowance by the court, and later, as Madame Kegel, caused a lot of trouble and considerable scandal. Her son saw her only once, when harsh words were exchanged between them. He reproached her with her dissolute life, to which she retorted by telling Don John that he was not the son of the emperor, but of an ordinary artillery man with whom she had been intimate and with whom she had deceived the man who John of Austria believed to be his father. It is probable, however, judging by his notes, that while still at Ratisbon, Charles had already reason to be displeased with the young Barbara. Be that as it may, Charles was in good form at the end of that spring and seems to have overcome the worries occasioned by his ill-health, harbinger of old age.

The adjournment of the Diet, on 24 July, was merely a simple formality. As early as the beginning of June in a letter to the Regent of the Netherlands, the emperor had expressed his conviction that from now on all attempts at peace were useless and that war remained the only means of ending the religious divisions in Germany. 'Moreover (he added), such action is justifiable in view of the violation of the Imperial Constitution of which Philip von Hesse and Johann-Friedrich of Saxony are guilty, by reason of their attack on the Duke of Brunswick.'

Despite an abundance of arms and careful preparation, the campaign might still have taken a catastrophic turn for the emperor if the Protestant states had not suffered from the hereditary malaise of all coalitions – they 'had as many opinions as they had heads'. Schertlin, the commander-in-chief, was prepared to bar the passage of the Alps to the imperial troops coming up from Italy. However, the war council of the League recalled him just at the moment when his manœuvre had every chance of succeeding, and he only managed to force the Italian units to proceed via Innsbruck and descend the Inn to Kufstein, instead of taking the shorter route by the Fern pass. Moreover, the Schmalkalden League, as the emperor himself recognised later, had had both the time and the opportunity to capture him at Ratisbon. Faced with such a threat, the emperor had retired to Landshut on the Isar, where on 13 August he was joined by the papal troops. On the following day, 14 August 1546, the League, in the old traditional style, dispatched a herald to challenge the emperor to battle. Thus it was the Protestant princes who officially initiated the war at a moment when the sovereign was still hesitating to announce the imperial ban on the Landgrave of Hesse and the Elector of Saxony.

The principal problem facing Charles was to unite his forces as quickly as possible with the other armies coming from the Low Countries, commanded by Maximilian Buren, the son of Egmont Buren von Isselstein. This talented general was able to cross the Rhine without having to force a passage, and then advanced rapidly by Miltenberg to meet the main army, leaving the enemy troops far in his rear.

In the meanwhile, on 31 August, Charles had crossed the Danube to the east of Ingoldstadt and had had his first encounter with the Schmalkalden soldiery. Once again, his coolness very much impressed the troops, whose own courage had been somewhat shaken by a particularly violent enemy cannonade. This incident inspired an army song, proof of the emperor's popularity in Germany at the start of the civil war there.

While this was going on, the two main armies entrenched themselves and after a few skirmishes the Protestants retired without risking an attack. Thus the imperialists gained the first psychological victory. The Danube campaign, however, was not over; the Protestants withdrew to the west and closed in on the city of Ulm, which was an important link with Swabia, from which the League obtained most of its military supplies. However, thanks to this manœuvre, the imperial forces were able to join up with Buren's troops from the Netherlands, without a fight. But their adversaries were also reinforced by the units of the Princes' army which had been detailed to defend the passage of the Rhine, but which, having failed in their task, now rejoined the main army of the League.

Von Ranke has tried to account for the Protestants' clumsy strategy on political grounds. According to him the princes had no aggressive intentions from a political point of view but were concerned solely to defend their faith, and so would naturally hesitate to embark on a full-scale military operation. But this line of reasoning is hardly conclusive: it was the League that had incited the emperor to battle, and it was the League that had declared war on him and told him categorically that he had forfeited the crown. If Ranke really believes that the Protestants stood to gain nothing from a military victory, he seems to have overlooked two major considerations: the tradition of princely rebellions and conspiracies, which had existed in the Germanic Roman Empire ever since the eleventh century, and with which the leaders of the Schmalkalden League were certainly familiar. And the fact that even if one accepts that to begin with they had no definite plans for the future – something in itself which is highly improbable – they would certainly have soon found a political line to follow. Having already announced in their Declaration at Landshut that Charles had forfeited his right to the crown they would no doubt have deposed him, together with his brother Ferdinand, and elected the King of France in their place. Thus, if the emperor had been defeated, the whole of Germany would have been shaken to its foundations and the last Catholic bastions destroyed. The partisans of the new faith would then have been able to reunite the National German Congress (*Versammlung teutscher Nation*), which for a long time had been considered as a sort of 'anti-Council', which would have voted a new imperial and ecclesiastical constitution.

The Protestant party, therefore, was certainly not lacking in ideas which would have been well served by a successful issue to the war. If, however, the League wasted precious time and thus lost the opportunity of achieving military success, this was in fact due to a lack of unity, mutual mistrust, and to the intrigues and selfish motives of most of its leaders. Moreover, in their subconscious minds, even when they were in open revolt, they still retained a certain respect for the Imperial Crown, and something like a belated recognition of the medieval concept of the Empire, revived under Charles v. Also to be taken into account was the diffusion of his own personal authority which became enhanced as the years went by. Even his most inveterate enemies could not deny the influence of a man who united immense knowledge, long experience and great wisdom with physical courage, a sense of responsibility and absolute moral rectitude. It was in the possession of these qualities that Charles differed from other ruling princes of his day. Indeed, in comparison with his adversaries, who, to use the words of Walther von der Vogelweide, 'were a poor lot of kings' (*arme Küngen*), Charles was a real Emperor, invested with the highest position in the western world.

The imperialists pursued the army of the League by short stages as far as the region between Donauworth and Nordlingern. On 4 October 1546, they were nearly engaged in a battle when the Habsburg forces mounted an attack on the flank of the enemy columns which were proceeding along the crest of a hill. It is not out of the question that on this day, the feast of St Francis, the emperor may well have recalled a prophecy widespread throughout Germany, according to which the saint would one day give him the Crown of France. Nevertheless, always prudent and ready to take advice from his experts, Charles accepted the views of his generals and recalled his forces, judging that the enemy's position was too favourable and that a battle under these conditions might well lead to disaster. However, ten days later, while advancing deep into hostile territory with a reconnaissance patrol, Charles was surprised by the enemy and nearly taken prisoner. Meanwhile, the Duke of Alba and the landgrave were engaged in an exchange of insulting and provocative messages, which seem an anachronism in what was a relatively modern war, which had started with an intensive artillery duel. The Spaniard invited the landgrave to come down from the heights and give battle as befits a man, to which Philip retorted that he had waited in vain near Ingolstadt for the imperialists to attack but that they had been too cowardly to leave their entrenchments.

These comings and goings and minor tactical manœuvres were by no means a waste of time. For Charles, the main front was elsewhere, and he awaited with impatience news of the great diplomatic offensive with which Ferdinand had been entrusted. On 4 October, Maurice of Saxony visited Prague, and although he still hesitated to assume the title of Elector which he had been promised, he was leaning more and more to the side of the emperor. When finally the news was received on 8 November 1546 that Maurice had signed an alliance, Charles ordered his artillery to fire a victory salvo.

While the emperor was waiting to hear the results of these diplomatic discussions, the season was already drawing to a close. The imperial army had suffered severe losses from sickness, particularly dysentry; furthermore, when Cardinal Farnese left, several thousand Italians followed him. They complained of the harsh climate and the sacrifices that war demanded of them; the Spaniards, on the other hand, put up with the rains, snow and cold without flinching.

On 21 November 1546, the landgrave and his demoralised forces retreated northwards by way of Heidenheim, thus leaving the whole of southern Germany in the hands of the emperor. The defection of young Maurice of Saxony was unquestionably the principal reason for the landgrave's decision, for Philip von Hesse had in no way under-estimated the danger with which he was threatened by the new elector who, indeed, was not only his son-in-law but also his disciple in Machiavellian intrigue. For the emperor, on the other hand, Maurice's decision not only gave him military advantage but also a moral victory: once an important Protestant had left the camp of his co-religionists to side with the crown, there could be no further accusations of religious persecution levelled against the emperor.

William of Orange once declared that only persistence in the face of adversity could assure success in any major enterprise. Few campaigns prove the truth of this adage better than the Schmalkalden War. Charles v, having once made up his mind, always acted with assurance and without hesitation, even in the most discouraging circum-stances – for example at Ratisbon, where he found himself almost unprotected; or at Ingolstadt, faced with the superior artillery power of the enemy or again, in camp at Sontheim, beset by difficulties on all sides. The principal reason for his confidence was the feeling of political superiority. Von Ranke, a practising Lutheran, who thanks to his conscientious and objective view of history has given us a remarkable account of this campaign, wrote: 'There is also such a thing as political strategy; it was this that defeated the Protestants even before the war had begun.'

Without hurrying, the emperor first of all reinforced his position in southern Germany. Once again he gave the impression of having plenty of time at his disposal. The general situation in Europe continued favourable to him. Naturally he could not know that within the next two years his principal rivals, François I and Henry viii, would be dead; but these two men had already lost much of their force and drive. The King of France, once so pugnacious, had become cautious; Charles's advance across his country up to the walls of Paris had made a deep impression on him. Moreover, Charles, despite his need of English support on military issues, had managed to refuse a demand made by Henry which could have had politically dangerous implications without giving any offence. Henry had in fact requested that he should be acknowledged as *Defensor Fedei* – head of the Catholic Church in England. Charles replied that his respect for a friendly country prevented him from interfering in a purely internal political matter, and that for him Henry would remain as ever, King of England and his most faithful ally.

In Germany, the time of year was unfavourable to the continuation of the campaign; it was better to wait for the spring. The letters Charles wrote to Ferdinand which, like a large proportion of his correspondence with his brothers and sisters, have very much the character of monologues, reveal his thoughts concerning the conduct of the war and the peace to come. In a plan to which he was to revert on many occasions, both now and later, Charles envisaged the formation of a 'Grand League', a veritable empire within the empire. By voluntary and contractual contributions, this League would provide the necessary means to conduct a *realpolitik*. This instrument of government would effectively replace the old administrative machine, already clogged by a whole lot of out-dated privileges and condemned to stagnation.

Charles's correspondence does not disclose to what extent he owed his ideas to the Spanish *Hermandades*, or even to the Swabian League, but he had probably taken them as models.

As a war measure, Charles proposed to blockade the recalcitrant cities which still adhered to the Schmalkalden League. He came up against the stubborn opposition of Queen Marie who was anxious to maintain peace in the Low Countries. She even went so far as to threaten to renounce the regency if her advice was not followed. This crisis shows once again the modernity of Charles's political and strategic ideas; but these ideas, too advanced for the times, could not be put into effect with the constitutional means at his disposal. As a realist, Charles was always ready to give way whenever he was presented with reasonable objections to his policies.

On 23 December 1546, Johann-Friedrich of Saxony invaded the territory of his cousin Maurice. The emperor made no move; a struggle between the two branches of the House of Wittin served his policy very well, for conflicts, in heightening the hostility between the two, helped to reduce the risk of treason on the part of Maurice – at least for the duration of the conflict. The situation would have only become serious for Charles had Johann-Friedrich invaded Bohemia where there was already disaffection among Hussite nobles and a certain section of public opinion hostile to the Habsburgs. But, in fact, Johann-Friedrich halted his advance before Leipzig; nevertheless, he achieved one major success when Albrecht-Alcibiades von Brandenburg, who had hastened to the help of Maurice, was defeated and taken prisoner. This resulted in a further split in the Protestant ranks which redounded to Charles's benefit.

About the new year of 1547, Charles was faced with other major worries apart from his military involvements. On 13 January, the council at the demand of the Curia debated the edict devoted to justification by faith alone. Thus, any expectations of favourable concessions being made to the Protestants on an essential theological point were completely destroyed.

On 22 January the pope recalled his troops from Germany. Never yet had the ineptitude of papal policy of the time been so apparent. While Charles was fighting in Germany to re-establish a united Church and bring back to it those who had strayed far away, the pope was actually undermining the sovereign's military operations.

At the same time, by using the council, not as a means to put an end to abuses, but above all to raise barriers of dogma against all further understanding, the pope was preventing all possibility of a peaceful agreement between Catholics and Protestants. Such unfortunate behaviour once again made evident the fact that Paul III was more concerned with furthering the interests of the House of Farnese than those of the Universal Catholic and Apostolic Church of which he was the head. In the course of the year 1547, Paul III was moreover to show himself not over-scrupulous in the means he employed to achieve his ends. The famous Fieschi conspiracy of Genoa in January 1547 is typical of many historical events which have become entirely distorted through literature and drama, especially by Schiller. It was in fact a dangerous enterprise fomented by partisans of the Farnese against the emperor and his great admiral, Andrea Doria. Ferrente Gonzaga must be given all due credit for crushing the plot. In September of the same year, Pier-Ludovico Farnese, Duke of Parma, lost his life in a conspiracy among the nobles. His subversive activities gave the emperor more than sufficient excuse to retain the duchy for himself, a decisive measure which impressed Paul III considerably more than any of the emperor's protests against papal schemes, such as the transference of the location of the council. In January 1547, the tension became such that Charles finally lost his temper in front of the Papal Nuncio. This was one of the very few occasions in the sovereign's life when he was to lose patience and despite the self-control which he had practised all his life, he so far forgot all precepts of moderation as to offend the person of the pope. This incident, however, had no aftermath.

During the first months of the year 1547, Ferdinand's situation deteriorated. On 4 March, therefore, the emperor dispatched an army to the north, and on the tenth of the month informed his brother of his decision to attack Saxony. He left Nuremberg on 28 March. Once again he displayed not only his very acute organising ability, but also his subtle understanding of the relation between politics and military strategy. Instead of advancing directly on Thuringia, where he would have been trapped between the armies of Johann-Friedrich and the Landgrave of Hesse, he chose the region of Tirschenreuth as a rallying point in which to join up with the forces of King Ferdinand and Duke Maurice. By this manœuvre he not only strengthened the ties by which the latter was attached to him – which was always essential – but he also provided the Bohemian nobles with an impressive display of Habsburg military might, and proof of his determination to adopt the cause of his brother, Ferdinand.

The emperor advanced on Plauen by way of Eger, and thence slowly descended towards the Elbe. Johann-Friedrich, whose troops were in the neighbourhood of Meissen, realised just in time the dangerous position in which this manœuvre had placed him, for he now ran the risk of being cut off from his own country. On 11 April, therefore, he marched in the direction of Wittenberg, following the right bank of the Elbe. He considered that the river afforded him sufficient protection, because, as he believed, the imperialists lacked the necessary bridging equipment to effect a crossing. The two armies thus marched parallel to each other on either bank. The emperor, approaching from Colditz and Leisnig, directed his advance towards the Saxon's flank. From careful preparations made before the campaign, Charles had learnt that there was a ford near Schirmenitz in the region of Mühlberg, which could provide a practical crossing place for his army. This was wide enough to allow the passage of cavalry, seven abreast, and the bottom was sufficiently sound to take the weight of men, horses and vehicles, and every sort of military equipment. The elector, however, was convinced that neither the emperor nor his officers were aware of the existence of this ford.

On Sunday, 24 April 1547, Charles struck camp at a very early hour in the morning while Johann-Friedrich was celebrating divine service. A thick mist enveloped the river and its banks. Charles, accompanied by Duke Maurice, was with the advance forces, while the main body of the army followed with the Archduke Ferdinand and Archduke Maximilian, then aged twenty. Towards ten o'clock the mist cleared, and the two armies found themselves face to face. Curiously enough, Johann-Friedrich, although sure that he only had a small hostile force on his flank, did not immediately attack and destroy the enemy while they were still manœuvring for position. This would have been all the easier since he had pontoons available to carry his troops over to the opposite bank, while his cavalry could have used the ford. On the contrary, he attempted to withdraw to a large neighbouring forest, under cover of which he hoped to reach the fortified town of Wittenberg. At the same time, there were differences of opinion among the imperial headquarters staff. Some feared that the numerically superior enemy had destroyed the troops that had already crossed the river. Charles, himself, however, was determined on a battle and pushed forward. His presence in the firing line inspired the Spanish soldiery to heroic feats of arms. Some leapt into the river with their equipment; others, stripped, with sword in mouth, swimming and wading, attacked the pontoons from which the elector's infantry opened a sustained fire. Soon the pontoons were captured. Some peasants pointed out to the imperialists another ford by which the cavalry could cross, while a temporary bridge was rapidly made to allow the main body of infantry to reach the farther bank.

The battle thus actually started in the form of a pursuit, which Melanchthon was to describe later as more of a *desertio* than a *fuga* on the part of the Protestant forces. Johann-Friedrich did his utmost to reach the forest with the larger part of his troops, while at the same time he ordered a cavalry unit – too weak for the purpose – to make a diversionary attack on the enemy. The superior dash and bravery of the Spanish and the aggressive spirit of the imperialists was demonstrated to the full. The elector was literally swallowed up in the mêlée and taken prisoner. He was led by the Duke of Alba in front of the emperor. When Johann-Friedrich prepared to dismount from his horse, the emperor signed to him to remain in the saddle, saying: 'Do you now

174

recognise me as Emperor of the Romans?' The elector replied that he was only a poor prisoner and begged that his rank should be respected. 'I will treat you as you would have treated me,' replied Charles, to which Ferdinand added: 'You have declared that you would drive me and my children out of my country and separate me from my compatriots.' The Bishop of Hildesheim, a great warrior in the sight of the Lord, who had crossed the Elbe in his armour, was to recount later how overjoyed he had been to see 'the wild boar captured', and added that he would not have missed being present for hundreds of ducats.

Maurice, who, at the beginning of the battle, had made Johann-Friedrich a last offer to negotiate, which the latter had refused, only arrived at headquarters very late in the evening. He had been more than twenty hours in the saddle and several times in danger of his life. He owed his life, on one occasion, to a happy stroke of fortune when a gun aimed at him had misfired. The electoral dignity, which from this day was really his, was to remain in the Albertine branch of the House of Wettin until the end of the Holy Roman Empire, when the Elector of Saxony, with Napoleon's help, took the title of King.

The emperor spent the night on the left bank of the Elbe. Certainly he must have been extremely satisfied with the results, particularly as his military casualties were minimal – less than fifty dead. Folk stories and Avila's *Commentarium de bello Germanico a Carolo Quinto Caesare Maximo gesto*, ascribe to him a Christian variant of Julius Caesar's famous words: 'I came; I saw; and God conquered', which adequately interprets his state of mind. Popular imagination was not slow to seize on this memorable occasion. It was said that an eagle had hovered over the Spanish army, and, as in the time of Joshua, God had prolonged the day to allow victory to be won; that a blood-red sun had risen higher into the heavens than usual.

Charles was fully aware of the importance of this day. The great picture of Titian shows the victor of Mühlberg, clad in steel, with lowered lance, mounted on a nervous jet-black charger. The background is filled with a reddish twilit sky, reflecting the fires of the battlefield. Contrary to the custom of the period, we are shown no corpses, prisoners, or fleeing enemies – the outward symbols of a great feat of arms. But this victory was no less glorious than that of Pavia. However, this time, the emperor, who had learnt his lesson, was wiser than he had been twenty-two years earlier. He was determined to exploit his victory. This at the time seemed so great and its consequences filled with such possibilities, that Charles might have well believed that an enduring peace was assured, and that his dreams of Christian unity and a combined crusade by the west against the Grand Turk would at last be realised. In his hour of glory, it was easy to believe that the dream of the Burgundian knights was at last to come true. Symbolically, on this triumphal day, Charles had not carried the colours of Spain or Austria, but the red and gold of Burgundy and the Golden Fleece.

8

The Empire Beyond the Seas

One of the most important chapters in the reign of Charles V was the foundation of the American Empire of the House of Habsburg. In general, this achievement has not been given the attention it deserves; it is seen as a series of adventures and campaigns; and its political significance has been neglected. But if we are to place the emperor of the west – a man whose influence has extended to our own day – in his proper historical perspective, it is essential that we should not overlook the part he played overseas.

Charles V never visited his Spanish possessions in America – the New Indies, as they were called – but, nevertheless, it would be unjust to suppose that he regarded them merely as an exotic appendage to his European empire. If he did not visit them, it was because European affairs were too pressing, voyages too slow, and the transmission of news so difficult, that he could never have found the time or leisure to absent himself for such a length of time.

The emperor's interest in overseas affairs had been apparent from his youth, when he followed with such attention the Portuguese explorer Magellan's expedition, an enterprise that was undertaken under the patronage of the Crown of Castile on 22 May 1518. On 10 August 1519, that is to say twenty-seven years after Columbus himself had set sail, Magellan had sailed from Seville with five ships. On 8 September 1522, one solitary vessel returned to the same port under the command of Lieutenant Sebastiano Elcano: it bore the symbolic name of *Victoria*.

It is fortunate for historians that amongst the survivors was the expedition's chronicler, Pigafetta; thanks to him the vicissitudes of the voyage are well known to us. At the cost of enormous difficulties the ships had succeeded in negotiating what they thought to be the southern tip of India – what are today called the Straits of Magellan. Favourable winds then drove them across the ocean towards the north-west where they finally reached comparatively smooth seas. They called this immense ocean the 'Pacific'. They discovered the islands to which they gave the name they still bear today, the Philippines; these remained Spanish for a long time and were one of the last overseas possessions of that country – it was only in 1898 that they were wrested from their mother country by the United States. Magellan lost his life in an encounter with the inhabitants, who had at first appeared to be friendly. The expedition suffered much from the attention of the Portuguese, but nevertheless they were able to bring back exotic spices from these islands; cloves in particular. The cargo which the *Victoria* alone brought back to Spain was worth five times more than the total cost of the expedition. During the last stage of the journey, the Portuguese again gave chase to the ship, but were unable to overtake it before it reached Seville. The first act of Elcano and his men on arrival was to walk barefoot from the harbour as far as the Cathedral of Our Lady, to thank the Blessed Virgin for having brought them home. It was only after they had rendered homage to God that they reported their valiant deeds and adventures to the king.

This first circumnavigation of the world contributed very considerably to Spain's expansion beyond the American continent. In fact, Magellan's long and complicated journey rendered obsolete the agreement of 1494, which had established the boundaries of Portuguese and Spanish territories. Furthermore, its scientific importance far surpassed that of any previous voyages.

The American possessions were soon to present serious problems of conscience, first for Ferdinand and Isabella and later for Charles. News arrived in Spain telling of the ill-treatment inflicted on the natives by the conquistadores, and by their Catholic Majesties' officials. The indigenous population, who had lived in a primitive, almost paradisial state, were unable to tolerate work in the mines. Slavery induced a curious decrease in the birthrate, and furthermore, they had no resistance to new illnesses and epidemics which the white men had brought to their country. At an immense distance beyond the seas, in lands which were almost unknown, inexplicable acts were being perpetrated which Charles was determined to remedy, but these territories were beyond his immediate personal control. The sovereign was dependent for his information on often contradictory reports, and was unable to see things for himself. On the one hand, officials, even those holding high positions, did their best to make excuses to the king for the excesses. They described the situation as tolerable, while on the other hand, members of religious orders bitterly complained and accused the authorities of unjustifiable cruelty. Alexander von Randa, who describes this epoch in American history as the 'fulfilment of a universal evolutionary process', speaks of a veritable 'revolt of the monks'.

The tragedy of Charles (and for Spain) did not only lie in the fact that the king was powerless to enforce his good intentions as fully and speedily as was desirable; the dossiers, which record with the utmost frankness the indictments of the Spanish monks and the energetic measures taken by the king against the abuses of traders and colonial officials, were exploited to create the 'Black Legend'. Widely disseminated during times of political and religious strife by the Anglo-Saxons, and to some extent by the Germans, this 'Black Legend' was based on material obtained from official documents and, while describing the 'horrors of Spanish colonial rule', entirely disregarded the efforts made by the king to put an end to the abuses and the great achievements of the royal régime overseas. Naturally, there was never any mention of the cruelties and massacres perpetrated by Anglo-Saxon conquerors, among whom, as a general rule, there was not the slightest attempt to assure a minimum of justice to native populations. Here, unlike the Spanish monks, there were no defenders of the oppressed.

The first reaction against these abuses dates back to the years preceding the accession of Charles v to the throne. On the fourth Sunday of Advent, 1511, a Dominican, Brother Montesinos, preached in front of an audience of señors of the European Colony of Española – what Professor Randa calls 'the first colonial society on American soil'. He called the dignitaries whom he addressed 'a generation of vipers'.

By what right do you oppress the people of this island? By what right have you reduced them to slavery, tortured and murdered them, humiliated them by forced labour, letting them die of hunger or fall victims to disease? What have you done that they should acknowledge their Creator? Are not these unfortunate wretches men like you? Have they not souls like yours? Do you hear nothing? Do you feel nothing? Does your conscience sleep? Know ye, that if you continue to act as you do now, you cannot save your souls from eternal damnation. Your fate will be that of the Moors and Turks who know not the Word of Jesus Christ.

179

After this veritable declaration of war by a Dominican, the colonial administration sent a Franciscan, Alonso de Espinal, to King Ferdinand to forestall Montesinas, should the latter lodge a complaint. Furnished with the highest testimonials, Espinal found all doors open to him, whereas to begin with Montesinas was unable to gain access to the sovereign. On a personal level, Espinal was not a dishonest man, but he was simple and trusting, and knew scarcely anything of America. Herein lay the danger, because the statements made by this worthy man might readily induce the king to believe the accusations made by the Dominicans were exaggerated, if not an outright lie. But Montesinas refused to be intimidated by the courtiers and eventually by dint of patience and energy succeeded in obtaining an audience with Ferdinand of Aragon. In simple and direct words, he reported to the king what his fellow Dominicans had charged him to say and the things he himself had observed. Ferdinand was certainly no sentimentalist; in the course of a long reign he had more than once been obliged to take strong measures – for example, in his proceedings against the Moriscos. However, he was profoundly shocked and moved by the Dominican's report. When the latter enumerated the misdeeds of officials and Spanish mercenaries and asked the Sovereign if this was his will, Ferdinand exclaimed, 'No, by God, in all my life I have never given such an order.'

The king was not content with making useless declarations; in 1512 the *Laws of Burgos* were promulgated, which provided for the protection of natives from exploitation. The documents bore the seal of the Archduchess Joanna, because Ferdinand could not govern his Castilian territories except in the name of his widowed and mentally incapacitated daughter. The *Laws of Burgos* already contained the fundamental ideas of the *New Laws* which were to be formulated by Charles V, and which, under Philip II, were to establish a system regulating all political, social and economic life in overseas territories.

The *Laws of Burgos* laid down that Indian labour was only legal providing that the work was not detrimental to the health of the natives or the good of the 'Republic', as the state was referred to in the documents. The Indians had the right to days of rest, their salaries were to be paid in foodstuffs or household equipment, and their possessions were not to be seized from them. The duty of Europeans was to take an interest in the natives' welfare and to initiate them into Christian faith.

Thus the Dominicans had gained an initial success. Soon, however, it was recognised that it is easier to make laws than to enforce them. The new continent was vast, and executive power rudimentary. Often the guilty parties were in fact the officials in charge, who should thus have meted out punishment on themselves, too much to expect of any man.

One of the most loyal supporters of the Dominicans overseas was the head of their Order, Father Caetano, known in German history as one of Luther's most formidable opponents. He is often described as a harsh doctrinarian, lacking in human sensibility. But this image is far from being the truth. On the contrary, he was a brave and good-hearted man, as is shown by his understanding attitude to his brothers-in-religion, and by his bold criticism of Ferdinand I, whom he reproached for pursuing a policy essentially unchristian.

Montesinos's adversaries and their followers employed arguments which were often wilfully false and hypocritical. For example, to justify their use of force to make the Indians work, they claimed that only by this means could they overcome the native's natural tendency to laziness, and in support of their argument, quoted St Paul: 'He that worketh not, shall not eat.' They also described the natives as incapable of governing themselves, and that they were therefore in need of firm and severe handling. Ferdinand, in spite of his initial show of goodwill to the Dominicans, could not always resist these oblique arguments, and after their first successes the missionaries were not always able to gain their point. Nevertheless, as Von Randa said, 'the revolt of the monks' had unleashed powerful moral forces. 'The Dominicans [he wrote] created the concept of the good Indian', something totally contrary to the later Puritan idea that 'the only good Indian was a dead Indian'.

From the moment he ascended the throne, the young King Charles had decisive views on the subject. The Burgundian knight who set foot on Castilian soil in 1516 to receive the crown, came, as already indicated, from a medieval world. He faced the Indian problem with understanding, and appreciated that any solution to it was largely dependent on a sense of chivalry, justice and good faith. By moral standards, Charles was considerably in advance of others among his contemporaries, who had been brought up in the new plutocracy.

In the meanwhile, Montesinos, who was only a simple monk without much influence, had found a successor better equipped to continue the struggle. This was Brother Bartolomé de Las Casas (1474–1566), the descendant of a knightly family of Crusaders of French origin. With the stalwart behaviour characteristic of his family, Brother Bartolomé was always courageous and studiedly impartial, even though he became obstinate and headstrong towards the end of his life – he reminds one of Coriolanus, but without the latter's ambition. However, his tendency towards exaggeration did more harm than good to his cause and his country.

It was a memorable day when Las Casas appeared for the first time before the king at Molina del Rey in Catalonia to make his report. Preceding him, the Bishop of Tierra Firme had spoken. The latter had at first refused to speak, and had finally only consented to give his point of view when ordered to do so by the king; he obviously was reluctant to engage in a public debate with someone he knew to be his superior. He ended his speech with the following cynical remarks:

> As far as the Indians are concerned, I can only say from my own personal experience that they are natural slaves. They appreciate the true worth of the gold they own, and therefore strong measures have to be taken to extract it from them.

Las Casas answered with a harsh speech which lasted almost an hour:

> My Lord Bishop, you have sinned a hundred times, nay, a thousand times. You have drunk the blood of your flock. If you do not repent of your misdeeds, you will be as incapable of saving your soul as once was Judas.

After this biting retort he continued:

> What I know, I have seen with my own eyes, not learnt from books. Terrible atrocities have been committed against the peaceful inhabitants of the Indies. These crimes have been perpetrated for no reason, unless from an insatiable thirst for gold.

Las Casas, like Montesinos before him, was able to report numerous details of the extortions made by the soldiery in villages. He told, for example, how a young Indian, mortally wounded in an ambush, had died in his arms. He had dragged his tortured body up to the Dominican, clutching his entrails. Father Bartolomé spoke proudly even to the king himself. He had not come from the Indies, he said, at the king's command. He had no desire for any special grace or favour. If he served the king, it was simply an act of civil obedience.

I have come to fulfil the Word of God. The unhappy people over the seas, my Lord King, are quite capable of recognising Christ. They are by nature free nations, and if the Reverend Bishop of Central America says, in the words of the philosopher Aristotle, that they are born slaves, I am obliged to say that everything the worthy ecclesiastic has said on the subject is as far removed from truth as Hell is from Heaven. Aristotle may have been a great philosopher, but he was a pagan and has been burning in Hell for a long time. Our faith, on the other hand, is the same everywhere and speaks to all peoples of the world. We have no right to deprive these souls of their liberty and reduce them to slavery, for it was for them also that our Lord Jesus Christ died on the Cross.

Other witnesses confirmed what Las Casas said. When at the end the Bishop of Tierra Firme once again demanded leave to speak, he was informed, after Charles and de Croy had conferred together briefly, that he should put in writing whatever he wished to add.

The impression which Las Casas' speech had made on Charles soon bore fruit. Before leaving Corunna for the Low Countries in 1520, the king prepared the ground for the foundation of an order at whose head he hoped to place the Dominican. This brotherhood was to consist of *hombres modelos*, exemplary men, who, to gain the confidence of the Indians, were to give the impression that they did not belong to the same race as the conquistadores. They were to wear a white cloak with a red cross, signifying that their duty was not only to convert, but to protect the Indians. In a document dated 19 March 1520, in which Charles conferred on Las Casas apostolic responsibility for all newly discovered countries in the Western Indies, he speaks of the 'evangelical road' which the knights of the order were to pursue. By a historical coincidence, at the same time in Germany, the monk, Martin Luther, justified his own act of rebellion against the pope, and later against the emperor, by claiming that he, too, was commanded by his conscience to follow an 'evangelical road'.

Las Casas was a contradictory character. He had the generous nature of an apostle and superabundant enthusiasm, but, nevertheless, his often excessive fervour and his judgements made in the heat of the moment, and a lack of foresight, often led him to commit errors no less great than his virtues. He himself recognised in his *History of the Indian Countries* that his own bad advice had been responsible for opening the way to the traffic in slaves. This infamous trade was to provoke innumerable injustices, and for centuries was a disgrace to the white races and a tragedy for the black. Las Casas wrote:

183

In these days a great misfortune has stricken us: negro slaves are being despatched to the Indies, and I was the first to have suggested it. I did it to protect the Indians and because of the poverty of the Spanish colonists. Had I known the conditions under which these men were captured in Africa, nothing in the world would have made me give such advice. The Flemings were in agreement with me that I should demand freedom for the Indians. They asked me how many slaves would be required in America. As I did not know, they questioned the Council of the Indies. The latter estimated that for the four islands of the Antilles [West Indies] four thousand workers would suffice. What sorrow all this has caused: In their place we should have sent [Flemish] peasant families and in this way we could have established an exemplary republic, the most peace-loving and Christian in all the World.

Another error of Las Casas was perhaps even more disastrous, and in this case he could not plead the excuse of ignorance. Charles, who in spite of his youth saw things in their widest perspective, had held to the idea of establishing a real peasant colony in the New World. With this end in view, he invested Adolphe de Veere, Admiral of Flanders, with the first *terra firma* to be discovered in his name. This was the peninsula of Yucatan. Soon a contingent of Flemish peasants was sent in five ships to San Lucar de Barrameda, the port of embarkation for the Indies, to become the pioneers in a systematic establishment of European farmers in hitherto uncultivated lands. It is a curious fact that Las Casas, probably blinded by an excess of nationalism, saw this enterprise as an intrigue on the part of his enemies. He allied himself with Admiral Diego Colon, the son of Christopher Columbus, who protested against the investiture of Adolphe de Veere, claiming that this privilege had belonged to his father. The emperor gave way, fearing that he had in fact violated legitimate rights. On this occasion Las Casas exhibited the kind of inhuman harshness which is characteristic of fanatics. He remarked, with a triumph which could scarcely be termed Christian: 'Some of the peasants brought from Spain died on the way and only a minute number were able to return to their native Flanders. This was the result of the bad advice of the Spaniards who wished to do me harm.'

In the meanwhile, the overseas empire was rapidly extending through its own dynamic impulse, as it were, without active assistance from the government of the mother country. The extraordinarily rapid growth of the territories brought about fresh difficulties, and it was practically impossible to consolidate any form of jurisdiction which would not continually have to be modified.

On 20 February 1519, only a few weeks after the death of Maximilian I, Fernando Cortez, who was completely free of any control by his hierarchical superiors, undertook his adventurous march into the Aztec Empire. Within only a few years, he was able to conquer a large part of the vast continent for the emperor. The conquistador, who was courageous to the point of heroism, but quite unscrupulous, had only about five hundred men at his command, and a little more than two dozen cannon when he put into land at what is today the town of Vera Cruz. From here he embarked on what is probably the most fantastic adventure in the whole of colonial history. He pushed forward with no knowledge of either geographical or climatic conditions, nor any knowledge of the real strength of the enemy he would meet. He stormed into the interior of the country and defeated the Aztecs, not so much because of his military superiority as by the profound effect made on the Indians by his armaments and personal courage.

This conqueror, who seemed the incarnation of all the theories of his contemporary, Machiavelli, and who had every opportunity of turning traitor to his king, always remained loyal to the sovereign, even when he acted contrary to Charles's intentions. His attitude was completely the opposite to that of Las Casas, who was always ready to rise against the king who loved him, who constantly forgave him and continued to confer on him the most important positions. Cortez, on the other hand, brought Charles an empire which, had he so wished, he could have conquered for himself. Furthermore, it was he who was the first to call the newly discovered lands a 'second empire'. He wrote as follows to the emperor: 'Your Majesty henceforth may be considered Emperor of these lands, with the same rights as in Germany, the crown of which, by the Grace of God, your Majesty possesses.' This was an idea which was to remain alive in the minds of Charles's successors, and in contemporary documents we often find the term 'Emperor of America and Europe'. The concept appears, for example, in the writings of Jaime Valdez (1600), but it is not given final expression in a legal form or an official title.

As a diplomatist, Cortez displayed the same qualities which enabled him, as a general, to conquer the Aztec Empire. Courageous, able and unscrupulous, he triumphed over all plots hatched against him by his Spanish rivals. Nevertheless, he too acted imprudently and provoked the Indians to a religious revolt. In the presence of the Emperor Montezuma and the nobility of the Aztec Empire, he smashed the golden mask of their principal god in the temple of Tenochtitlan, turned over other idols and placed statues of the Virgin and saints on their altars, which up to then had been used for human sacrifice. In a report on the subject, he noted with a certain naïvety that his action 'had saddened the Aztecs'.

However, I declared to them that there was only one God who had made Heaven and Earth and all that is therein; He was their Creator just as He was ours; He was without beginning and immortal. Henceforth it was He they must worship and in whom they must believe.

These acts were followed by the formal prohibition of child sacrifices as being contrary to the law and Charles's will. Cortez made it known that anyone who continued to practise these bloody rites would be condemned to death. On this occasion, the conquistador was hardly acting as a man of his time but rather as a crusader, the spiritual heir of numerous generations of hidalgos and caballeros who had given their lives in the struggle against the Moors. Moreover, he was well aware of the danger he ran by his action, recording that 'something must be risked in the name of God'.

To begin with, the Mexicans did not dare to revolt, but they soon became aware of divisions in the Spanish camp and determined to take advantage of the situation. With the authority of Cardinal Adrien van Utrecht, who was acting as regent during Charles's absence, the Governor of Cuba dispatched an army to free Montezuma from the hands of Cortez. The personal aura which surrounded the great adventurer, however, proved more powerful where the troops were concerned than discipline, and the soldiers deserted to the side of the man they were supposed to capture. The Aztecs, however, realised that Cortez's assertions did not all necessarily correspond with reality, and that it was manifestly obvious that the quasi-divine monarch of the vast overseas empire did not possess only faithful and obedient servants, and that perhaps even he was not so powerful as Cortez had claimed. They decided, therefore, to attack the palace of the conquistador. An enormous crowd of Indians hurled themselves against the handful of Spaniards with a veritable hail of arrows and set fire to the citadel of the conqueror. Montezuma himself, who tried to act as mediator, was wounded and died of a haemorrhage, according to contemporary writings, after having torn off his bandage. Only half of the Spaniards managed to escape from the island city during that notorious *noche triste.* In the plain of Otumba they were forced once again to give battle. The situation seemed desperate until Cortez managed to seize the great banner of the Aztec Empire and kill their commander-in-chief. This action demoralised the vast Indian army, who then let themselves be overpowered by the little group of Spaniards. In the course of these dramatic days, Cortez's prowess completely surpassed any of the exploits described by Xenophon during the retreat of the Ten Thousand, or the greatest feats of the Crusaders, and he demonstrated his outstanding courage and tactical sense. Now, after this victory, his skill as a diplomatist became manifest. Aided by his greatly enhanced prestige, he was able to form a league of Indian tribes and lead them into battle against Quatemozin, the last of the Aztec Emperors. And in this way he achieved the impossible: the submission of an entire country.

Returning from Germany, Charles had wondered in all conscience if he could honestly approve of what was happening, and if the right to rule over New Spain was really his. Only after he had learnt of the setback to his plans for the foundation of a new religious order, did he make up his mind. Las Casas had reported to him that the Indians made no distinction whatsoever between 'bad whites' and those who came with the sole purpose of aiding them. The natives had lost all faith in the God of the Europeans; the white cloak emblazoned with the red cross was not sufficient to convince them. Such a state of affairs seemed to justify Cortez's action, and under the circumstances Charles decided to ratify his conquest. He explained his decision in a letter containing a profession of faith, truly imperial in character and motivated by the highest of ideals of western Christianity.

Above all, we must remember our duty to God and obey the provisions of the papal bull. It is not necessary to save the souls of the Indians by force. Human sacrifices and cannibalism must be stopped; idols and their temples must be destroyed. Our Lord created the Indians, not as slaves, but as free men. In Little Spain (i.e. in the Caribbean Islands) they have died in consequence of ill-treatment and forced labour. The same thing must not happen again in New Spain. The Indians must adhere to our faith only of their own free will. Between Spaniards and Indians only free trade is authorised. It is forbidden on pain of severe punishment to seize anything belonging to the Indians; nothing must change hands without adequate payment. We must meet them in a spirit of love and friendship and always keep our promises . . . Under no circumstances must war be made on them unless they themselves are the aggressors. Only in this

187

case may war be declared. This declaration must be repeated three times by a Christian who speaks their language.

Charles did not confine himself to these edicts. He was determined to win Mexico a second time without recourse to violence; Von Randa speaks of a veritable *conquista* of souls. Charles delegated monks for the task and appointed at their head a man in whom he had the utmost confidence and whom he regarded, it was said, almost as his own son – Peter of Ghent. Furthermore, it was not the intention of the emperor's envoys to make converts according to the system often practised in eastern Europe, that is to say, by first converting the princes and then baptising their subjects to order. In Mexico, on the contrary, it was considered most important that every Indian, before baptism, should be genuinely convinced of the truth of the new faith. Naturally the missionaries tried, in particular, to win over the Indian nobility and, above all, the House of Montezuma. At his death, the Aztec Emperor had asked that Charles v should take care of his children, and it was his son who founded the line of the Counts of Montezuma and Tula. In 1700, a descendant of this Christian Indian Dynasty was still a viceroy of the House of Austria in New Spain.

Although during the course of the following years the emperor was fully occupied in Europe with wars, diplomacy and religious affairs, not to mention numerous journeys, America was not overlooked by him. He strengthened the position of the Dominicans in the *Consejo Real y Supremo de las Indias* and appointed as general of the order and president of the council, his own father confessor. In order to prevent corruption or nepotism, the emperor ordained that no member of the council should possess any territory overseas and forbade their sons to receive any sinecures or benefices. At the time of his marriage to the Infanta Isabella of Portugal at Seville, Charles once again declared: 'I wish the Indians to be free and not slaves.'

While respecting the qualities of Cortez, whom he went to see at Toledo when the latter was ill, Charles did his best never to identify himself with the policies which the conquistador had pursued in Mexico. When Cortez, who had remarried towards the end of his life, wished to revisit Mexico, he was denied entry to the capital, where his presence might have awakened unpleasant memories among the populace. Charles appointed Antonio Mendoza as Governor and Viceroy of New Spain, a very different type of man, who, by his good works and unflagging devotion, earned himself the title of 'king of the poor'. Owing to their rapid expansion, the colonies, as we have already observed, were constantly outgrowing the systems of administrative control and native protection which had been established by the Council of the Indies and the emperor himself. This naturally led to further deplorable abuses. The conquest of Peru, for example, led to irregularities far surpassing any committed in the past by Cortez in Mexico. Once again, the missionaries protested and a second veritable 'rebellion of monks' culminated in further indictments which they laid before the emperor in the third decade of the century. Without allowing himself to become discouraged by these incidents, Charles remained constant to his ideals. Whenever he felt the occasion demanded, he intervened and issued imperial edicts or took direct measures to put an end to injustices.

Las Casas found in Brother Francisco de Vitoria (1483–1546) an assistant with far greater knowledge and political acumen than he himself had ever possessed. Vitoria, a famous jurist and professor at the University of Salamanca, worked out a theory legitimising Spanish colonialism, a theory based, not on the territorial or sovereign rights of the pope, nor on the imperial dignity of Charles, but on the missionary duty with which the Pope had entrusted the Spanish and Portuguese. Resurrecting an old saying derived from Roman Law (de jure gentium), Vitoria proclaimed the rights of the Indians in their own country, and thus, by his reversion to an original premise, this great scholar can be considered today as having re-established the rights of man.

Continually faced with fresh difficulties Charles promulgated new legislation, the Leyes Neuvas. Far wider in scope than the bounds of colonial policy, this work codified the points of law concerning the legal position and treatment of the Indians. Severe penalties were to be imposed for any infringements. The former privileges of the Indian nobility were to be respected in the same way as was the status of kings, princes, republics and communes.

At the time of this reform, Charles tried to assure Bartolomé de Las Casas of much greater authority by offering him the Bishopric of Cuzco. The monk, however, preferred a small and poor diocese in Guatemala. As a result, relations, already strained between Charles and the 'Apostle to the Indians', only deteriorated still further, especially when the emperor, under pressure from both military and civil officials, was obliged to amend certain clauses in the *Leyes Nuevas*. Las Casas felt that he had been personally insulted; nothing could pacify him. The emperor sent Pedro de la Gasca, a theologian from Salamanca, to America to reassure him but, not in the least bit appeased, Las Casas started a campaign which surpassed all bounds, and which finally culminated in action destructive to his own country. One might even say that Las Casas became a traitor to his motherland towards the end of his life. True, he was motivated by noble aims, but he was also actuated by pride and senile obstinacy.

It was only after Philip II had succeeded Charles that a way was found to impose the new laws in the true spirit in which they had been conceived and to realise in a practical manner the emperor's ideas. These had embraced the problem from every point of view; the social angle receiving particular attention – as is exemplified by the fact that pearl-diving was prohibited as being harmful to the health of the natives. Philip, following in his father's steps, recalled what the latter had said when he forbade the use of forced labour: 'We respect the lives of Indians more than the profit we derive from their labour'. It is a remarkable fact that the right of workers to share in the profits of an enterprise and the principle of an equitable wage, were already incorporated in Spanish legislation at that time, that is to say, centuries before they were promulgated in the encyclical, *Rerum novarum*, the Christian political and social charter. In 1593, a legal working day of eight hours was introduced in America. Alexander von Randa, the greatest contemporary authority on Austro-American relations and on the subject of privileges granted to the Austrian missionaries, and on comparative social legislation, maintains that there is an obvious connection between the eight-hour day introduced into America by Philip II and similar legislation, which had existed since the fifteenth century in the hereditary Austrian States and Franche-Comté. Thus, for the first time in history, the Habsburg Empire had inaugurated social measures which were only rediscovered and applied in the great industrial countries many centuries later. Philip also imposed controls on all journeys and immigration to America. Nevertheless, influenced by religious struggles, he imposed in contradistinction to the decrees of his father certain restrictions hitherto unknown. Another innovation made it illegal to separate negro families, a matter whose importance is reflected in certain grim aspects of our twentieth century.

Besides social legislation, Charles was also interested in the administrative and legal organisation of his new empire. He did not regard his territories in the new world merely as provinces or colonies in the imperialist sense of the word. For him, they were independent states, often referred to as 'republics' governed by viceroys. Once peace was established in a region, the Spaniards instituted forms of government which for those times were very modern. Thus, in several of the southern American States we find elected legislative bodies, known as *Cabildos*, similar to those functioning in the Canary Islands.

Charles also attached great importance to cultural development and soon established the first university in America at San Domingo in the Island of Hispaniola. In 1551, still during Charles's lifetime, the University of Mexico was founded, to be followed by a whole series of educational establishments elsewhere on the American continent. A tradition for research and learning was thus developed in Latin America which was in no way inferior to that of many European universities. At the end of Charles's reign, of the ten million inhabitants in his Spanish possessions there were only some hundred thousand Europeans – one per cent of the total population. The Americas, in fact, had all the conditions necessary for the foundation of a powerful and, for the period, modern empire, strongly imbued with the Christian spirit.

From an economic point of view, the New Indies did not bring in the fabulous sums of money and riches which the conquistadores had spoken of. However, Charles, sooner than most, realised the possibilities which these territories might offer in the long run. He supported the meritorious efforts of the Spanish administration in interesting other parts of his European Empire in the development of the new countries. The attempt to establish Flemish settlers in Yucatan has already been mentioned. In 1528, the emperor signed a contract with the great Augsburg banking house of Welser for the recruitment and settlement of German miners to develop the silver mines of Venezuela. To begin with, the Welsers transported twenty-four mining specialists from Joachimstal in Bohemia to South America. At the same time, this great commercial house obtained a licence to import coloured slaves. The Welser's colonisation programme was under the direction of Henry Ehinger and Jérôme Sailer. Henry Ehinger, the brother of Ambrose Ehinger, the Welser's agent at San Domingo, became the first Governor of Venezuela. His successor, Nicolas Federmann of Ulm, a more energetic and less scrupulous man than Ehinger, however, roused the hostility of the Spanish conquistadores, who, having arrived before him in the country, considered the Germans as intruders. The Welser enterprise did not last long – it was no more than an adventurous expedition without a sequel. One of the results of the rapid expansion of Spanish territories overseas was more than likely Charles's decision to substitute the device *Plus Ultra* for the mottoes of *Non plus ultra* and *Nondum*, which he had formerly borne in Burgundian and Spanish journeys. His desire to go always further, which this motto expresses, was not confined to purely territorial expansion: Charles never lost sight of his imperial duty as Defender of the Faith and to restore Christian unity in the west. The badge which surrounded the device of *Plus Ultra* represented the two Pillars of Hercules, which, in antiquity had marked the end of the world. Now the Spanish had broached these confines; they had circumnavigated the world and conquered vast territories. From now on, the Pillars of Hercules were emblematic of Spain's imperial duty to protect all its people and spread the gospel among all the nations of the world. Charles VI, the last Habsburg in the male line and also the last of his House, and third of that name to be King of Spain, retained the symbol; the Pillars of Hercules were incorporated in the façade of the Church of Saint-Charles Borromée built by him in Vienna; they commemorate the tradition of his great ancestor which henceforth would be continued in the centre of the European continent.

It was also in the reign of Charles V that a Spanish officer of Basque origin, Ignatius Loyola, founded the Jesuit Order, which was officially recognised by the pope in 1540. Although the order had no official connection with the emperor and his policies, Ignatius Loyola nevertheless imbued it with the spirit of the Spanish army, in which he himself had served and which was both representative of the faith which had sustained the *Reconquista* and of Burgundian chivalry. This is reflected in the organisation of the order on military lines, in its discipline and obedience, and in the courage of its members in the face of death. The Jesuit ideal, the desire to take an active part in the unification of the church and to devote itself to the greater glory of God throughout the world, certainly found more inspiration in Charles's attitude than in that of the Curia of that time. Also, their scientific interests, their researches in the field of natural sciences, their cultural initiatives – particularly by the establishment of numerous colleges and universities – united the Jesuits with the humanist ideals held by the emperor and which were encouraged by his court. On a spiritual level, the Jesuits served the ideal represented by Charles's device, *Plus ultra*, in his overseas dominions. Only death prevented St Francis Xavier, whose device was *Amplius* – which recalls so vividly that of the emperor – from entering China in 1552.

If under Charles's successors the concept of a Universal Christian Empire seemed on several occasions to be on the point of realisation, this was due in part at least to the activities of the Society of Jesus in China, Japan and South America.

It was not for nothing that the maps of the world at that time were surmounted by the imperial eagle. Philip II was to be called on to govern an empire which circled the earth. A Universal Christian Empire beyond the seas was already beginning to take shape. At such a time, one might well have believed that the victor of Mühlberg would succeed in realising his ambition of uniting the Holy Roman Empire.

9

Twilight Over the West

THE INTERIM DIET OF AUGSBURG
OR
THE 'CONGRESS IN ARMS'

The lightning advance of the imperial troops after the battle of Mühlberg had brought them right up to the walls of Wittenberg. On 19 May 1547, the town was obliged to capitulate under conditions which seemed very like a peace treaty. Negotiations with Charles's prisoner Prince Johann-Friedrich, which began immediately, were made all the more difficult because like François I at Madrid he obstinately refused to co-operate. Finally the emperor had recourse to a procedure which was hardly typical of his usual conduct: he convoked a special tribunal to try the Elector of Saxony. This so-called Court of Justice, exceeding its powers of authority, condemned Johann-Friedrich to death. Charles had never had the slightest intention of putting this sentence into execution – in his eyes it was simply a means of putting pressure on the elector – but this does not excuse the trial. Sentence was officially suspended, but the elector remained the emperor's prisoner and was only granted his liberty some years later at a very critical point for Charles.

The real winner in all this was Maurice of Saxony. His title to the electoral dignity confirmed, he rapidly became the most powerful of princes in Saxony, once Johann-Friedrich had divided the territories of which he had been ruler among his heirs.

Negotiations were much more easily concluded with the Landgrave Philip of Hesse. The imperial victory made such an impression on Philip that he capitulated without there being any need for further force. At their first meeting, Charles treated him with severity and made only one concession – he would not be imprisoned for life. With other prisoners, he accompanied the emperor to the Diet of Augsburg.

Although appearing advantageous, the emperor's situation was already deteriorating. Charles, in fact, was not seeking to humiliate his enemies, but above all to reorganise the empire and unite the church. But this objective, which for a moment had seemed within his grasp, was visibly disappearing into the distance.

Already, the imperialists had become aware shortly after the surrender of the landgrave that it was easier to defeat territorial princes than subdue big cities, capable of enduring prolonged sieges. The main centres of resistance in north Germany were Magdeburg and Bremen. Unlike the cities of the south, with their restricted territories, these northern strongholds had access to the sea. In order to capture Magdeburg, it was necessary to cut its lines of communication provided by the Elbe, while it was impossible to take Bremen without having control of the sea and the mouth of the Weser. Charles, always a realist, rarely embarked on a seemingly impossible task. In north Germany, therefore, once the Duke of Brunswick had been reinstated in his country, there was no military action worthy of the name, with the exception of some very bitter engagements in the vicinity of Bremen, in which the followers of the emperor suffered decisive defeat.

However, the principal obstacle to success, notwithstanding the difficulties of subduing the cities, was less strategic than psychological. In Protestant German territories (notably those in which the Reformation had been introduced a quarter of a century ago) the concessions which the emperor now contemplated, and which even twenty years earlier might have brought an end to religious strife, were no longer sufficient. Problems like the marriage of priests, or the taking of both bread and wine at Holy Communion, were things of the past. A new generation had grown up in the doctrine and customs of the new faith, and only knew those of the old by hearsay. For many years now the principles of Luther and his disciples had been accepted; not only were they an integral part of the everyday speech of preachers, but had become part of the fundamental Protestant faith. The Catholic liturgy, veneration of the Virgin Mary, prayers to saints, confession and the Mass, which in the time of Luther were still under debate, were, in the eyes of the younger Protestant generation, no more than so much paganism, idolatry and blasphemy.

Luther had died in his native town of Eisleben in the autumn of 1546, where he had come to arbitrate in a family dispute of the Dukes of Dessau, and he was buried in the chapel of the castle of Wittenberg. Henceforth, both parties were to be the poorer for the lack of his authority and conciliatory spirit. Melanchthon was apparently ready to make concessions which he had previously repudiated, but now, without the support of the Master, he was unable to put over his point of view to the new generation of Protestant theologians. One of the most distinguished of these was Mathias Flacius Illyricus of the Magdeburg faction, whose moving spirit had been Nicholas von Amsdorf. This community was soon to gain a reputation as the theological centre of Protestantism – 'the Chancellory of Our Lord God'. It was significant that Flacius's pamphlet, *Schmach- und Schmah-büchel*, was directed as much against the emperor as against Melanchthon. As a consequence of the presence of Spaniards in Germany, theological resistance had become dangerously reinforced by nationalist feelings of resentment. For the greater mass of ordinary Protestant people, the religious war was now transformed into a war against the foreign intruders, of which there were now many more, since Charles, in order to break down the resistance of the towns, in particular those of southern Germany, had quartered many troops there, including a large number of Spaniards.

Anti-imperialist broadsides, illustrated with engravings, which were distributed during the Schmalkalden war and particularly during the campaign along the Danube, represented the emperor as the prisoner of the 'Infernal Whore of the New Babylon', or again as Hercules deceived by the Roman Omphale. After Mühlberg, on the other hand, he was depicted as a modern Varus, leading his Roman legions against Germany, and it was predicted that his fate would be no different from that which had awaited the consul of the Emperor Augustus in the Teuteberg forest.

Even before he opened the Diet of Augsburg, the emperor knew that he would have to abandon his dream of re-establishing a united church. He would have to contemplate instead new interim solutions. His brilliant military victory had no doubt discouraged the enemies of the empire, but it had come too late. If Charles had been able to gain a similar triumph some ten years earlier, he might perhaps have achieved his goal. To a certain degree, he was now suffering as a result of his past forbearance and indefatigable attempts to unite the two faiths by peaceful means, and also because of his illusion that the internal dissensions in the empire would be healed by a common desire to form a united front against the Turks. It might well be concluded that one reason for Charles's failure in Germany was because he decided too late to have recourse to force, and then only when provoked by the princes of the Schmalkalden League.

Finally, a short while after the surrender of Wittenberg, Charles was obliged to decrease his military forces under the necessity of sending back Ferdinand's armies to put down a rebellion in Bohemia, where some of the nobility and towns had conspired against the Catholic rule of the Habsburgs. The insurrection, however, was only half-hearted and unsupported by the populace in general and Ferdinand was therefore able to suppress it quite quickly. On 2 June 1547, he arrived at Prague furnished with the military means to reduce the capital. The city surrendered without a blow. On the following day, 3 June, he ordered the rebels to come to Leitmeritz, where, with an impressive display of armed strength, he demanded their pardon. Thenceforth, Bohemia found itself once again placed firmly under the control of the dynasty.

On 1 September 1547, the Diet of Augsburg was opened. It is known to history as the 'Diet under Arms', because until its adjournment on 30 May 1548, its sessions were dominated by the blow inflicted to the Protestant cause by the imperial victory over the Schmalkalden League. But even before this event, the emperor found himself again caught between two stools; on the one side there was the pope, on the other the recalcitrant German princes and cities. After the departure of the papal troops, relations between Charles and Paul III had first become embittered and then finally overtly hostile. The pope, who had been sorely tried by events in Genoa and Parma, lost all sense of proportion when his son, Pier Luciano Farnese, was assassinated. He invited France to declare war on the emperor and occupy Naples; he tried to revive old quarrels in Italy, and eventually even went so far as to enter into negotiations with the Turks with a view to forming an alliance between the papacy and the Turkish government against the emperor. It seemed, for a time, that the pitiless struggle between the two highest authorities in Christendom had been resuscitated; the papacy even went so far as to compare Charles v with Frederick II of Hohenstaufen. The emperor was tempted by the possibilities: several German princes had suggested that he should place himself at the head of the council, re-establish it at Trent and force the pope into a secondary role. Charles would have been able to take command of the whole German nation, concede the

Protestants everything they wanted, and lead a great imperial army into Italy. Just as he had marched northwards less than a year ago, with an army of Italians and Spaniards, so now he could march to the south. But Charles resisted the temptation. He saw the problems confronting him from a universal point of view, a point of view that embraced the interests of the whole of western Europe, and not just his duties towards Spain and the Low Countries. He took into consideration the dissensions which existed in Germany and the situation in England and France following the deaths of their respective kings. His comprehensive outlook, and above all his fidelity to the Church of Rome, made him aware of the dangers of unilateral action. Only by genuine agreement, by an arbitrated settlement, could unity – at least political unity – be re-established in the Christian Church.

The *Interim* which he conceded the Diet was strongly recommended by his confessor and by other theologians faithful to Erasmus's spirit. By this gesture the emperor hoped to encourage the return of those who had become separated from the old church. This resolution admitted in principle communion with both bread and wine, recognised the validity of the marriages of priests which had already been solemnised, but it demanded that the whole of the empire should return to the Catholic rites which would be officially protected.

Inspired by the intransigent attitude of Leonhard von Eck, the Catholics refused. At the same time, the Protestant resistance hardened, particularly in southern Germany. The emperor was forced to call on the army to force the town of Constance to abide by the laws of the empire, an act which aggravated dislike of the Spaniards. In north Germany also, the Protestants sabotaged the projected compromise and replaced the *Interim* of Augsburg with what they termed the *Interim* of Leipzig. Only Melanchthon, the wisest of all the Reformers, was prepared to find a basis for an agreement, even being, it seemed, prepared to recognise the pope. Unfortunately, as already mentioned, he had not sufficient authority to win over to his point of view the evangelical estates, preachers and theologians.

We have already spoken of the imperial league of which Charles dreamed. It was to be composed of the imperial estates which had remained loyal – towns in particular – together with the emperor as representative of the Low Countries, and Ferdinand in the name of Austria. The league would appoint only one military commander-in-chief, and there would be a federal treasury and one supreme court.

Under these conditions, the old constitution of the empire would remain the same as before, at least on paper, but in practice nothing would be decided without first obtaining the consent of the league. The election of the emperor and the convocation of diets would be a pure formality. This project, however, came to nothing because of dissension in the Catholic camp. Right from the preliminary talks, Bavaria, activated always by Leonhard von Eck, opposed this plan with the same energy as it had opposed any *rapprochement* with the Protestants.

At the same time as he was working on these projects, the emperor was also occupied with plans for a new order of succession to the throne and, in consequence, a revision of his agreements with his brother, Ferdinand. He proposed to make the latter sovereign of the imperial throne. In other words, Ferdinand would not be succeeded by his son, Maximilian, but by Philip of Spain, who, in his turn, would be succeeded by the heir to the Austrian domains. The emperor summoned the Infante Philip to Augsburg to take a personal part in drawing up the treaty. His action displeased the princes of the empire as well as Ferdinand, who regarded it as an act of disloyalty. In other words the idea was neither workable as far as the empire was concerned, nor even within the House of Habsburg itself.

That Charles should waste his time on such speculative schemes can only be explained by his ultimate aim, which was to arrive at a common agreement which would oblige all the signatories to participate in a united war against the Turks. The emperor was convinced that Germany, and *à fortiori*, Austria, were by themselves incapable of resisting the forces of Islam. He knew from his own experience the importance of Spanish aid in moments of difficulty. On the other hand, his expeditions to north Africa had shown him that Spanish policy in the Mediterranean needed the support of the Danube basin. The idea of establishing a common European strategy and maintaining the Madrid–Vienna–Brussels axis as the basis of continental policy in face of the threat from the east was his constant preoccupation.

The death of Paul III in 1549 greatly helped the emperor's position as far as Italian and ecclesiastical affairs were concerned. Julius III, the new pope, authorised the re-establishment of the Council of Trent and he even consented to the presence of Protestant speakers. This concession, however, was made too late; the Protestants completely rejected the council whose dogmatic decisions in the first stages of the sessions had caused an irreparable breach.

In the meanwhile in Germany, the emperor's position continued to deteriorate. The opposition of the princes extended from Brandenburg and Prussia to Bavaria, and even to Ferdinand of Austria himself, who had taken the emperor's new plans of succession in very bad part, and was insisting that his son, who was in Madrid at the time, should return to Germany. However, the real danger threatening the emperor came from a quarter where he had anticipated active assistance. Already since the campaign in the Danube Valley, Charles had had the idea of attracting to his side the younger generation of princes, particularly the Protestant princes, and of discarding the old incorrigibles like Johann-Friedrich and the Landgrave Philip. The merits of this policy were confirmed by Granvelle's and Ferdinand's diplomatic work in obtaining an alliance with the young elector, Maurice of Saxony, in whom the emperor had the greatest confidence. When Maurice declared himself ready to crush the opposition in Magdeburg if charged with the execution of the imperial ban, his allegiance seemed confirmed.

In the meanwhile, however, Maurice was secretly preparing a reversal of alliances. On 3 October 1551, together with other Protestant princes, he concluded an agreement with Henri II of France. On 15 January 1552, the Treaty of Chambord was signed, whereby the princes agreed that Henri II, in his capacity as vicar of the empire, should be given possession of the Lorraine dioceses of Metz, Toul and Verdun, together with the Bishopric of Cambrai. The importance of this event far exceeded any purely tactical manœuvre or treacherous action by an elector against his emperor; it was to influence the policies of the empire and German states for centuries to come. The truly revolutionary aspect of this treaty has already been commented upon in a preceding chapter, inasmuch as the transference of these territorial possessions was excused on the grounds that as French was the language of these dioceses, they were logically subject to France. This was the first time in history that an international document had given precedence to 'nationality'. On this count, the whole raison d'être of the Holy Roman Empire would dissolve into nothingness. Once the idea of a national state was admitted, the inescapable consequence would be the secession of the Low Countries and imperial territories in Italy, and for a very long time to come the western part of central Europe would be in turmoil. Open war with Maurice of Saxony was not long delayed and a lightning stroke was aimed at the emperor himself. Charles, at the time, was residing at Innsbruck, whence he could simultaneously keep an eye on events in Germany and the Council of Trent. For this reason, he had virtually no troops with him. In March of 1552 Maurice, followed by units of the Hessian army, thrust through Saxony to Augsburg and thence advanced directly on Innsbruck, while, at the same time, the King of France, without warning, occupied the dioceses promised by the princes. Charles was within an inch of being captured. Precipitately, and with almost no military protection, he took refuge in Villach. The work of the Council of Trent was suspended and the delegates decamped in all directions. Johann-Friedrich of Saxony, who until now had remained the emperor's prisoner, was freed.

King Ferdinand once again entered into negotiations with Maurice at Passau, and once again there was talk of a peace that would be everlasting. But, however, this time the word did not have its original connotation – the establishment of a united faith in Germany – but contained the accepted implication of dualism, or the coexistence of two distinct forms of worship within the empire.

The emperor's main preoccupation during this time, however, was the expulsion of the French from Lorraine, where they controlled the passage of the Meuse and Moselle and so cut the direct route between the Netherlands and Alsace. Moreover, if the French succeeded in advancing beyond the Moselle to the Rhine, the kings of France, sooner or later, would have laid claim to the imperial crown. With the assistance of the Low Countries, Charles was able to raise an army sufficiently strong to undertake a siege of Metz. Probably he was unwise to embark on an enterprise of such importance so late in the season, for it was not until 19 October 1552 that the imperial forces took up their positions before the city. However, the Duke of Alva, who commanded the operation, had assured the emperor that the fortress would be taken before the rigours of winter set in.

But the emperor was now faced with a new and serious danger from Germany, which he was only able to avert by a last-minute move. The great marauding campaign, organised by Albrecht-Alcibiades von Brandenburg, with ten thousand men at his command, represented a very real threat. Albrecht-Alcibiades, one of the last of the robber barons, conducted his operations on a grand scale. In some ways he was reminiscent of Franz von Sickingen, who, at the beginning of Charles's reign, had played such an important role and whose life of brutality and violence had inevitably led to his tragic death beneath the ruins of

Landstuhl, his castle stronghold. The baron of Sickingen, however, did not dream solely of pillage and plunder, he still belonged to that generation of knights for whom, in spite of their defiance of authority, the concept of the emperor and the empire itself still had a profound significance and inspired them with what might be called an innate sense of loyalty. The Margrave Albrecht, on the other hand, was nothing more than a marauder and a scoundrel, who made war with no other thought than that of material gain. In 1552 he swept through Franconia, pillaging and burning, respecting neither the territories of the Catholic Bishop of Bamberg, nor those of the Protestant free imperial city of Nüremberg; he then devastated the diocesan territories of Wurtzburg, and finally invaded Alsace, with the intention of linking up with the French army. To prevent this old murderer from allying himself with his enemies and falling on the rear of the imperial army entrenched before Metz, the emperor had no alternative but to buy his services. Contemporary records quote Charles's remarks on this occasion, which express his disgust with the transaction and for the character of his new partner, but they also show that he had no choice in the matter.

The imperial forces had brought very powerful siege artillery with them to breach the walls of Metz. About twenty-five cannon opened fire on the south side of the fortress, and on 25 November the wall between two large towers collapsed, forming a breach about twenty feet wide. The imperial army was exultant and the infantry prepared to attack. Only then was it discovered that behind the breach there was a second line of defence, strongly held by units of sharp-shooters. It was impossible to mount an assault. This was a bitter blow to the morale of the troops, which had already been severely tried by the raw winter weather, and the epidemics which had broken out in the ranks of the Spaniards and Italians. At the beginning of 1553, the siege had to be raised, the Duke of Alva being strongly criticised for this setback to their plans by headquarters who considered him responsible for it.

The campaign against the Turks in Hungary, which was being fought at the same time, brought no appreciable results. Here, Maurice of Saxony had once again rallied to the imperialists, but Ferdinand, not without reason, placed no confidence in him, and the allies' action was thereby paralysed. At the same time, very fierce battles were being fought in Italy where a Turkish fleet, in conjunction with French galleys, was ravaging the coasts of the Spanish possessions there.

In Germany, an already complex situation became further complicated by a fresh outbreak of hostilities between Albrecht-Alcibiades von Brandenburg and Maurice of Saxony. As the former was still technically in the service of Charles, it might have been thought that the war between these two Protestant princes was an act of retaliation by Charles against Maurice. In fact, this was not the case, particularly as in the meanwhile the Elector of Saxony had been fighting in Hungary at the side of the Habsburgs. On 9 July 1553, Maurice succeeded in decisively defeating the Brandenburgers at Sievershausen, where the Hohenzollern troops were annihilated. The victory, however, cost him his life. Maurice fell on the field of honour at the age of thirty-five. There is no doubt that this was a blessing for Germany, for had he lived, this courageous, talented, but unscrupulous prince would certainly have led his country into many other disasters. Nevertheless, it is to his credit that the articles of the religious peace treaty, which was eventually concluded two years after his death, had been formulated during the negotiations which the young elector had conducted at Passau with King Ferdinand.

Charles, who after his setback at Metz, retired profoundly depressed to his native Netherlands, did not remain inactive for long. Reverting to old traditions, he conceived the idea for a new marriage. Once more the old adage, *Bella gerant alii, tu felix Austria nube* (Let others make war, you, happy Austria, marry!) was to be revealed in all its truth. In 1554, the emperor was able to arrange a marriage between Mary of England and the Infante Philip, eleven years her junior. Mary had become heir to the English throne after the premature death of the young king, Edward VI. According to contemporary documents, it would seem that for Mary, at the age of thirty-eight, this was a real love match, but letters from the emperor to his heir point to the fact that Philip only accepted this sacrifice because of the service he thus rendered to religion and imperial policy. Despite the somewhat inauspicious prospects, the marriage, which lasted only four years, turned out to be a happy one. Nevertheless, the essential purpose of this union – the establishment of an Atlantic Habsburg Empire – was invalidated when Mary remained childless. Philip had succeeded in making himself accepted as Prince Consort in England, despite the difficulties which the queen's Catholicism and the link which this established with Spain had created. One major reason for Philip's initial success was probably because the Reformation in England, unlike that in Germany, was not the affair of the people in general, but rather a whim on the part of Henry VIII. The revolutionary passion which animated the small evangelical sects did not find favour in the eyes of the High Church – indeed Anglicans and Catholics alike regarded them with hostility. Anglicanism, moreover, was not really consolidated until after Mary's death. It was only in the reign of Elizabeth that Catholics were as cruelly persecuted as were the followers of the Evangelical sects. It was official propaganda that dubbed Mary, after her death, with the name of *Bloody*, in the hope of thus justifying Elizabeth's illegal accession to the throne and religious intolerance.

If Philip and Mary had had children the consequences would have been incalculable. A union of the crowns and estates which would have thus been created to the advantage of the House of Habsburg, would also have assured it of complete supremacy over its continental rivals, and protected the maritime flank of the empire.

The history of the overseas territories would also have run a different course. By the third decade of the century, French and British navigators had already crossed the Atlantic. In the face of this competition neither Portugal nor Spain were strong enough to defend their rights north of the Gulf of Mexico, which were still based on the ruling of Pope Alexander VI. It is difficult to imagine the vast prospects that would have been open to England and Spain had they been united and the overseas territories from the St Lawrence to Cape Horn thus under one crown. One can imagine the feelings of the ageing emperor who, after so many brilliant victories and strokes of fate, might now hope that his great work was at last about to be realised. But he was soon to be cruelly disappointed. By 1555 it was certain that there was to be no heir from the Anglo-Spanish marriage. It is possible that it was this disappointment, just as much as the frustration to his hopes at the Diet of Augsburg in 1555, that finally decided him to retire from public life.

ABDICATION AND LAST RETREAT

It is not easy to determine the exact moment when Charles V first decided to abandon the cares of state and spend his last years in contemplative retreat. In a letter dated 17 December 1552, the Bishop of Arras notes: 'The emperor talks of abandoning everything and retiring to Spain.' This ambiguous statement might be merely descriptive of the emperor's despair after the failure of the siege of Metz, but it already had a deeper and graver significance.

In 1550, while travelling by boat on the Rhine from the Netherlands to south Germany, the emperor had already started to dictate his memoirs. His personal secretary, Willem van Male, who was to remain with him until his death, took down notes from dictation. However, it is more than probable that he also had access to the emperor's writings, particularly his campaign diaries. Charles did not wish to meditate on the past. The record of his life is not one long apologia, he makes no attempt to defend himself or his motives, but he seems to have wanted to present events as they actually were. Nowadays there are too many actors on the public stage in the habit of writing autobiographies even before they have accomplished anything worth recording. It is all the more difficult, therefore, to think of someone living at the time of Charles v writing his memoirs solely with the purpose of saying farewell to everyday life and to reassess, in a spirit of calm before departing this world, the ups and downs of a public life. It is thus valid to think that in 1550 the emperor, at least subconsciously, had already decided to put his house in order during his lifetime, and to retire from active politics.

The decisions reached at the Diet of Augsburg, for which Charles no longer wished to take any responsibility and against which he made a solemn protest, were probably ultimately responsible for the emperor's decision to abdicate. The religious peace of Augsburg had been established on the basis of the acceptance of two confessions within the empire, both with absolute equality in law. The principle of *cujus regio ejus religio* was proclaimed, which gave each territorial sovereign the right to violate the conscience of his subjects. Such a decision was intolerable to a man whose moral education had been based on the ideals of Adrien van Utrecht and Erasmus of Rotterdam. What is more, the sovereign found inadmissible the recognition of the theft of ecclesiastical property, by which the more unscrupulous princes had enriched themselves on the pretext of becoming converted to the new faith. Charles protested against these decisions which he foresaw would 'offend, injure and weaken our old, true, Catholic, Christian religion'.

King Ferdinand had given way at Augsburg because he was obsessed by the Turkish threat, in face of which he wished to retain the support of the Protestant princes. What is more, he did not feel strong enough to continue the struggle alone once his brother decided to retire from the affairs of the empire. The younger Habsburg – more prepared to compromise than his brother – did not have the equanimity and perseverance with which Charles had maintained, for thirty years, his struggle for religious unity. In order to obtain Protestant consent to his *Reservatio ecclesiastica*, Ferdinand made further major concessions by the *Declaratio Fernandea*, according to which Protestant subjects of Catholic states would not be forced to return to the old faith. Both these dispositions made at Augsburg were, however, to be later violated, and lead to fresh religious wars which only came to an end with the Peace of Westphalia.

While still in expectation of an heir from Philip's marriage to Mary of England, the emperor, on 6 June 1554, finally established the order of succession to the throne. For Spain he decided to retain strict rights of primogeniture; Philip's son, Don Carlos, would therefore be the lawful heir-apparent. On the other hand, the children by Philip's English marriage would succeed their father to the Netherlands; in this way Charles hoped to create the same powerful combine which was to exist for a short time under William III of Orange and Mary of England. Burgundy would become the link between Habsburg domains.

Once again, in 1554, Charles was obliged to take the field when the French invaded the Low Countries. The most remarkable action among the defensive battles which followed was the raising of the siege of Renty on 15 August 1554. Despite the physical pain he was in, the emperor took command of this operation, which was to be his last military engagement. When later an artist who was working on a painting representing this victory referred to the 'rout' of the French, Charles called him to order and insisted that this was not a word to be applied to what had been a perfectly orderly withdrawal. Even in the smallest details, the emperor always insisted on historical accuracy.

In Italy, after many vicissitudes, the imperialists at last succeeded in defeating Siena, a victory which re-established the balance of power in the peninsula. On the other hand, after 1555 further political difficulties arose when Pope Paul VI of the House of Caraffe was elected to the throne of St Peter. He was to prove a more tenacious and dangerous enemy of the Habsburgs than either Clement VII or Paul III.

In the history of the popes, the reign of Paul IV marks a period of transition. He was no worldly Renaissance pontiff, ambitious and pleasure-seeking, but rather a true representative of the period of the counter-Reformation, which already foreshadows the Baroque. Pious and imbued with religious fervour, he favoured reform, but although he had an aversion for politics, he was still incapable of ridding himself of a thirst for power, typical of his predecessors. The means employed by the pope against the emperor, his intrigues to assure French predominance throughout the whole of Italy, and the haughty way in which he addressed Charles v, forced the latter to send the Duke of Alva as his special envoy to the papal court. In Rome, the duke make it clear that the emperor was determined personally to put an end to the machinations of the Curia if His Holiness himself was not strong enough to keep his cardinals in order.

One of the greatest paradoxes of Charles's life is that one who had done so much to preserve the papacy as a universal institution should number among his most bitter enemies the popes themselves, and that, until the moment of his death, he should have lived on bad political and personal terms with the leaders of his church.

On 13 April 1555, Joanna the Mad died. Only then did Charles become the sole ruler of Spain.

On 22 October of the same year, the emperor resigned his position as head of the Order of the Golden Fleece. This was the first of a whole series of ceremonies in which he abdicated his rights and functions one after another. The Chapters of the Order had had occasion more than once to criticise the emperor, and often in an almost cruel fashion they had reproached him for his indecision and procrastination, which they attributed to apathy. However, it was one of the privileges of the knights of this illustrious company to pass judgement on the sovereign, and Charles had always accepted their censure without anger, unlike Marguerite's violent reaction, when the seigneurs of the Golden Fleece, headed by her young nephew, had protested at the arrest of Don Manuel.

The great spate of activity engaged in by the emperor during the year 1555 seemed to confirm the doubts which had been raised concerning his decision to abdicate, but his resignation on 22 October from the Golden Fleece proved to the world that his decision was irrevocable.

Three days later, on 25 October, in the Great Hall of the Château de Bruxelles, he handed over the government of the Low Countries to King Philip. Charles appeared in mourning, surrounded by knights of the Golden Fleece, councillors and governors, and leaning on the arm of William of Orange – a symbolic gesture in the light of events to come. Queens Eleanore and Marie, the Duke of Savoy, the Archduke Ferdinand of Austria, and the Duchess Christina of Lorraine took part in the solemn ceremony. The proceedings were opened by the Councillor, Philbert de Bruxelles, who announced the decision of the emperor. Then Charles spoke. He had made notes of several dates and various points on a slip of paper which he held in his hand, and with the help of these he summed up the whole of his career. He recalled how forty years ago his majority had been declared in this same hall, and how later he had succeeded his grandfathers – Ferdinand in Spain and Maximilian in the empire; he mentioned that the most serious threat with which he had to contend was the great Christian schism and the constantly renewed alliances of his enemies from which he had to protect his territories. Then he enumerated his various journeys – he had travelled nine times to Germany, six times to Spain, four times to France, twice to England and twice to Africa. His departure for Spain, for which he was now preparing, would be his last. He noted with sorrow that the peace which he had tried to bring about during his long reign had finally eluded his House and his Estates. He had never rested and often he had risked his life; now he had reached the end of his strength – already he had felt himself to be at death's door a number of times. Then he reverted again to the attempt of his enemies to take him prisoner at Innsbruck and referred to the siege of Metz and its unfortunate sequel, the recollection of which, he said, was more painful than any other that he would take with him in his retirement. Once again he insisted that the setback had been due to bad weather conditions. Reading this passage and comparing it with the honesty with which he habitually recognised his own mistakes, one is forced to conclude that in introducing this justification Charles was really defending one of his most loyal servants, the Duke of Alva, who had been so severely censured for his conduct of the campaign. The emperor went on to remind his audience that success and defeat equally were both in the hands of the Almighty, and thanked God that He had helped him so often.

In conclusion, he stressed once again that it was only because he was worn out that he was obliged to hand over his countries to King Philip and place the empire in the hands of King Ferdinand. He asked his son to remain loyal to the faith of his fathers, and always to maintain law and order. He admitted that he had often been in the wrong and blamed his errors in the main on his youth, and his own obstinacy and weakness. His last words of all were the most moving; he had never, he said, intentionally infringed the rights of anyone; if he had done so, he asked their forgiveness. It was only after this that he sank down exhausted on the throne.

Those present were unable to hide their emotion; women wept openly, and the tears were even pouring down the face of the prematurely aged emperor, who asked pardon for such a display of emotion. King Philip threw himself at his father's feet and promised that he would never forget the words his father had just spoken. He remained faithful to his oath, in fact there are few sons in history who have retained such obedience to the memories of their fathers. After he had been embraced by his father, Philip, apologising for his inability to speak the language of the country, left the Bishop of Arras to read a proclamation in his name. It seemed an ill omen for the future; the new master of Burgundy, unlike Charles, had neither been born nor brought up in the country, and therefore lacked the deep understanding of it which was such a characteristic of his father. It was now the turn of Queen Marie to make her farewell, as she wished to accompany her brother back to Spain. The emperor, on his part, thanked her for faithful services to him.

Karl Brandi, the historian, has very properly stressed the unique character of this historical event. Nevertheless, it is impossible to follow him all the way in his attempts to explain the occasion as characteristically 'High Renaissance', for this is only a half-truth. There is too much of the Christian Middle Ages in this abdication ceremony, even already too much which presages the piety of the Baroque to call it typically Renaissance. In fact, what took place at Brussels was very much in keeping with the character of the central figure in the drama, and characteristic of the innate courage which distinguished Charles, and also of the great changes taking place at this period which he himself had helped to bring about.

The renunciation of Castile, Aragon, Sicily and the New Indies took place a few months later, on 16 January 1556. The official ceremony took place in the emperor's private apartments in the presence of only a few witnesses. On this occasion, the sovereign emphasised – typically for him – that in old age God was better served in solitude. When he handed Philip the casket containing his last will and testament, he added that he would avail himself of the days remaining to him, to repent his sins and salve his conscience.

The new king, Philip, was solemnly proclaimed throughout Spain.

Don Carlos, as yet a child, paid homage to his absent father, and when the royal standard was held above his head, shouted *'Castilla, Castilla, por el Rey Don Felipe!'*

It was at this time that Charles, at one of the last audiences he was to hold in an official capacity, received the Admiral of France, Gaspar de Coligny, on being presented with the latter's credentials. Coligny was later to fall a victim of the wars of religion, which France could perhaps have avoided had she not played so active a part in preventing the emperor from establishing a united church in Germany. In the course of conversation with the admiral, the emperor again expressed (as he had already done in his youth) his pride in being descended from the House of Valois.

The Archduke Maximilian, who had married Charles's daughter Marie – a marriage by which the Austrian line of the Habsburgs and the Habsburg–Lorraine dynasty are directly descended from the great sovereign – arrived in the Low Countries with his wife to take leave of the emperor. The latter would have liked to have seen his brother Ferdinand once again, but this was no longer possible, and it was therefore by letter that he invested the King of the Romans with the imperial dignity on 12 September 1556. The elector-princes, however, did not officially recognise the abdication, and they did not proclaim Ferdinand emperor until February 1558.

On 28 August 1556, in his native city of Ghent, Charles parted from Philip, never to see him again. With a fleet of fifty-six vessels the emperor and his suite put to sea and on 28 September cast anchor in the little port of Laredo. At his express wish, no one was to receive him publicly, excepting the Infante Carlos. From Laredo, the sovereign went to the castle of Jarandilla. On 25 November (the autumn was particularly mild that year, and flowers were still in bloom) Charles came for the first time to Yuste, the Hieronymite monastery, to the west of Toledo. The country house, which he had ordered to be built, was not quite ready, but already on 5 February 1557, Charles and his small following had established their permanent quarters there. There are many legends concerning this last retreat which history has never unravelled. However, there is an abundance of authenticated sources concerning the last phase of Charles v's life. The monks wrote detailed accounts of the sovereign's habits, and there are the numerous letters written by his entourage and his own personal correspondence to give us a faithful picture of his way of life and principal preoccupations.

Charles's life at Yuste was not that of a monk or hermit; he was no penitent, mortifying himself and suffering from pangs of conscience. Nor did he devote himself exclusively to his large collection of watches, although it is said that the first man to see him in the mornings was his clockmaker whose duty was to regulate them. Such stories are in fact fantasies, invented in bad faith by ill-informed chroniclers. In reality, Charles, on his country estate, lived the life of a grand seigneur who, after an eventful life and years of incessant strain, wanted peace and calm to follow his inclinations and enjoy the small pleasures of life.

The house in which he lived had only one upper storey, which, like the ground floor, was divided into four spacious rooms, furnished in very good taste with *objets d'art*, but these rooms were in no way comparable with the great state apartments of palaces of the period. The villa was built in the style of the Renaissance on a simple geometric plan, with no useless crannies or decoration. It stood in the middle of a garden with one wing built up against the monastery, in such a manner that from his room the emperor could see the high altar of the church, and follow divine service or listen to the chanting of the monks.

The day started in church with a mass for the dead queen, which the emperor did not attend. He only arose about ten o'clock – as was the custom in Spain. His servants helped him dress and he then passed the day in reading or in conversation with Willem van Male, his secretary and reader. He often took walks beneath the trees or in the flower garden, conversing or meditating. If he had taken communion in the morning, he also attended high mass, and in the afternoon he liked to listen to a sermon.

Of course, he also had visits from the outside world, but as a general rule, he preferred not to be disturbed; he enjoyed his solitude, the beautiful countryside and the monastic silence. His court consisted of some fifty persons, only a small number of whom had daily contact with him. The emperor's permanent attendants were his medical adviser, Doctor Mathys, a Fleming; his reader, van Male; Martin de Gaztelu, his secretary, and lastly his confessor, Juan de Reglas.

The latter, who was the son of poor peasants, had at first serious misgivings and wondered if his limited horizons would ever allow him to reach an understanding of such problems as occupied the emperor. Charles, however, reassured him; he had already discussed questions concerning his abdication with his confessors in Brussels and had received absolution; now, once and for all, he had put any conscientious doubts on this score behind him. Juan, therefore, would only be concerned with sins the emperor might commit in his retreat. Nevertheless, Charles was continually dogged by one particular question: had he not, perhaps, opposed the heretical doctrines too late and acted without sufficient energy? He still felt responsible for the religious schism in Germany, and the messages which he sent to his nearest relatives, to Philip and to his sisters, Eleanore and Marie, show that he was seriously disturbed by this problem.

Other regrets which Charles might have manifested are not attested to with the same precision. The emperor may have reproached himself for not remarrying after the death of the Empress Isabella, out of love for his son, and for having sinned in consequence. But such self-criticism is improbable, since opinion of the time was very tolerant of sins of the flesh; moreover, Josef Lortz, historian of the Catholic church, praises the purity of Charles's life and speaks of his exemplary conduct as a husband. In noting a few of his peccadilloes, Lortz adds that from the point of view of Christian morals, the emperor's conduct was far superior to that of the majority of his contemporaries, whether Catholic or Protestant, ecclesiastics or laymen.

The emperor's majordomo was Luis Mendez de Quijada, Señor de Villagarcia, whose wife, the Lady Magdalena Uloa, took care of Jeronimo, the emperor's son by Barbara Blomberg. Imagining that the child was the issue of a love affair between her husband and a German woman, she brought him up as she would her own, and became very attached to this little boy, who had curly blond hair and blue eyes. When she followed her husband to Yuste, Jeronimo, then twelve years old, joined the emperor's suite as a page, certainly not without the latter's consent. The child pleased the old man, and it was from that moment that his noble origins were made known and that he was recognised officially as Don John of Austria.

A visitor with whom the emperor often had long conversations was the Jesuit, Francisco de Borgia, Duke of Gandia, who had formerly been chamberlain to the Empress Isabella. It is possible that it was this pious man who suggested that the emperor should cut short his memoirs at the year 1549. To the emperor's question whether it were not a sin to devote his time to the past and exalt his own brilliant actions, he would reply that any attachment to what has gone before was nothing but idolatry, and added, 'God is present, here and now'.

The queens, Eleanore and Marie, also visited Yuste. Charles tried to persuade Marie to reassume the Regency of the Low Countries, and she refused. But the emperor did no less, when his son begged him to leave his solitary retreat and re-enter active politics. Philip was disturbed by papal intrigues and by the threat of a new alliance between the Vatican and France. The emperor, however, maintained that the danger was exaggerated and that there would be a favourable outcome. Future events were to prove him justified.

In 1557, Philip succeeded in capturing Saint Quentin. The emperor, nevertheless, upbraided him for not having given battle in open country. On 13 July 1558, the Comte d'Egmont defeated the French at Gravelines and so decided the struggle for the frontier district of Flanders in favour of Spain. In Italy, the Duke of Alva reduced the papal strongholds, and the emperor was extremely angry when Philip, acceding to the demands of the pope, later restored these places to him and even begged his pardon.

During the year 1557, the emperor's health and morale were particularly good. He enjoyed the landscape with its groups of chestnuts and cedars, orange and lemon trees planted round his country house. The vivid green of the foliage gave him immense pleasure, and he often took short walks in the countryside. He distributed alms generously to the neighbouring villagers, despite the complaints of his courtiers that they frequently stole the royal Swiss cows and threw stones into the garden. He also had difficulties with the Spanish exchequer, which, only after repeated demands, agreed to pay the estimated allowance of twenty thousand ducats for the maintenance and needs of the emperor's court.

From the sovereign's library, and reports made by his entourage, we are able to get an exact idea of his literary and scientific tastes at Yuste. He read (or had read to him) the philosophical and theological works of Boetius and St Augustine, as well as the writings of Spanish mystics. He also read with critical interest the memoirs of the French statesman, Philippe de Commynes, visibly rejoicing in the author's candour. In his library was one of his favourite books, the *Courtier* by Balthazar Castiglione, and he always had to hand such historical works as Caesar, Polybius, Tacitus and Thucydides, as well as chivalric romances, telling of the noble deeds of Charles the Rash. With the help of his books on astronomy and atlases, the emperor was happily able to plot again the course of his own journeys and campaigns.

After a very severe winter, the summer of 1558 brought with it a period of excessive heat and drought, when there were many cases of sickness and even death among the emperor's entourage. It is unlikely, however, that the illness from which Charles was to die was due to these climatic conditions, particularly since reports tell us that Charles generally felt very well at the hottest times. During that August, his condition visibly weakened, and on the evening of the thirty-first, after having spent the afternoon on the terrace, he complained of a feeling of discomfort saying, *Malo me sienta*. Accounts of this day, which were later distorted, have given rise to the story that he ordered his requiem mass to be celebrated while he was still alive, and that he himself was present at the service. Actually, there was a memorial service, but this was held for his father and grandfather.

From 1 September the emperor was confined to his bed. His condition became so aggravated that Quijada summoned Carranza, Archbishop of Toledo, to administer the last sacraments. The patient, who was perfectly conscious, participated in the ceremony with all the seriousness and interest with which he always treated the Catholic liturgy, and he prescribed the exact order of the psalms and prayers to be recited. He also sent a last message to his son, by Luis Quijada, asking him to be good to his followers and in particular to take Gila, his barber, into his service.

On 20 September, the emperor's condition was worse, and neither he nor his entourage doubted the issue any longer; death was approaching and it was now only a question of hours. Archbishop Carranza comforted the dying man and assured him that by the Passion of Christ on the Cross, his sins would be redeemed and he would attain eternal life. The monks, who were present, were shocked by these words, which seemed to them to be alluding to Lutheranism and recalled the *sola fide* of the German reformer. This incident was later to play an important part in the charge of heresy that was brought against Carranza, who was to end his days in the Inquisitor's dungeons. The emperor himself had given the archbishop far too much latitude, which eventually rebounded on him. Charles had even asked for a special dispensation from the Inquisition to use a French translation of the Bible at Yuste.

Relieving Carranza, Brother de Villalba comforted the emperor in his anguish. He spoke to him of St Matthew, the apostle whose saint's day it was, and reminded him that he was the brother of the emperor's patron saint, Mathias, and promised that these two great protectors

214

would accompany him beyond the grave to eternity. In the early hours of 21 September 1558, the emperor died. His last word was 'Jesus'.

To know the dying emperor's thoughts during the last hours of his life is beyond the capacity of the historian. Perhaps Karl Burckhardt was not far wrong when, following the dictates of his imagination rather more than tradition, he wrote as follows of the end of the emperor's life:

The balance sheet which Charles might have drawn up on his death bed, recording his thoughts and examination of conscience, must surely have been summed up in the words: *in vain*. Each time his enemies had been defeated, they had become stronger ... Often during his last weeks, at the peaceful hour when twilight gathered over his gardens, the Emperor had sat contemplating Titian's glory, the great painting of the Judgement of Heaven, in which, as one of the great concord of a universal hierarchy (*faisant partie de la grande harmonie d'une hiérarchie universelle*), he is depicted as a suppliant before the throne of God, taking all responsibility on his shoulders. Perhaps at such moments, the emperor realised that the seeds of his actions would one day burgeon, but unlike the seeds sown in terrestrial fields, at no specific time or place and in no predestined shape, but in some place somewhere, and under some form impossible yet to imagine.

IO

The Emperor's Personality
and Place in History

When King Philip II tried to persuade his father to leave his retreat at
Yuste and re-enter the political arena, he wrote that it would be
sufficient for the emperor to show himself in public and announce his
decision to resume at least some of his former duties, to re-establish
order in the world. At the time which he sent this letter, Philip was
already thirty years old, and as history was to prove, he had the
true spirit of a king and great moral courage. But in his relations
with his father, he always remained the dutiful son, convinced of the
gulf that separated him from such an exceptional personality as his
parent.

The extraordinary aura which surrounded the emperor is all the
more remarkable since he did not have imposing stature, which popular
tradition expects of an emperor. His armour, which can be seen in
several collections, is that of a small man with a slim, neat figure, almost
like an adolescent's. He certainly did not correspond to the ideal of
masculine beauty which existed at the time, and his appearance had
none of the theatricality or stateliness characteristic of other rulers of his
day. If we compare the portraits of François I, Henry VIII, Maurice of
Saxony, and even the Renaissance popes, with those of the emperor, we
are immediately aware of the striking difference.

Charles's simplicity, however, did not preclude him from having
both dignity and elegance. This is obvious, not only from the first
portrait made of him by Titian, in which the sovereign is depicted in
very elegant garb, with a hound at his side, but it is also evident from
portraits showing him simply dressed in black, slightly stooped, and
looking like some prosperous burgher from Amsterdam or Augsburg,

and finally, from the magnificent picture of the emperor on the eve of the Battle of Mühlberg. All these works, though painted at different ages and under very different circumstances, portray the same characteristic features – a face always stamped with a serious expression; an almost absent-minded look as he concentrates on his inner thoughts – very different from the usual image which Renaissance rulers wished to leave to posterity.

The portraits made in his youth clearly reveal Charles's main physical characteristics – the firm protuberant chin and half-open mouth. These traits, which seem to have been handed down from the Zimburgis of Masovia, must have developed through numerous inter-family marriages until at last they become almost caricatured in following generations of Habsburgs; however, they disappear almost completely in the sons of Leopold I. The beard Charles wore once he was a grown man and which he kept until his death, partially concealed this scarcely flattering aspect of his face. Changes in his appearance and dress do not date from the time of his great break with official life, but from the most important moment in his reign – his coronation. From that time on the aura surrounding him increased in brilliance. The evolution which had started with the Diet of Worms continued right up until his triumph at the Battle of Mühlberg. The emperor's dignity, wisdom and constancy of purpose, his unrivalled experience acquired in the course of a long rule, left their impression on all. The world no longer saw him as a hesitant and inexperienced young man, but as a true ruler, possessed of that intangible but very real quality known as intrinsic authority. His flight from Innsbruck and defeat at Metz changed nothing. A ruler who can suffer such reverses and misfortunes without diminishing in stature is indeed a true sovereign; he is what he is; a usurper on the other hand is always vulnerable.

The gulf separating Charles from his peers on the thrones of Europe, and even more, from the princes of the empire, continued to grow ever wider. Hajo Holborn, the American historian, remarks that Charles 'had a strong contempt for the princes, and the knowledge of their perversity greatly strengthened his conviction that he would ultimately be victorious. He awaited with heroic patience the hour of his triumph which he knew to be inevitable.'

The dominant trait in the character of the emperor, and one which is apparent in all his writings and actions, was without doubt his self-control and resolute mastery over his feelings. In the course of a long public life, during which all his actions were carefully noted by his contemporaries, the occasions on which he displayed anger or scorn are extremely rare. His will-power and patience were allied to his absolute confidence that God would never desert him, and it was this belief which enabled him to accept adversity as being the will of the Almighty. He was master of himself, as of others.

It is said that when he assumed his armour, his whole body trembled, but that this weakness vanished as soon as he descended into the lists for a tourney or into the bull ring, and, above all, when he marched into battle at the head of his troops. When action was under way, Charles was always to be found with the advance guard or in the heart of the battle. However, he himself never referred to his exploits in his letters or reports, limiting himself solely to objective factual accounts. In fact he went so far as to forbid his chroniclers to mention his personal acts of bravery or feats of arms. In his eyes, they were not worth recording.

We lack evidence of Charles's intimate life. Had he followed the style of the times, his memoirs would have depicted him as the master of the world, the victor of many battles, as an erudite and cultivated prince and great orator. Quite contrary to such a picture his writings, although providing an excellent source whereby we can follow the chain of events and giving us precise and detailed accounts of the emperor's campaigns – in fact indispensable documents from the historians' point of view – tell us little or nothing of his loves and sufferings, nothing of his joys and sorrows or inner thoughts.

In reading objectively the writings which the sovereign has bequeathed to us, we find without much difficulty the key to what has been called the mystery of Charles v. His almost inhuman detachment in relation to his station in life stems from a conscious effort to make the person disappear behind the robe. He had, from his ancestry and from the upbringing given to him notably by Adrien, Mota, and later Gattinara, a boundless respect for the dignity with which he had been invested, and believed it was his duty to ignore the simple human being who wore an eternal crown. Firmly convinced that the person could never attain the heights of the ideal, he imposed upon himself an iron control and sought to eliminate the human factor even in his correspondence. In his own eyes, he was no longer Charles of Burgundy, a man and mortal, but the Emperor who never dies.

His letters to his brothers and sisters enable us to retrace the beginnings of his political ideas. His mode of working derives from the lessons of Adrien of Utrecht; Gattinara also had taught him much. Faced with a specific problem, he first of all analysed the question, looked for the way to a solution, weighed the pros and cons, ready to study and accept objections, in order finally to come to a decision. In the course of these arguments, however, he never betrayed his own conscience, even if he sometimes battled for weeks and even months to reach a conclusion.

We know that Charles was a lover of the arts and like most members of his family he loved music. At Yuste he used to listen with enjoyment to the church choirs and was able to distinguish voices of individual monks so well that in the evening he would smilingly tell one father or other in which part of the office he had sung out of tune. Charles was also an expert connoisseur of painting, as can be seen by his preference for Giorgione and Titian. After he had retired to Yuste, he often had pictures brought from his collection in order that he might contemplate them carefully and in detail. Indeed, such was his concentration that both his doctor and his confessor advised him to desist from this practice in case it over-taxed him. The same anecdote is told of Charles V and Titian, as of Maximilian and Dürer. In both cases, the emperor had picked up the brush which had slipped from the painter's hand, saying that in the domain of the spirit, a great artist was also a prince and the equal of the sovereign. But the emperor's view of art was an austere one. With his medieval outlook, artistic creations were for him nothing less than a service to God, and not, as they were for the Renaissance humanists and patrons of the arts, the apotheosis of the human form. Charles's profound religiosity followed the same logical pattern. It is difficult to know how much of his sense of religion he owed to his parental heritage, or to his education and own personal studies. But his education in the Low Countries and the influence of Adrian van Utrecht's *Devotia moderna*, together with his own further studies, lent his thoughts many of the traits of Erasmus's humanism. This was the cause of the criticisms levelled at him by churchmen, the most conservative amongst whom reproached him for not rendering himself completely immune to the Reformation and all heretical trends. On the other hand, Josef Lortz calls Charles the only true Catholic rival to Luther, inasmuch as a reform of the church was concerned. He fully subscribes to the opinion of Castiglione who affirmed that the emperor was the finest Christian he had ever met, either in the secular world or among members of the clergy. Lortz even goes so far as to write, 'Discounting saints and penitents, Charles was the greatest servant of his time the Church possessed.'

Despite its political aspects, Charles's fight for the unity of the church was prompted by his own faith. From a religious point of view he could not conceive of anything other than the complete subordination of political aims to the most important of all laws, that is to say, the preservation of the faith of his forefathers, and with that the one and only Catholic church. On this subject, the judgement of the Protestant historian, Leopold von Ranke, is significant:

> Kings, like the King of England, could think of schisms; such an idea never tempted the emperor. His authority was derived from its ecclesiastical character. It was only in the exercise of this ecclesiastical duty that his position had any real meaning.

There is no doubt whatsoever that on many occasions the immediate aims and fundamental ideas of the emperor were much closer to those of the Reformation than those of some elements of the Curia. Indeed, the latter often refused to make concessions to the Reformers who were anxious to put an end to abuses and make a fresh start. The Curia also opposed for too long the convocation of a council. However, it must be recognised objectively that this unfortunate attitude was sometimes prompted by a fear – justified by certain historical events – that ecclesiastical assemblies at a time of crisis often only aggravated confusion and led to further schisms. Despite all his disappointments, Charles always remained persuaded that the conflict could only be resolved by those who had temporarily seceded from the church returning to its bosom. On this point Ranke remarks:

> His supreme aim was no doubt political, but essentially it was religious, in the Catholic sense of the word. It was this that allowed him to form his own opinion independently of the mood and emotions of the masses.

Holborn maintains that Charles was never influenced by passion: 'On his political chess-board [he writes], emotions had no place.' It was this attitude of mind which gave him his independence and made him resistant to the trends of the times – to what is known as 'the spirit of the age'. Thanks to this attitude he often seemed to be controlling events with the lever of an Archimedes, far removed from his immediate world.

Religion for Charles was intimately connected with his respect for the law. The law was a sacred institution for him, and inseparable from the notion of the empire itself. He interpreted the motto on his coinage (*As the sun rules in the sky, so the Emperor rules on Earth*), not as recognising his unlimited power but, on the contrary, as meaning that he was invested with a legal right founded on natural laws. He was profoundly influenced by such considerations – unlike most of his contemporaries – and firmly believed in the royal maxim of the Visigoths: *Rex eris, si recta facis; si autem non facis non eris* (You will be king if you rule justly; otherwise you will no longer be king). Moreover, the same thought is expressed in the device of the Iron Crown of Lombardy, *recta tueri*. Personally, he suffered a great deal when forced to make decisions which were purely dictated by political expediency, like alliances with men such as Albrecht-Alcibiades von Brandenburg, whom he profoundly despised. We also know of his deep concern with seeing that justice was done in his American domains. In this case, one of his greatest disappointments was to see Las Casas, in whom he had had so much confidence, assuming at the end of his days a destructive attitude, instead of working constantly to put an end to existing abuses. Such thoughts preoccupied him to his dying day. This was why, towards the end of his life, he ordered a complete reappraisal of former litigation which had legitimised his rights to the Duchy of Parma.

In speaking of Charles's character, Cardinal Contarini remarked that although Charles had a sanguine side to his nature, his dominant characteristics were 'melancholic'. Lacking a comprehensive view of the emperor's life, many of his contemporaries confounded his taciturnity with resignation and his solemnity with melancholia. But the life of the emperor, up to the time of his abdication and even more during his last days at Yuste, shows that Charles, like a true Christian, had a positive attitude to life. He knew how to enjoy nature and the arts, he loved philosophy and the sciences; and he appreciated feminine beauty and the brilliance of both ecclesiastical and secular festivals and also the tensions evoked by trials of courage, by battle and by danger. Thus he had, as Brandi remarks, a singularly harmonious existence, which is all the more strange since as heir to long-forgotten traditions and the herald of an idea which his contemporaries were not yet sufficiently advanced to comprehend, his style of life was very different from that of other men of the Renaissance.

Some of the judgements passed on Charles have been conditioned by religious and nationalist prejudices, not to mention pseudo-historical theories, founded on a biassed view of the past; it is scarcely worth wasting time on their analysis.

The emperor has been reproached in particular for his so-called treacherous behaviour before the Schmalkalden war. But in fact Charles, like any other ruler, had to keep his military preparations secret; moreover, he showed himself willing, right up to the time of the outbreak of war, to refrain from force provided the princes agreed to accept a reasonable peace. Charles never let down or betrayed an ally. Lortz declared that the most important difference between the emperor and the majority of his contemporaries, not excluding the popes, was that unlike them he was always loyal. If ever there was a clash of duties, his allegiance to God and the Christian faith was his first concern.

In the light of these observations, it is impossible to accept Burckhardt's point of view without certain reservations. As we have seen in the preceding chapter, he creates the impression that the emperor must have considered his life to have been a tragic failure or all to no purpose. The contrary is proved by the emperor's writings, where he often remarks that all is decided by God for the best. It is true that his main objectives in the years between 1520 and 1555 were never attained; but Charles accepted the dictates of fate, even when they were incomprehensible to him, because he had confidence in Divine Wisdom. One can believe, therefore, that some of the ideas which Von Ranke expressed centuries later were not unfamiliar to Charles:

It seems inevitable that a prince with the traditions, world position and ideology of a man like Charles, should set himself the goals he did. His energy, of which he gave ample proof, his personal talents and the errors committed by his enemies, took him surprisingly far on his chosen path. Force of circumstances alone, prevented him from achieving his ends. He defended ideas like that of Christian unity, which was still alive in the hearts of men, but which in fact had become so enfeebled that it no longer dominated the minds of either party.

This remark admirably illustrates one of the emperor's characteristic traits – his ability to emancipate himself from the bonds which fettered his century. The epoch was not yet ready for ideas which it considered old-fashioned. It relegated those of the emperor to the 'barbarous

Middle Ages' or what was soon to be known as 'The Dark Ages'. The pride of those Renaissance men, who considered themselves to be living in a *nova aetas*, prevented them from understanding the mind of an emperor who was not a slave to the ideas predominant at the time; but who as a politician and soldier, and above all, as one who was invested with the highest non-ecclesiastical function of all Christendom, felt it incumbent upon him to see further than his day and age. Taking this into consideration one is forced to ask if Charles's tragedy was not perhaps inherent in the epoch, rather than being, as often wrongly interpreted, the emperor's own personal drama. Charles had unshakeable faith and confidence in God's wisdom and a profound understanding of the moral obligations imposed on him by history, which for him signified the realisation of God's will on earth. With such a spirit he must certainly have been in sympathy with the thoughts which the poet, Grillparzer, attributes to him: 'My house will survive because it is one with the spirit of the universe of which it is the centre, whence it can patiently await the return of erring spirits.'

Karl Burckhardt wrote:

It is a profoundly tragic moment when Charles learns that his own confessor, his spiritual guide and counsellor, is a follower of the new creed; when he sees sickly heirs succeeding him to the throne, and is forced to realise that it is the children who have been born to him of a momentary weakness of the flesh – Marguerite of Parma, who was later to become Regent of the Netherlands, and the son of the bourgeoise of Ratisbon, Don John of Austria, future victor of Lepanto – who were endowed with those same qualities of vigour and energy which he himself possessed when he was still the best horseman and finest swordsman at the court of Burgundy.

If at such a moment Charles was deeply moved, it was not that he despaired of God's mercy, but that he was lost in admiration at the miraculous ways of providence. *Omnia ad majorem Dei gloriam*, the motto of the Society of Jesus, filled his thoughts, and united there with St Benet's similar great dictum, *ut in omnibus glorifecetur Deus*, despite the fact that God's will is often incomprehensible to mortal man. That God could write even in curved lines was something that the Renaissance ignored, but which was recognised once again in the Baroque period, when the church rediscovered the road to the profound faith of the Middle Ages. But before this rediscovery, Charles himself had seen the truth; he never seems to have doubted it. It is certainly not by chance that no great literary dramatists of the mundane theatre has taken the life of Charles as a subject for a play. As a man, as a historical personage, he was not a figure of tragedy, but the image of an Emperor incarnate, *imago imperatoris*.

II

Historical Perspective

In periods of religious or national decadence historical facts are only too frequently distorted. This was the case in Germany in the sixteenth century when between 1559 and 1574 the *Magdeburger Centurion*, the first great history of the church written from a Protestant point of view, was published. This is a tendentious work, opposed both to the idea of the Empire and the Church of Rome. Its influence on German political thought was still apparent even as late as the nineteenth century, and its basic sentiments often reflected in the anti-Austrian writings of Prussian historians. It is notable, however, that Charles V is almost the only Catholic statesman of his period to whom these historians have not been altogether hostile. The worst they could find to say of him from their distorted point of view was that he had turned his back on his German origins to become a servant of Rome. It is unnecessary today to emphasise the absurdity of such allegations, although it is true that only within recent times has it been recognised that Charles and the popes seldom acted in concert.

During the decisive years of its development [*wrote Lortz*] the Protestant cause never received more tangible help than that accorded by certain papal measures – although from a religious and ecclesiastical point of view the popes were its mortal enemies – and by the support given to it by His Most Christian Majesty, the King of France.

It should not be forgotten either that until recently Protestant historians have found themselves in an ambiguous position when assessing the personality and works of the emperor. When they were honest with themselves, they had to recognise that the national evolution in

Germany would have taken a much smoother course had the emperor been able to realise his plans. For example Johannes Haller, the last important Protestant historian of the German Empire, has this to say of Charles v:

If we could change the course of history to suit our needs we would have chosen differently at this period. Had Charles succeeded in winning a lasting victory the Empire would have been strengthened internally, and the danger which threatened Germany from east and west would have been averted. There are even some people who believe that Protestantism should have been suppressed in order to establish a united nation.

Haller, nevertheless, fearing perhaps that he had gone too far in expressing these sentiments, later tries to justify himself in the eyes of his readers by adding that under the circumstances a victory for Charles would have meant subjugation of Germany by Spain; altogether too high a price to pay for a united empire.

It is not only German historians, however, who have had difficulty in fully understanding the political phenomenon of Charles. French and English authors have treated the question from a nationalist point of view, something which would have been quite foreign to the emperor. Even André Maurois, despite his great understanding of history, has described the period of François i and his successors as a period of struggles against German aggression. The debatable nature of such an opinion is only too apparent when it is realised that up to the time of the peace of the Pyrenees the so-called Germanic world was, from a military point of view, represented by Spain. Karl Wilhelm Nitzsch, the historian and economist, approaches more closely to the truth:

In Charles v we find united all the principal interests which preoccupied the world of his time – the direction of overseas conquests, the settlement of the American Indian problem, the burning question of ecclesiastical reform and the war against the Turks. But it is only in our day that history has done justice to the personality and work of Charles and has seen him as the personification of the imperial ideal which is an archetypal concept of humanity.

Royall Tyler and Alexander von Randa add that in the thousand years that elapsed between Charlemagne and Napoleon no ruler had more significance for Christianity than Charles, for his work in Europe and in America had an influence which can still be felt today.

This is particularly true of Spain. Shortly after the senior Habsburg line died out, Spain underwent a process of rapid degeneration; it was scarred by the miseries of civil war and its economic development was so retarded that only a quarter of a century ago it had hardly got beyond the feudal stage. For the Spanish, therefore, its splendour under the Habsburgs remains in their memory the 'golden age'. Charles's device of the double-headed eagle, the buildings which he has left us at Toledo, Granada and many other towns – and in particular the Escorial, whose architecture is a manifestation of the western imperial ideal – are all monuments which even today evoke the glories of the past. The cultural historian, Hans Sedlmeier, draws a striking parallel between the Escorial and the great imperial Baroque monasteries of Melk, Klosternneubourg and Göttweig. At first sight the austere Renaissance palace which Philip II constructed on the slopes of the Guaderrama seems to have little in common with the abbeys on the lush banks of the Danube. Nevertheless, the idea of integrating church and state, monastery and castle, of combining a royal sepulchre with a dwellingplace, such as the one Philip created in the Escorial and which Charles VI planned for Klosterneubourg, establishes an interrelationship between Spanish and Austrian Habsburg territories.

Charles V was the founder of modern Spain. The heritage which he bequeathed to the Iberian peninsula was one to which the Spaniards turned quite naturally when, after 1898, they started on the path which was to lead them away from their isolation and often fatalistic resignation and restore them to a place in history. We only have to read the works of Unamuno or Salvador de Madariaga to appreciate that the spirit of the new Spain was recreated in the image in which it had been left when the work of Charles V and Philip II was interrupted.

It would be a mistake, however, to restrict this historical phenomenon to the Iberian peninsula. It must not be forgotten that for the emperor there were no frontiers as we understand the word today. For him, Spain was not only the peninsula, but embraced the whole world of *Hispanidad*, the Philippines, as well as Spanish America.

It is not surprising, therefore, that the beginning of this century saw a revival of the Spanish spirit in the broadest sense of the term. The writings of Madariaga are evidence of the greatness of the cultural and historical commonwealth. The ideal of an *Hispanidad* has once again become an actuality on both sides of the Atlantic, and nothing much short of a universal cataclysm will curtail the influence which it is beginning to exercise on world events.

The discoveries of the Spanish conquistadors in central and south America, in the Pacific and the trading posts established by Spanish merchants, would not in themselves have been enough to give rise to a *realpolitik*. It was Charles's imperial concept in conjunction with the missionary zeal of the religious orders that started the evolutionary process, whose scope has only begun to be appreciated by the Spanish Americans and Spaniards themselves in the course of the last decades. If in our century Spanish language and culture and the links between Spain and her sister nations in central and southern America are once again united to form the equivalent of a British Commonwealth of Nations, and if the link across the South Atlantic has once again acquired a political significance, this is no more than a continuation of Charles's efforts in the sixteenth century. The emperor's discussions with Las Casas, his *Lois Novelles*, his interest in his overseas territories, of which he had a very exact idea despite the fact he never visited them, seem as close to us today as if the interim period of decline and economic ruin had never existed.

But even in Germany, where at least ostensibly the emperor's plans came to nothing, the memory of his struggle to achieve unity and a Christian entente and to revive the empire still survives. With the establishment of the *Reichsregiment* under Charles v, the development of the German constitution reached a decisive stage. It was not the emperor's fault as all historians agree – but rather lack of understanding or treachery on the part of the German princes which stopped the emperor from carrying out his work effectively. In the American work already mentioned, Holborn reminds us that before the Schmalkalden war Melanchthon had considered the chances of a Protestant victory very favourable although at the same time he believed he saw in the stars the warning of disasters to come. Holborn adds, 'These stars were in fact in the hearts of men unequal to their historic task.' Charles himself had had no wish to assume responsibility for the religious peace of Augsburg; he had no desire to associate himself with the continuation of the Schism, though it was he, nevertheless, who had created the conditions necessary for what one might call, to use a modern expression, peaceful co-existence in western Christendom.

The ecclesiastical policies of Charles v have an importance which far exceeds their time and place. Without exaggerating one can say that so great was the opposition from the pope and the Curia, as well as from the Protestants, that the council would never have been convoked had it not been for the emperor's indefatigable insistence. Luther maintained from the start that even the council did not constitute an absolute authority; only the dictates of an individual's conscience could do that. Illogically the reformer was trying to impose his own doctrine as the guiding rule which others should follow. Charles on the other hand, in the face of every possible sort of opposition, continued to uphold the idea of a universal council. He never ceased to hope that it might be possible by dint of patience to induce both the princes and the Protestant theologians not only to discuss the issues at stake but also to accept the council's decisions once they were made. Because of the attitude of Paul III, the council, when it finally did assemble, adopted quite a different line from the one Charles had intended. The interruptions to the sessions of the Council of Trent had weakened its oecumenical significance. At the same time, the pope's measures against the emperor, inspired purely by political interests, contributed in great measure to render the resounding victory he had gained by force of arms purely illusory.

Charles did not live to see the happy change of attitude which was to occur during the third session of the council, when despite opposition from high places an irresistible desire for reform finally prevailed. But nevertheless Charles can justly be claimed to be the father of the Counter-Reformation. The term 'Counter-Reformation', however, should not be interpreted in the sense given to it by certain biassed and over-imaginative historians, who have completely distorted the significance of what was an essentially spiritual movement. Despite his austere conviction, Charles never entertained the idea of making converts by force. What he desired for the church was a new sort of power which would cause all men of goodwill to be irresistibly drawn to it; something that would release the religious instincts that the Almighty has implanted in the hearts of all men. It was these efforts on the part of the emperor that contributed to the growth of the Baroque civilisation in Europe, which was soon to usurp the place of the old Catholicism and form a new link between Christians.

In our own day, the second Vatican Council has been a milestone in religious affairs; the church has entered on a new road which may finally lead it to the goal which the emperor had aimed for all his life. Thus we see the great advocate for Christian unity re-emerging from the obscurity of the past to serve as an example to our troubled world today. Herein lies one of the decisive factors to explain the close relationship linking Charles v with the second half of our twentieth century. Leopold von Ranke, speaking of the emperor, remarked:

There was no longer any room in the occidental world for the church he had envisaged: a church uniting religion and politics and embracing the whole of the western world. Never since Charles Quint, has any man clung to the idea of this united and uniting church with such strength.

The Protestant historian, who belonged to a century when the old faith was only too frequently replaced by nationalism, consoled himself in the belief that some other sort of community was springing up to replace religion. 'The common advance of European culture and power is replacing the unity of the church,' he wrote.

Today the grandeur of Europe is in ruins; the system of national states is revealed as the disastrous – perhaps even fatal – mistake that it is. European civil wars and two world conflagrations have led the continent to the brink of complete disintegration. Taking advantage of our weakness, a vast offensive has been unleashed. This movement with its anti-colonialism, dictated by the revolt of youth, openly supported, or at the least, exploited by the communists, has become a serious menace to humanity in the twentieth century. On its own side European civilisation, freed of the twin disciplines imposed by Christian morality and supra-national commonwealth, has produced, together with certain undoubted benefits, the means of collective suicide.

But reaction is setting in, and the notion of a united Europe is taking hold again. People are once again beginning to appreciate that religion and politics are indeed interdependent as well as the need to establish common economic markets and tariffs founded on a firmly ethical basis.

It is perhaps not surprising, therefore, to find Burgundy – the country where Charles was born and educated, where he learnt to understand the meaning of probity, and whose culture and spirit he absorbed and imported to Spain, Germany and Italy – as the key piece in the plans for a European entente in our day. It was only natural that Burgundy should be chosen when it was a question of selecting a centre for such supra-national organisations as The Coal and Steel Federation, the Common Market, Euratom and the Council of Europe.

Although the ideal of the Crusades is no longer a reality in its ancient form, the tradition of Burgundian chivalry, which finds its finest expression in the Order of the Golden Fleece, has lost none of its importance. To prevent the disaster of a nuclear war, it is not sufficient merely to balance the weapons of destruction on either side of the Iron Curtain; the only effective weapons at our disposal are spiritual and moral ones; only through faith and Christian charity can we stem the expansion of mechanistic and materialistic civilisation.

Charles embodied these ideals. He fought courageously for justice on earth and had respect for the integrity of man. His conception of the functions of the emperor and of the empire may at first sight seem to be linked with the institutions of his epoch, and consequently now outdated. But, in reality, his conception corresponds to the fundamental principles rooted in human nature, principles which must be reassumed and realised by each succeeding generation in a form appropriate to its epoch. As a historical personage he was no more than mortal. There remains nothing of his transient life on earth, only the dust in the marble sarcophagus in the Escorial; but inasmuch as he represents an eternal ideal, the Emperor, after more than five centuries, is still living among us – not only as our European ancestor, but as a guide towards the centuries to come.

Chronological Table
of Charles V's Reign

1500	Birth of Charles V at Ghent (24 February). Discovery of Brazil by Cabral.
1501	Capture of Naples by the French. Agreement on the future marriage between Charles and Princess Claude, daughter of Louis XII.
1502	Peasant Revolt in the Bishopric of Speier (the Bundschuh). Foundation of the University of Wittenberg by the Prince Elector of Saxony. Birth of the Archduke Ferdinand (future Emperor Ferdinand I) at Alcala. Foundation at Seville of the *Casa de la Contracion*, centre for the control of trade with overseas territories.
1504	Death of Isabella, Queen of Castile; Cardinal Ximenes appointed Regent of Castile. Death of Philibert of Savoy, second husband of Marguerite of Austria-Burgundy, daughter of Maximilian I. The French driven out of Naples by the Spanish (Gonzalvo de Cordoba).
1505	Acquisition of Naples by Spain. Marriage of King Ferdinand of Aragon and Germaine de Foix, niece of Louis XII of France. Martin Luther (1483–1546) enters the convent of the Augustinians at Erfurt.
1506	Death of Philippe le Beau of Austria-Burgundy; Queen Joanna of Castile goes mad; Guillaume de Croy, Seigneur de Chièvres, appointed Governor of Flanders. Beginning of the rebuilding of St Peter's, Rome.

1507 Emperor Maximilian entrusts Archduchess Marguerite with the education of Charles and appoints her Regent of Burgundy.

1508 Formation of the League of Cambrai by the Emperor, the Pope, Spain and France against Venice.
Plans for the marriage of Charles and Mary of England (after the French had broken off his betrothal to Princess Claude of France).
Foundation of the University of Alcalade Henares by Cardinal Ximenes.
Luther leaves Erfurt for Wittenberg.

1509 Death of Henry VII of England.

1509–47 Henry VIII, King of England; married to Catharine of Aragon; advised by Cardinal Thomas Wolsey.

1510 Luther visits Rome.

1511 Formation of the *Holy League* against France (Emperor Maximilian, Ferdinand of Aragon and Henry VIII).
Recapture of Navarre by the Spanish.

1512 Diet of Cologne: the Empire divided into ten spheres to preserve internal peace.
Second victory of the Emperor Maximilian at Guinegatte.
Death of the Medici pope, Julius II.
Speculation concerning the possible candidature of the emperor for the pontifical throne; election of Leo X (1513–21).
Luther at Wittenberg as professor and doctor of theology.
Balbao reaches the Pacific coast.

1514 Peasant Revolt in Württemberg ('Poor Conrad').
Chief of the Castilian faction in Burgundy, Don Juan Manuel, arrested by order of the Archduchess Marguerite.
Marriage of Princess Mary of England and Louis XII of France.

1515 Proclamation of Archduke Charles's majority.
Death of Louis XII of France.
François I of Orléans-Angoulême crowned King of France.

1515–1547 Victory of François I over the Swiss at Marignan; capture of Milan.
Double marriage between the Houses of Habsburg and Jagellon – Ludwig of Hungary and Bohemia with the

Archduchess Marie (granddaughter of Maximilian) and the Archduke Ferdinand (represented by his grandfather Maximilian) with Anne of Bohemia.

1516   Death of Ferdinand of Aragon (28 January); negotiations concerning the succession (Joanna, Charles or Ferdinand?).
Raising of the siege of Fort Peñon near Algiers by the victory of Diego de Vera; failure of the Spaniards to capture Algiers.
Concordat between France and the Papacy; the Pope exchanges his right to appoint bishops for payment of annual taxes.
Publication of Thomas More's *Utopia*.
Publication by Erasmus of the New Testament in Greek with Latin translation (the text used later on by Luther).

1517   Charles arrives in Spain.
Publication by Luther of the Ninety-five Articles, in particular against the sale of indulgences (31 October); beginning of his fight against the Church.
Meeting of Charles at Tordesillas with his mother Joanna and the youngest of his sisters, Catherine (4 November).
Death of Cardinal Ximenes at Roa (8 November).
Conquest of Egypt by the Turks.

1518   Charles in Catalonia; nomination of Mercurino Gattinara as Grand Chancellor of Burgundy.
Start of the struggle of Huldreich Zwingli (1484–1531) against the Catholic Church in Zürich.
Discussion between Luther and Cardinal Gaetano at Augsburg.
Philip Mélanchthon, Professor at Wittenberg.

1519   Death of the Emperor Maximilian I (12 January); struggle for the succession to the Empire; principal candidates François I and Charles of Austria-Burgundy.
Unanimous election of Charles at Frankfurt (28 June).
News of his election received by Charles in Spain (6 July).
Charles at Barcelona confronts the Catalan Estates; beginning of unrest at Valencia.
Debate of Leipzig. Luther confronts Eck and defends his thesis that the papal council is not infallible.
Eviction of Duke Ulrich of Württemberg from his State by the *Schwabische Bund*; acquisition of Württemberg by Austria.
Start of the expedition of Fernando Cortez for Mexico.
Departure of Ferdinand Magellan on his journey round the world from Spain.

1519—*continued* Death of Leonardo da Vinci (last years of life spent at the French Court).

1520   On the advice of the Dominican father, Antonio Montesinos, promulgation by Charles of the Laws of Burgos for the protection of the Indians.

Departure of Charles from Spain (26 May), after having obtained substantial financial aid from the *Cortès* at Corunna.

Nomination of Adrien of Utrecht, Cardinal of Tortosa, as Regent of Castile.

Start of the Revolt of the *Communeros*.

Formation of the *Holy Junta* by the *Communeros* (29 June).

Recognition of the Germania of Valencia by the Cardinal-Regent.

Papal bull condemning Luther (burnt by the latter); publication of three pamphlets by Luther to spread his doctrine in Germany.

Death of Raphael.

Beginning of the reign of Sultan Suliman II (The Magnificent) in Turkey (1520–1566).

1521   Diet of Worms: Luther's discourse before the Emperor and Diet (18 April); edict of Worms against the doctrine of Luther; the Reformer placed under the Imperial ban.

Luther secretly abducted to reside in the Wartburg.

Bestowal of the hereditary states of the Habsburgs in Germany on Ferdinand I.

Defeat of the *Communeros* near Villalar (24 April); imprisonment and execution of Juan de Padilla.

Defeat of the *Germania* of Valencia at Oropesa and Almenara (18 July); end of the revolt.

Death of Croy, Seigneur de Chièvres, tutor and counsellor of Charles.

Belgrade taken by the Turks.

Erasmus of Rotterdam (Prince of Humanists) establishes himself in Basle.

1522   Death of Pope Leo X. Election to the Papal Throne of Adrien of Utrecht, Cardinal of Tortosa, tutor of Charles (Hadrian VI).

Spanish victory over the French at La Bicoque; capture of Genoa by Pescara and Colonna.

Diet of Nuremberg; first negative reactions by the Estates regarding the edict of Worms.

Return of Luther to Wittenberg; restoration of order in Karlstadt among rebellious religious sects; publication of the Lutheran translation of the New Testament.
Revolution and terror in Majorca.
Completion of the Conquest of Mexico by Cortez.
Return of Captain Elcano to Spain with the one surviving ship of Magellan's expedition.
Surrender of Rhodes to the Turks after an heroic defence, departure of the Knights of St John.

1523   Proclamation of the Sixty-eight Articles of Faith by Zwingli (theses more radical than those of Luther).
Death of Pope Hadrian VI; election of the Medici Pope Clement VII de' Medici (1523–1534).
Death of Ulrich von Hutten on the island of Ufenau.
Death of Franz von Sickingen; end of the war of the knights against the territorial princes.
Re-establishment of peace in Majorca (3 June); execution of Joannot Colom and his companions in the castle of Bellver.

1524   Peasant Revolt in Germany over the Twelve Articles.
Polemical writing of Luther against the peasants.

1525   Victory over the French by the Imperial army at Pavia (24 February); François I taken prisoner.
Dissolution of the revolutionary movement of Thomas Münzer (Thuringia) after the defeat of Frankenhausen.
Luther's *De servo arbitrio* against Erasmus; break between Reformers and Humanists.
Creation of the Council of the Indies by Charles V.
Secularisation of the Teutonic Order by its Grand Master Albrecht von Brandenburg. Transformation of Prussia into a secular duchy under Polish sovereignty.

1526   Peace of Madrid between Charles V and François I.
Diet of Speier; increasing opposition of the Princes to the Edict of Worms.
Marriage of Charles V with the Infanta Isabella of Portugal.
Renewal of the war with France, following the refusal of François I, released from captivity, to recognise the Peace Treaty; formation of the League of Cognac (France, the Pope, Florence and Venice) against the Emperor.
Victory of the Turks at Mohacs; death of Ludwig II of Bohemia and Hungary. Bohemia and the western part of Hungary

CHRONOLOGICAL TABLE OF CHARLES V'S REIGN

1526—continued transferred to Ferdinand of Austria under the Agreement of Inheritance; Transylvania, under Turkish protectorate, refuses to recognise the Habsburg Kingdom.

1527 Birth of the Infante Philip of Spain (future Philip II).
Birth of the Archduke Maximilian of Austria (future Maximilian II).
Sack of Rome by the Imperial mercenaries under the command of the Constable de Bourbon; death of the Constable.
Clement VII imprisoned in the Castle Sant' Angelo.
Start of the Reformation in Sweden (Gustavus Vasa).
Foundation of the University of Marburg.
Death of Nicolo Macchiavelli.

1528 Intervention by Henry VIII in the war against the Emperor.
Agreement between Charles and the Welsers of Augsburg on the development of Venezuela (Little Venice).
Birth of Marie, daughter of Charles and Isabella, future wife of Maximilian II, and thus ancestress of the House of Habsburg-Lorraine.
Foundation of the University of Strasbourg.

1529 Siege of Vienna by the Turks; failure of Suliman II to take the city.
The Ladies' Peace of Cambrai, negotiated by the Archduchesses Marguerite and Louise, mother of François I.
Diet of Speier; renewal of the Edict of Worms; protest of the Evangelical States (origin of the name 'Protestant').
Religious debate between Luther and Zwingli at Marburg Castle.
Publication of Luther's Catechism.

1530 Imperial coronation of Charles V at Bologna by the Pope.
Diet of Augsburg (June–September); *Confessio Augustana*; *Confutatio*; *Apologia* by Melanchthon.
Death of the Grand Chancellor Gattinara.
Death of Cardinal Wolsey.
Death of the Regent Archduchess Marguerite.
Foundation of Protestant Princes' League of Schmalkalden.
Decree by the Empress Isabella forbidding the enslavement of the natives in the New World.

1531 Election and coronation of Ferdinand, King of Bohemia and Hungary, as King of the Romans; protest by the Elector of Saxony.

238

Death of Zwingli at the Battle of Kappel against the Swiss Catholic Confederates.
Nomination of the Dowager Queen Marie of Hungary as Regent of the Low Countries.
Beginning of the Conquest of Peru by Francisco Pizarro.

1532   Religious compromise at Nuremberg; freedom of worship for all creeds.
The Turks march against Vienna; advance of the Imperial armies under Charles and Ferdinand. Suliman avoids battle.

1533   Agreement between Suliman and Ferdinand of Hungary.
Beginnings of Anabaptist risings in Munster.
Death of Ariosto.

1534   Death of Pope Clement VII; election of the Farnese Pope, Paul III (1534–49).
England breaks with the Church of Rome.
Completion of Luther's translation of the Bible.
Return of Ulrich von Württemberg to his country with the assistance of the Protestant Princes.

1535   Expedition of the Emperor against Khair-ed-din Barbarossa; victory of La Goulette; fall of Tunis; liberation of thousands of Christian slaves.
Capture of Munster by the Prince-Bishop; massacre of the Anabaptists.
Execution of Sir Thomas More.
Death of Francesco Sforza. (Milan later passes to the Infante Philip.)
Foundation of Buenos Aires.

1536   Renewal of war with France; alliance of François I with the Turks.
Discovery of California by Cortez.
Death of Erasmus of Rotterdam.

1537   Refusal of the Protestant States to participate in the Council convoked by the Pope.

1538   Armistice of Nice between Charles V and François I; meeting of the two monarchs at Aigues-Mortes.
Foundation of the Holy League of Catholic Princes at Nuremberg.

1539   Death of the Empress Isabella.

1540   Official papal recognition of the Society of Jesus founded in
        1534 by Ignatius Loyola (1491–1556).

1541   Failure of Charles V's expedition against Algiers.
        Diet of Ratisbon: *Interim*
        Death of Nicolas Copernicus.
        Death of Theophrastus Bombastus Paracelsus.

1542   Beginning of the fourth war by France against Charles V; allies
        of France: the Turks, Denmark and the Duke of Cleves;
        England, the ally of Charles.
        Diet of Nuremberg.
        Failure to secularise the see of Cologne.
        Beginning of the colonisation of Chile.
        Leyes Neuvas for the protection of Indians (Bartolomeo de Las
        Casas).

1543   The Infante Philip nominated Regent of Spain; marriage with
        the Infanta Maria of Portugal.
        Meeting between Charles V and Pope Paul III (Alessandro
        Farnese) in Busseto.
        Dangerous situation in the Low Countries following the
        French offensive.
        Continuation of the Diet of Nuremberg.
        Cleves surrenders to the Imperial Army.

1544   Diet of Speier: approval of the financial means to prosecute
        war against France.
        Campaign under the personal command of the Emperor; great
        military success; advances to the Marne and towards Paris.
        Peace of Crépy: renunciation by François I of all pretensions to
        Burgundian and Italian territories of the House of Habsburg.

1545   Opening of the Council of Trent.
        Birth of Don Carlos, son of Philip; death of his mother, the
        Infanta Maria.

1546   Death of Martin Luther.
        Start of the Schmalkalden War; Maurice of Saxony supports
        the Emperor.
        Charles V in Ratisbon.
        Campaign of the Danube; operations brought to a victorious
        conclusion without a major battle thanks to the Emperor's
        strategic skill.

1547   Campaign of the Elbe. Victory of the Emperor near Mühlberg (24 April); Friedrich of Saxony taken prisoner; submission of the Landgrave Philip von Hesse; partition of the territories of the House of Wettin; the electorate passes to the Albertine line (Maurice of Saxony).
Death of François I; accession of Henri II (1547–1553) to the throne of France.
Death of Henry VIII of England. Accession of Edward VI (1547–53) to the throne of England.
Council of Trent transferred to Bologna.
Conspiracy of the Fiesco dynasty in Genoa against the Doria.

1548   Diet of Augsburg: new *Interim* (*The Armed Diet*).

1549   Death of Paul III; election of Julius III (1549–55).

1550   Magdeburg under the ban of the Emperor; execution of the Edict entrusted to Maurice of Saxony.

1551   Return of the Council to Trent.
Defection of Maurice of Saxony. New revolt of the Protestant Princes allied to France.

1552   Treaty of Chambord between Henri II of France and the Imperial Protestant Princes; agreement on the surrender of the Bishoprics of Metz, Toul and Verdun to France.
Advance of Maurice of Saxony against Innsbruck; the Emperor forced to flee.
Treaty of Passau between King Ferdinand and the rebel Princes.
Siege of Metz by Charles; French success.

1553   Victory of Maurice of Saxony at Sievershausen over Albrecht-Alcibiades of Brandenburg; Maurice killed in the battle.
Death of Edward VI of England; accession to the throne of his half-sister, Mary ('Bloody Mary').
Death of Lucas Cranach. (A *Madonna* painted by him accompanied Charles V on all his journeys and campaigns; it now hangs in the church of St Jakob in Innsbruck.)
Death of François Rabelais.

1554   The Kingdom of Naples ceded by Charles to his son Philip, who marries Mary, Queen of England. (The marriage was without issue.)

I

1555   Death of Queen Joanna.
Death of Pope Julius III; election of Marcellus and, after his sudden death, of Pope Paul IV Caraffa (1555–59).
Religious Peace of Augsburg: principle of *Cuius regio, eius religio*; permission to Nonconformists to emigrate.
Reservatio ecclesiastica (those States of the Empire which adopted the new doctrines must relinquish their sovereign rights), a principle limited by the *Declaratio Fernandea* (no retrospective application of the ecclesiastical reservation); equality of creeds in Imperial cities where the population held different beliefs.
Transfer of the Government of the Low Countries by Charles to his son Philip.

1556   Abdication of Charles V. Ferdinand I and the cadet (Austrian) line of the House of Habsburg succeed to the Empire; Philip II succeeds to the Crown of Spain, to Italy, the Low Countries and the overseas territories.
Charles retires to a country house on the estates of the Convent of St Jeronimo de Yuste.

1557–1558   Victory of the Burgundian and Spanish army over the French at St Quentin and Gravelines.
Death of Queen Mary; accession of Elizabeth to the throne of England (1558–1603).
Death of Charles V (21 September).
Death of Queen Marie of Hungary, Regent of the Low Countries (18 October).

1563   End of the Council of Trent. Reform of the Catholic Church and start of the Counter-Reformation.

1571   Naval battle won at Lepanto, a decisive victory over the Turks, won by Don John of Austria (illegitimate son of Charles V by Barbara Blomberg) in command of a combined Spanish, Venetian and Papal fleet.

1574   Philip II removes the body of Charles V to the crypt of S. Lorenzo in the Escorial.

Sources and Bibliography

We possess a wealth of material for the history of Charles V. The emperor ruled over Burgundy, Italy and Germany and journeyed untiringly through his domains. Wars and the politics of dynastic marriages involved him in continual negotiations with France and England; his influence extended overseas, and his Mediterranean policies brought him into contact with the Moslem world. Not surprisingly, the emperor is referred to in hundreds of contemporary documents and reports. Furthermore, chroniclers of the time, notably Sandoval, wrote biographies of Charles. Innumerable public and diplomatic documents relating to the policies of the emperor are scattered among the archives of Europe; many, no doubt, still awaiting discovery. Finally, the emperor has left us many writings – letters, notes, plans and a brief autobiography, either written by Charles himself or dictated. We have already noted the importance of his rich personal correspondence. Consequently the historian's problem, far from being a lack of material, lies in selecting from among an overwhelming mass of documents. Unhappily, few critical surveys exist of source material, a deficiency deplored by Alfred Morel-Fatio in his *Historiography of Charles V*. This erudite and conscientious author was moved to admiration for the historian with the temerity to attempt a life of the emperor before some order had been imposed on the material; his comment was particularly inspired by the work of Hermann Baumgarten, planned to cover four volumes, but of which only three appeared between 1885 and 1892.

Compared with the wealth of source material, published lives of Charles are surprisingly few. There was little serious interest in the emperor before the beginning of this century, when a series of studies, beginning with Armstrong's first work in 1902, culminated in the remarkable works by Peter Rassow and Karl Brandi's great biography. In my opinion, Rassow has gained the deepest insight into the personality of Charles, but it must be kept in mind that his book was published at the height of Hitler's power. The writings of Brandi contain many latent criticisms of the Nazi régime and of Hitler in person, and the fact that his book even though too specialised for the general public, went into four editions between 1937 and 1942, indicates the important role it played in German writings of the Nazi era. Seeking escape from an intolerable present, intellectuals took refuge in the past, revealing where their sympathies lay by their interest in personalities opposed to the ideals of National Socialism. Any writer of that period seeking to exercise political influence was bound, in fact, to be cautious and could only express dangerous opinions by indirect comment. After the Second World War there was an increased interest in Charles. The idea of a united Europe recalled the figure of the last ruler of the Holy Roman Empire who strove to unite Christendom. Of recent years interest has revived in the Papal Council and Reform of the Church; Charles worked all his life in support of an ecumenical council and was one of the instigators, if not the principal promoter, of the Council of Trent. Now, at this moment, when history is not just being made by the Nation States of Europe and the United States of America, but is moving into a universal era, it is only natural that the Habsburg policies of the sixteenth century so brilliantly depicted by Alexander Randa should attract attention. Finally, research into the background of the life of Charles has been greatly facilitated by recent studies, in which historians have used modern methods of approach to the cultural, religious, social and economic life of the period. In this category one work above all demands mention, *The Decline of the Middle Ages*, by Johan Huizinga, which is fundamental reading for any research into Burgundian history. The American, Royall Tyler, shows a remarkable understanding of the emperor, while the choice and presentation of the iconography in the great work of that doyen of Belgian historians, Vicomte Charles de Terlinden, are indispensable to anyone seeking the man behind the actions and the documents.

ALLEN (P.A.): *The Age of Erasmus*. Oxford, 1914.
ANDREAS (Willy): *Deutschland vor der Reformation. Eine Zeitenwende*. Stuttgart, 1948.
ANDRES (Marcos, T.): *Vitoria y Carlos V en la soberania hispano-americana*, in *Acta Salmanticensia*, t. I, n°. 1.
ARMSTRONG (Edward): *The Emperor Charles V*. London, 1910.
BABELON (Jean): *Charles Quint*. Paris, 1947.
BALESTEROS y BERETA (A.): *Historia de España*, IV. 1, 1943.
BATAILLON (Marcel): *Erasme et l'Espagne*. Paris, 1937.
BRADFORD (William): *Correspondence of the Emperor Charles V, and his Ambassadors*. London, 1850.
BRANDENBURG (Erich): *Kaiser Karl V*. 1922.
BRANDI (Karl): *Kaiser Karl V, Werden und Schicksal einer Persönlichkeit und eines Weltreiches*. T. I. München, 1942; t. II. Quellen und Erörterungen, 1941.
BAUMGARTEN (Hermann): *Karl V und die deutsche Reformation*, 1889.
BURCKHARDT (Carl J.): *Gedanken über Karl V*. München.

CHAMPION (Pierre): *Le Règne de François Ier*. Paris, 1935.

COSSIO (Francisco de): *Carlos V*. Madrid, 1941.

FERDINANDY (Michael von): *Karl V*. Tübingen, 1964.

FIEDLER (J.): *Relationen venetianischer Botschafter über Deutschland und Österreich im XVI. Jahrhundert*, dans *Fontes Rerum Austriacarum*, XXX, 1870.

FRANZ (Günther): *Der deutsche Bauernkrieg*. Darmstaft, 1956.

GACHARD et PIOT: *Collection des Voyages des Souverains des Pays-Bas*. Tome III. *Expédition à Tunis*. Bruxelles, 1881–1882 (also contains *Expédition à Alger*).

GACHARD (P.): *Correspondance de Charles Quint et d'Adrien VI*. 1859.

GARCIA-ONTIVEROS (Eduardo): *La Politica norteafricana de Carlos I*. Madrid, 1950.

GRANVELLE (Cardinal de): *Papiers d'Etat*, pub. Ch. Weiss, vol. 1841–1852.

HÄBLER (Konrad): *Geschichte Spaniens unter den Habsburgern*. Gotha, 1907.

HARE (Christopher): *A Great Emperor, Charles V (1519–1558)*. London, 1927.

HEIDRICH (Paul): *Karl V und die deutschen Protestanten am Vorabend des Schmalkaldischen Krieges*. Frankfurt, 1911.

HENNE (Alexandre): *Histoire de Belgique*, T. III. Bruxelles, 1907.

HERRE (Paul): *Barbara Blomberg*. 1909.

HÖFLER (Constantin von): *Zur Kritik und Quellenkunde der ersten Regierungsjahre Kaiser Karls V*. Wien, 1876.

HUIZINGA (Johan): *Erasmus*. 1936.

— *Herbst des Mittelalters*, 1952.

ILLESCAS (Gonzalo de): *Carlos Quintos en Tunis*. Madrid (vers 1550).

LANZ (Karl): *Korrespondenz des Kaiser Karl V*. 4 vol. Leipzig, 1844–1845.

— *Staatspapiere zur Geschichte des Kaisers Karl V*. 1845.

LEVA (Giuseppe di): *Storia documentata di Carlo V in correlazione all'Italia*. 5 vol., Venezia, 1863–1894.

LEHNHOFF (Otto): *Die Beichtväter Karls V*, Gött. Diss. Alfeld, 1933.

LOPEZ DE GÓMARA (Franceso): *Annals of the Emperor Charles V*. Oxford, 1912.

LORTZ (Josef): *Die Reformation in Deutschland*, 2 vol. 1949.

MALE (G. van): *Lettres sur la vie intérieure de Charles Quint*.

MENENDEZ PIDAL (Ramon): *Idea imperial de Carlos V*. Madrid, 1940.

MEXIA (Pedro): *Historia de Carlos Quinto*. 1530. new éd., Madrid, 1940.

MIGNET (François): *Rivalité de Francois Ier et de Charles Quint*. Paris, 1876.

MOREL-FATIO (Alfred): *Historiographie de Charles Quint*, and *Mémoires de Charles Quint*, Bibliothèque de l'école des Hautes Études, 202. Fasc. Paris, 1913.

PASTOR (Ludwig von): *Die Reunionsbestrebungen während der Regierung Karls V*. Freiburg i. Br. 1879.

PIRENNE (Henri): *Histoire de Belgique*. 3 vol., Bruxelles, 1907.

RANKE (Leopold von): *Die Osmanen und die spanische Monarchie*. Berlin, 1837.
— *Die römischen Päpste, ihre Kirche und ihr Staat im XVI und XVII. Jahrhundert.*
3 vol., 1900.
— *Deutsche Geschichte im Zeitalter der Reformation*. 6 vol., 1925–1926.
RASSOW (Peter): *La Primera Firma de Carlos V*, in *Investigación y Progreso*.
Madrid, 1927.
— *Die Chronik des Pedro Giron und andere Quellen zur Geschichte Kaiser Karls V.*
Breslau, 1929.
— *Die Kaiser-Idee Karls V. dargestellt in der Politik der Jahre 1528–1540*. Berlin,
1932.
— *Die politische Welt Karls V*. München, 1946. trans from Spanish: *El Mundo
político de Carlos V*. Madrid, 1945.
— *Forschungen zur Reichs-Idee im XVI. und XVII. Jahrhundert*. Köln, 1955.
— *Karl V. Der letzte Kaiser des Mittelalters*. Göttingen, 1957.
ROBERTSON (William): *History of the Reign of the Emperor Charles the Fifth.*
London, 1769.
SANDOVAL (Prudencio de): *Historia de la Vida y Hechos del Emperador
Carlos V*. Pamplona, 1618.
SCHNEIDER (Reinhold): *Philipp der Zweite oder Religion und Macht*. Köln,
1957.
SCHUTZ (A.): *Der Donaufeldzug Karls V*. Tübingen, 1930.
SCHWARZENBERG (Gertrude von): *Karl V. Ahnherr Europas*. Hamburg,
1954.
TERLINDEN (Vicomte Charles de): *Das Goldene Vlies* dans *Virtute Fideque,*
Festschrift für Otto von Habsburg. Wien, 1965.
— *Charles Quint, Empereur des Deux Mondes*. Bruxelles, 1965.
TREVOR-DAVIES (R.): *The Golden Century of Spain*. 1937.
TYLER (Royall): *The Emperor Charles the Fifth*. London, 1956.
WINKER (Will): *Kaiser Maximilian I zwischen Wirklichkeit und Traum.*
München, 1950.
LEWIS (Wyndham): *Emperor of the West*. London, 1934.

Index

Ackermann of Bohemia, 58

Acuna, Antonio de, Bishop of Zamara, 94

Adorno, Antonio, 105

Adrien of Utrecht, and education of Charles, 30; as privy councillor, 34; as Regent in Spain, 35, 45, 90, 92, 94, 186; attitude of Spanish to, 45, 90, 94, 97; influence of, on Charles, 65, 84, 218, 219; character of, 90, 92, 101–2; during rising in Castile, 92, 94, 97; elected pope, 101–2; death of, 102

Africa, North, Spanish interest in, 36, 38, 42, 136–7, 139, 143–4, 157–6; corsairs in, 38, 141, 143, 155; Portuguese interest in, 135; Turks in, 137, 139, 140, 143–4, 156–177

'Against the Hordes of Peasant Bandits and Assassins', 119

'Against the Papacy of Rome founded by the Devil', 161

Alba, Duke of, 169, 174

Albrecht, brother of Friedrich, Emperor, 7

Albrecht, Duke of Austria, 2, 3, 5

Albrecht II, Emperor, 5, 6

Albrecht-Alcibiades von Brandenburg, 172, 201, 203, 221

Albrecht of Bavaria, 163

Albrecht of Brandenburg, Archbishop of Mainz, 78, 85

Alcantara, Order of, 39

Aleandro, Girolomo, 82

d'Alençon, Duke of, 107

d'Alençon, Dowager Duchess of, 110

Alexander VI, Pope, 37, 204

Algiers, 72, 137, 144, 148, 156–7

Allstedt, 118

Almenara, 98

Alva, Duke of, 156, 201, 202, 207, 208, 213

Ampfing, battle of, 3

Amsdorf, Nicholas von, 196

Anabaptists, 94, 151

Anchiata, Juan de, 30

Angoulême, Comte de see François I

Anne of Austria, 161

Anne of Bohemia and Hungary, 163

Anne of Jagellon, wife of Ferdinand I

Aquinus, St Thomas, 130

Aragon, geographical position of, 35–6; and France, 35–6, 42, 135; and Castile, 134–5; Mediterranean policy of, 134–5; renunciation of, by Charles, 209 see also Spain

Arras, Bishop of, 204–5, 209

Arras, Treaty of, 19, 20

Augsburg, Diet of, 7, 75, 131, 194, 197–8, 205, 206

Augustinians, 65, 84

Austria, 4–5, 54, 181, 119, 163

d'Avalos, Hernando, 91

Avignon, 12

Avila, 92

Aztec Empire, 185–7

Babenburg dynasty, 1

Baglioni, Malatesta de, 128

Balancon, 30

Balboa, Vasco Nunez de, 37

Ball, John, 114

Bamberg, Bishop of, 202

Barbarossa, Khair-ed-din, 135, 137, 140, 141, 143, 144, 155, 159

Barbarossa, Horuch, 137

Basle, Council of, 88

Bavaria, 131, 132, 150, 163, 199, 200

Bavaria, Duke of, 121

Bayard, 48